The State Economic Handbook

The State Economic Handbook
2008 Edition

Anderson Economic Group, LLC
Scott D. Watkins, Editor
Patrick L. Anderson, Executive Editor

palgrave
macmillan

THE STATE ECONOMIC HANDBOOK 2008

This book contains data obtained from original public and private sources. All materials from copyrighted sources have been reprinted with approval. Business climate rankings from Forbes Magazine are reprinted by permission of Forbes Magazine © 2006 Forbes Inc. Tax climate rankings from the Tax Foundation are reprinted by permission of The Tax Foundation © 2006. Tax climate rankings from Anderson Economic Group were originally published in the firm's report "Benchmarking for Success: A Comparison of State Business Taxes," August 2006, and are reprinted with permission. Voter participation and presidential election results are reprinted by permission of Dave Leip's Atlas of U.S. Presidential Elections, http://www.uselectionatlas.org (December 2006). All other data presented are from works by the U.S. government, other sources in the public domain, or Anderson Economic Group, LLC.

First published in 2007 by
PALGRAVE MACMILLAN™
175 Fifth Avenue, New York, N.Y.10010 and
Houndmills, Basingstoke, Hampshire, England RG21 6XS
Companies and representatives throughout the world.

PALGRAVE MACMILLAN is the global academic imprint of the Palgrave Macmillan division of St. Martin's Press, LLC and of Palgrave Macmillan Ltd. Macmillan® is a registered trademark in the United States, United Kingdom and other countries. Palgrave is a registered trademark in the European Union and other countries.

ISBN-13: 978–0–230–60049–2
ISBN-10: 0–230–60049–2
ISSN: 1938–4939

A catalog record for this book is available from the Library of Congress.

A catalogue record for this book is available from the British Library.

Design by Newgen Imaging Systems (P) Ltd., Chennai, India.

First edition: September 2007

10 9 8 7 6 5 4 3 2 1

Printed in the United States of America.

Table of Contents

Acknowledgments

This book could not have been completed if not for the assistance of the staff at Anderson Economic Group, LLC who spent time collecting and organizing data, maintaining databases, analyzing and checking figures, and researching each of the fifty states.

Those deserving particular thanks are: Lisa Asmus, who provided great assistance with this first edition, and Andrea Chroniewicz, who assisted on the initial drafts of the book. Cameron VanWyngarden for creating the maps used in the book, and for assisting in checking data and proofreading. Nicole Funari, Alex Rosaen, Caroline Sallee, and Jeff Smith also assisted with checking data and proofreading. Becky Scott of PS Publications in Lansing, Michigan, is thanked for her assistance in developing the XML scripts used to automate much of the data formatting and publishing.

Introduction

Many of our most important decisions center on "where?" Where is the best market for my services? Where should my family move? Where will my target customers be located 20 years from now? And the list goes on.

There are troves of data available to help us make informed location decisions. The problem, however, is navigating the endless series of data that are available and properly comparing data on different places.

The experts at Anderson Economic Group, LLC have prepared this book to help navigate the way. For each state we present important information about population makeup, workforce and industry, voter behavior, taxation, and more. These data, which come from various federal agencies, Forbes Magazine, Anderson Economic Group, the Tax Foundation, and other such sources, have not been assembled in any other single volume. We selected the data in this book based on what our business, government, and nonprofit clients actually use to make decisions in real-world situations.

This volume is intended to serve both as a quick reference for top-level decisions, and as a starting point for more in-depth research. It includes carefully selected variables that give a broad picture of the economic, demographic, and political environments in each state. It also carefully documents the sources of the information, allowing readers to find the original source if necessary.

Organization of the Book

This book provides a concise look at key economic, demographic, and political information for each of America's 50 states. Data are presented on a state-by-state basis, and the states are ordered alphabetically, from Alabama to Wyoming. There is also a State Ranking section at the end of the book to present a clear look at how the states compare. Following the ranking section is a brief discussion on the data sources used in the book, as well as a glossary of terms that provides a clear understanding of what each variable presented really means.

Each state's section begins with a map of the state showing its major population centers, the main road network, the capital city, and where the state is located relative to others. A narrative is provided to highlight key demographic and economic trends, and to assess the state's economy and demography relative to the nation as a whole.

In addition to the maps and the narrative there are five data sections for each state. First is demographic and socioeconomic data from 2000 and 2005, including population and income figures. This is followed by a section on workforce and industry, which covers the labor force, education attainment, and employment and payroll information. It also includes a listing of the state's top-10 industries in terms of 2004 employment.

The third data section for each state presents tax and business climate information. Tax revenues, by type of tax, are presented for the 2001–2 and the 2003–4 fiscal years. Business climate rankings, as reported by Anderson Economic Group, LLC; Forbes Magazine; and the Tax Foundation; are also provided. The number of firm births and terminations in 2002–3, as reported by the Census Bureau, is also included in this section.

Voting behavior and elected officials is the next data section for each state. Included is voter turnout, popular vote, and electoral vote data for the past four presidential elections. Information on Gubernatorial and Congressional office holders is also provided.

The last data section for each state presents the names and websites for four business and economic agencies in the state. The agencies selected for listing were the state-level chamber of commerce, the state's economic development agency, the state office or agency for small business development and assistance, and the state office for business and corporate registrations.

About Anderson Economic Group, LLC

This book was prepared by Anderson Economic Group, LLC, a consulting firm specializing in economics, finance, public policy, and market assessments. The firm assists businesses, state and local governments, and nonprofits with location analyses, market strategies, economic development, and policy analyses, often relying on the data presented in this book.

Scott D. Watkins, a consultant with Anderson Economic Group, is the editor of this publication. His work focuses on economic, public policy, and education finance. Recent reports by Mr. Watkins include "Economic Impacts from 2006 Detroit Tigers' Game Attendance," "Automation Alley's Second Annual Technology Industry Report: Driving Southeast Michigan Forward," The Economic Impact of North-Central West Virginia's Technology Industry," and "Benchmarking for Success: Education Performance among the American States." Mr. Watkins holds an M.B.A. from the Eli Broad College of Business at Michigan State

University. He also has a bachelor's degree in International Relations from the James Madison College at Michigan State University.

Patrick L. Anderson, Principal and CEO at Anderson Economic Group, is this book's executive editor. Mr. Anderson is the author of more than 100 published works on economics, finance, and public policy, and his views are often cited in news reports throughout the United States. His first book, *Business Economics and Finance,* was published in 2004, and his paper on "Pocketbook Issues and the Presidency" was awarded the Edmund Mennis Award for the best contributed paper in 2004 by the National Association for Business Economics.

Prior to founding Anderson Economic Group, Mr. Anderson served as the Chief of Staff of the Michigan Department of State, and as Deputy Budget Director for the State of Michigan. He was also an officer in Alexander Hamilton Life Insurance, an economist for Manufacturers National Bank of Detroit, and a graduate fellow with the Central Intelligence Agency in Washington, DC. He is a graduate of the University of Michigan, where he earned a master's degree in Public Policy and a bachelor's degree in Political Science.

Contacting Anderson Economic Group

For more information on Anderson Economic Group please visit the company's website at http://www.AndersonEconomicGroup.com.

To offer suggestions for future editions of *The State Economic Handbook,* or to notify us of a typographical or data error, please email statehandbook@AndersonEconomicGroup.com. Any errata or significant data notes will be available on the State Economic Handbook page at http://www.AndersonEconomicGroup.com. Please note that minor data revisions, especially of demographic data, occur regularly and may be the cause of small differences in data reported at a later date.

Alabama

Demographics and Socioeconomics. Alabama, located in the East South Central region of the United States, has a population of 4.4 million people, making it the twenty-third most populous state in 2005. The state's population decreased by 4,542 people from 2000 to 2005 but is projected to increase to 4.8 million by 2025. This 0.4 percent projected annual growth rate compares to the projected national average of 1.0 percent. The state's 2005 per capita personal income of $29,623 was the eleventh lowest in the United States, some $4,872 below the national average. Per capita income in Alabama grew at an average annual rate of 4.5 percent from 2000 to 2005, compared to 2.9 percent nationally.

Workforce and Industry. In 2004 the state's largest industry in terms of employment was manufacturing, followed by retail trade. The fastest growing industry was professional, scientific, and technical services, with 40.3 percent growth from 1998 to 2004. The state's workforce is generally less educated than that of other states: 80.3 percent of the state's adult population has graduated from

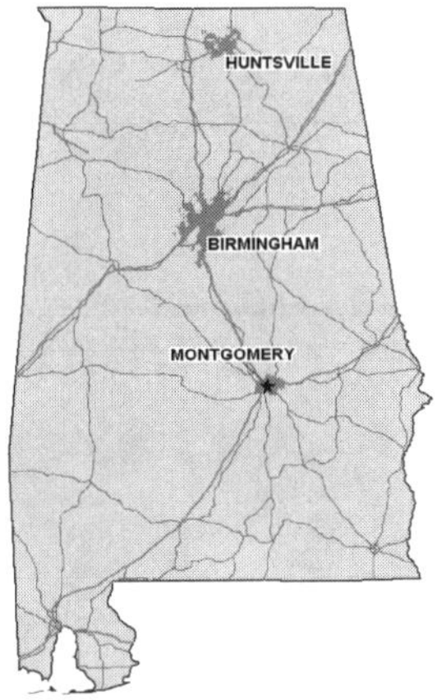

★ State Capitol

Major Urban Area

Major Roadway

Demographic and Socioeconomic Profile

Demographics and Socioeconomic Figures		
Population and Households	**2000**	**2005**
Total Population	4,447,100	4,442,558
Number of Households	1,737,080	1,788,692
Average Household Size	2.5	2.5
Age and Ethnicity		
Median Age	35.8	37.4
Population 18 Years of Age and Older	3,324,488	3,356,850
Population 65 Years of Age and Older	580,028	572,684
Caucasian Population	3,161,671	3,153,627
African-American Population	1,153,044	1,144,330
Hispanic Population	72,627	99,040
Asian Population	29,908	38,444
Foreign-Born Population	87,772	120,773
Income		
Per Capita Personal Income (USD)	$23,764	$29,623
Median Household Income (USD)	$34,135	$36,879
Individuals below Poverty Level	16.1%	17.0%

Data: U.S. Census, American Community Survey; U.S. Department of Commerce, Bureau of Economic Analysis

high school, compared to an 84.2 percent national average; 21.4 percent hold a bachelor degree or higher (national average is 27.2 percent); and 7.9 percent hold professional or graduate degrees (national average is 10.0 percent).

Tax Profile and Business Climate. In fiscal year 2003–4 Alabama had total tax revenues of $10.5 billion. The largest share was generated from sales and gross receipts taxes, followed by individual income taxes. In terms of business taxes, the state ranked fourteenth in a 2006 report by Anderson Economic Group. Forbes Magazine and the Tax Foundation ranked the state's business climate fortieth and twentieth, respectively.

Population Projections

	2010	2015	2020	2025
Total Population	4,596,330	4,663,111	4,728,915	4,800,092
Median Age	38.5	39.4	40.3	40.9
Population 18 Years of Age and Older	3,504,146	3,574,114	3,642,576	3,706,831
Population 65 Years of Age and Older	648,889	739,580	842,607	953,727

Data: U.S. Census Bureau

Workforce and Industry Profile

Workforce

	2000	2005
Civilian Labor Force	2,047,100	2,137,629
Labor Force Participation Rate	59.8%	61.8%
Unemployment Rate	4.1%	4.0%
Average Earnings per Job (USD)	$29,041	$32,310
Education Attainment (Population 25 Years and Older)	**(%)**	**(%)**
High School Graduate or Higher	75.3	80.3
Bachelors Degree or Higher	19.0	21.4
Graduate or Professional Degree	6.9	7.9

Data: U.S. Census Bureau, American Community Survey; U.S. Department of Labor, Bureau of Labor Statistics

Industry Overview

	1998	2004
Total Employees	1,604,110	1,629,141
Total Payroll ($1,000)	40,330,597	49,772,829
Total Establishments	100,316	100,802
Establishments with 1–19 Employees	86,193	85,838
Establishments with 20–49 Employees	8,791	9,429
Establishments with 50–249 Employees	4,558	4,778
Establishments with 250–999 Employees	674	657
Establishments with 1,000+ Employees	100	100

Data: U.S. Census Bureau, County Business Patterns

Major Industries (Ranked by 2004 Employment; Payroll in $1,000s)				
Industry	1998 Employment	2004 Employment	1998 Payroll	2004 Payroll
Manufacturing	352,422	273,967	10,341,656	10,068,273
Retail Trade	226,485	237,633	3,651,939	4,547,641
Health Care and Social Assistance	201,111	226,910	5,738,000	7,614,450
Accommodation and Food Services	127,254	141,442	1,175,671	1,491,409
Admin., Support, Waste Mngt., Remediation Services	100,378	107,523	1,706,594	2,351,832
Construction	101,007	104,672	2,635,107	3,232,887
Professional, Scientific, Technical Services	65,195	91,498	2,519,999	4,470,329
Other Services (except Public Admin.)	80,060	82,869	1,219,639	1,496,849
Wholesale Trade	79,147	76,123	2,540,100	2,992,934
Finance and Insurance	67,933	75,700	2,554,861	3,742,804

Data: U.S. Census Bureau, County Business Patterns

Taxes and Business Climate

State and Local Taxes		
Combined Revenues ($1,000)	2001–2	2003–4
Revenue from Property Taxes	1,473,554	1,661,855
Revenue from Sales and Gross Receipts Taxes	4,799,669	5,217,009
Revenue from Individual Income Taxes	2,126,559	2,344,266
Revenue from Corporate Income Taxes	322,636	292,051
Revenue from Other Taxes	996,409	1,020,185
Total Tax Revenue	9,718,827	10,535,366
Per Capita Taxes		
Property Tax per Capita	331	367
Sales and Gross Receipts Tax per Capita	1,079	1,153
Individual Income Tax per Capita	478	518
Corporate Income Tax per Capita	73	65
Other Taxes per Capita	224	225
Total Taxes per Capita	2,185	2,328

Data: U.S. Census Bureau; Anderson Economic Group, LLC

Business Climate Measures	
Anderson Economic Group: 2006 Business Tax Ranking (1 is Best)	14
Forbes Magazine: 2006 Best States for Business Ranking (1 is Best)	40
Tax Foundation: 2007 Business Tax Climate Ranking (1 is Best)	20
2002–3 Employer Firm Births	9,563
2002–3 Employer Firm Terminations	8,991

Data: Anderson Economic Group; Tax Foundation; Forbes Magazine; U.S. Census, Statistics of U.S. Businesses

Voting Behavior and Elected Officials

Voter Registration and Turnout (%)

	1992	1996	2000	2004
Registered Voters Who Voted	76.4	62.1	66.1	72.5
Citizens Age 18+ Who Voted	55.2	47.7	50.3	55.5

Data: Dave Leip's Atlas of U.S. Presidential Elections

Presidential Election Results (Nationwide Winner Listed First)

2004	Popular Vote (%)	Electoral Votes
George W. Bush (Republican, Incumbent)	62.5	9
John Kerry (Democrat)	36.8	0
Other	0.7	0
2000		
George W. Bush (Republican)	56.5	9
Albert Gore (Democrat)	41.6	0
Ralph Nader (Green)	1.1	0
Other	0.8	0
1996		
William Clinton (Democrat, Incumbent)	43.2	0
Robert Dole (Republican)	50.1	9
H. Ross Perot (Reformist)	6.0	0
Other	0.7	0
1992		
William Clinton (Democrat)	40.9	0
George H. W. Bush (Republican, Incumbent)	47.7	9
H. Ross Perot (Independent)	10.9	0
Other	0.6	0

Data: Dave Leip's Atlas of U.S. Presidential Elections

Governor and U.S. Congressional Seats				
Governor	**Party**	**Year Term Began**	**Term**	**Max. Consecutive Terms**
Bob Riley	R	2003	Second	2
U.S. Senators	**Party**	**Year Elected**	**Term Expires**	
Jeff Sessions	R	1996	2009	
Richard C. Shelby	R	1986	2011	
U.S. Representatives		**Republican**	**Democrat**	**Other**
		5	2	0

Data: National Governors Association, U.S. Senate, U.S. House of Representatives

Business and Economic Agencies

Agency	Website Address
Business Council of Alabama	www.bcatoday.org
Alabama Development Office	www.ado.state.al.us
Alabama Small Business Dev. Consortium	www.asbdc.org
Alabama Secretary of State	www.sos.state.al.us

Data: Various Agency Websites

Alaska

Demographics and Socioeconomics. With a population of 641,724 people, Alaska was the fourth least populous state in the United States in 2005. From 2000 to 2005 the state's population increased by 14,792 people, and is projected to increase to 820,881 by 2025. This 1.2 percent projected annual growth rate is just over the projected national average of 1.0 percent. In 2005 Alaska had a per capita personal income of $35,433. This was $938 above the national average and the fifteenth highest in the country. The state's per capita income grew at an average annual rate of 3.5 percent from 2000 to 2005, compared to 2.9 percent nationally.

Workforce and Industry. Alaska's largest industry in terms of 2004 employment was health care and social assistance. The fastest growing industry was management of companies and enterprises, with 51.4 percent growth from 1998 to 2004. The state's workforce is generally more educated than that of other states: 91.0 percent of the state's adult population has graduated from high school, compared to an 84.2 percent national average; 27.3 percent hold a bachelor

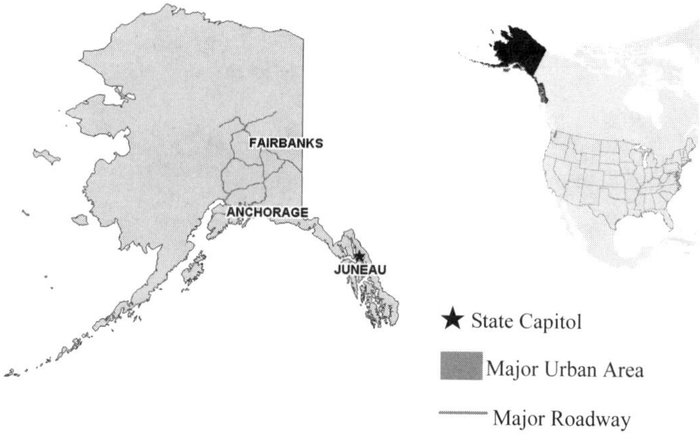

Demographic and Socioeconomic Profile

Demographics and Socioeconomic Figures		
Population and Households	**2000**	**2005**
Total Population	626,932	641,724
Number of Households	221,600	233,252
Average Household Size	2.7	2.8
Age and Ethnicity		
Median Age	32.4	33.9
Population 18 Years of Age and Older	436,425	454,226
Population 65 Years of Age and Older	35,093	42,156
Caucasian Population	434,225	443,874
African-American Population	21,968	22,103
Hispanic Population	25,765	30,843
Asian Population	25,496	28,838
Foreign-Born Population	37,170	34,368
Income		
Per Capita Personal Income (USD)	$29,867	$35,433
Median Household Income (USD)	$51,571	$56,234
Individuals below Poverty Level	9.4%	11.2%

Data: U.S. Census, American Community Survey; U.S. Department of Commerce, Bureau of Economic Analysis

degree or higher (national average is 27.2 percent); and 10.1 percent hold professional or graduate degrees (national average is 10.0 percent).

Tax Profile and Business Climate. Alaska's total tax revenue was $2.4 billion for fiscal year 2003–4. The largest share of tax revenue in 2003–4 was generated from property taxes, followed by other taxes. There was no revenue from individual income taxes. In terms of business taxes, the state ranked forty-seventh in a 2006 report by Anderson Economic Group. Forbes Magazine and the Tax Foundation ranked the state's business climate forty-seventh and third, respectively.

Population Projections	2010	2015	2020	2025
Total Population	694,109	732,544	774,421	820,881
Median Age	32.5	32.3	32.9	33.3
Population 18 Years of Age and Older	510,126	533,371	555,795	584,703
Population 65 Years of Age and Older	56,548	75,023	96,388	115,135

Data: U.S. Census Bureau

Workforce and Industry Profile

Workforce	2000	2005
Civilian Labor Force	309,485	330,672
Labor Force Participation Rate	71.3%	70.9%
Unemployment Rate	6.2%	6.8%
Average Earnings per Job (USD)	$35,142	$42,740
Education Attainment (Population 25 Years and Older)	**(%)**	**(%)**
High School Graduate or Higher	88.3	91.0
Bachelors Degree or Higher	24.7	27.3
Graduate or Professional Degree	8.6	10.1

Data: U.S. Census Bureau, American Community Survey; U.S. Department of Labor, Bureau of Labor Statistics

Industry Overview	1998	2004
Total Employees	196,135	223,153
Total Payroll ($1,000)	6,883,920	9,124,830
Total Establishments	18,212	19,387
Establishments with 1–19 Employees	16,424	17,317
Establishments with 20–49 Employees	1,212	1,402
Establishments with 50–249 Employees	486	573
Establishments with 250–999 Employees	85	83
Establishments with 1,000+ Employees	5	12

Data: U.S. Census Bureau, County Business Patterns

Major Industries (Ranked by 2004 Employment; Payroll in $1,000s)				
Industry	1998 Employment	2004 Employment	1998 Payroll	2004 Payroll
Health Care and Social Assistance	28,919	38,242	1,061,078	1,587,451
Retail Trade	32,186	34,274	743,092	882,875
Accommodation and Food Services	20,086	23,382	343,467	472,551
Construction	12,915	17,599	642,928	1,117,227
Transportation and Warehousing	17,005	17,473	745,246	900,820
Admin., Support, Waste Mngt., Remediation Services	9,881	12,877	289,675	516,262
Professional, Scientific, Technical Services	9,497	11,867	446,785	616,147
Other Services (except Public Admin.)	9,991	10,124	211,565	262,736
Manufacturing	12,117	10,081	352,818	395,766
Wholesale Trade	7,040	8,167	275,492	365,830

Data: U.S. Census Bureau, County Business Patterns

Taxes and Business Climate

State and Local Taxes		
Combined Revenues ($1,000)	2001–2	2003–4
Revenue from Property Taxes	830,011	859,056
Revenue from Sales and Gross Receipts Taxes	310,584	358,186
Revenue from Individual Income Taxes	0	0
Revenue from Corporate Income Taxes	269,273	339,564
Revenue from Other Taxes	660,040	818,825
Total Tax Revenue	2,069,908	2,375,631
Per Capita Taxes		
Property Tax per Capita	1,324	1,306
Sales and Gross Receipts Tax per Capita	495	544
Individual Income Tax per Capita	0	0
Corporate Income Tax per Capita	429	516
Other Taxes per Capita	1,053	1,244
Total Taxes per Capita	3,301	3,610

Data: U.S. Census Bureau; Anderson Economic Group, LLC

Business Climate Measures	
Anderson Economic Group: 2006 Business Tax Ranking (1 is Best)	47
Forbes Magazine: 2006 Best States for Business Ranking (1 is Best)	47
Tax Foundation: 2007 Business Tax Climate Ranking (1 is Best)	3
2002–3 Employer Firm Births	1,977
2002–3 Employer Firm Terminations	1,720

Data: Anderson Economic Group; Tax Foundation; Forbes Magazine; U.S. Census, Statistics of U.S. Businesses

Voting Behavior and Elected Officials

Voter Registration and Turnout (%)	1992	1996	2000	2004
Registered Voters Who Voted	82.1	58.2	60.3	66.2
Citizens Age 18+ Who Voted	65.4	56.9	65.4	68.0

Data: Dave Leip's Atlas of U.S. Presidential Elections

Presidential Election Results (Nationwide Winner Listed First)		
2004	**Popular Vote (%)**	**Electoral Votes**
George W. Bush (Republican, Incumbent)	61.1	3
John Kerry (Democrat)	35.5	0
Other	3.4	0
2000		
George W. Bush (Republican)	58.6	3
Albert Gore (Democrat)	27.7	0
Ralph Nader (Green)	10.1	0
Other	3.6	0
1996		
William Clinton (Democrat, Incumbent)	33.3	0
Robert Dole (Republican)	50.8	3
H. Ross Perot (Reformist)	10.9	0
Other	5.0	0
1992		
William Clinton (Democrat)	30.3	0
George H. W. Bush (Republican, Incumbent)	39.5	3
H. Ross Perot (Independent)	28.4	0
Other	1.8	0

Data: Dave Leip's Atlas of U.S. Presidential Elections

Governor and U.S. Congressional Seats				
Governor	**Party**	**Year Term Began**	**Term**	**Max. Consecutive Terms**
Sarah Palin	R	2007	First	2
U.S. Senators	**Party**	**Year Elected**	**Term Expires**	
Ted Stevens	R	1970	2009	
Lisa Murkowski	R	2002	2011	
U.S. Representatives		**Republican**	**Democrat**	**Other**
		1	0	0

Data: National Governors Association, U.S. Senate, U.S. House of Representatives

Business and Economic Agencies

Agency	Website Address
Alaska State Chamber	www.alaskachamber.com
Alaska Department of Commerce, Community, and Economic Development	www.dced.state.ak.us
Alaska Small Business Dev. Center	www.aksbdc.org
Division of Corporations, Business, and Professional Licensing	www.dced.state.ak.us/occ

Data: Various Agency Websites

Arizona

Demographics and Socioeconomics. Arizona is located in the Mountain region of the United States. Arizona has a population of 5.8 million people, making it the sixteenth most populous state in 2005. The state's population increased by 699,207 people from 2000 to 2005, and is projected to increase to 9.5 million by 2025. This 2.5 percent projected annual growth rate is one of the highest in the nation and compares to the projected national average of 1.0 percent. Per capita personal income in Arizona was $30,157 in 2005, ranking the thirteenth lowest in the country and $4,338 below the national average. From 2000 to 2005 per capita income in Arizona grew at an average annual rate of 3.3 percent, compared to 2.9 percent nationally.

Workforce and Industry. The state's workforce is generally less educated than that of other states — 83.8 percent of the state's adult population has graduated from high school, compared to an 84.2 percent national average; 25.6 percent hold a bachelor degree or higher (national average is 27.2 percent); and 9.3 percent hold professional

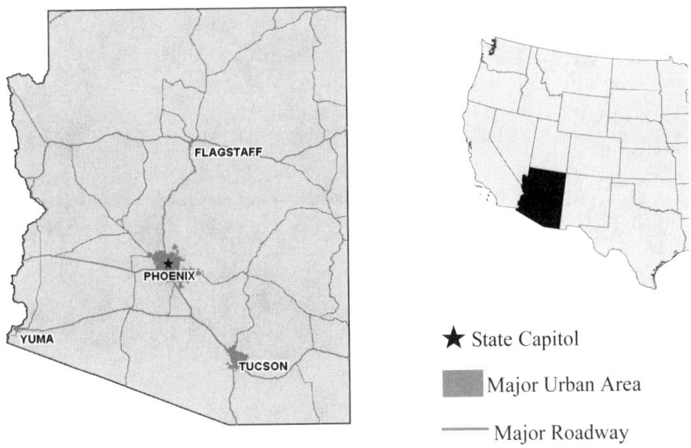

Demographic and Socioeconomic Profile

Demographics and Socioeconomic Figures		
Population and Households	**2000**	**2005**
Total Population	5,130,632	5,829,839
Number of Households	1,901,327	2,204,013
Average Household Size	2.6	2.7
Age and Ethnicity		
Median Age	34.2	34.5
Population 18 Years of Age and Older	3,767,931	4,255,951
Population 65 Years of Age and Older	667,607	735,397
Caucasian Population	3,871,715	4,440,804
African-American Population	154,316	180,769
Hispanic Population	1,295,317	1,668,524
Asian Population	91,223	129,197
Foreign-Born Population	656,183	843,296
Income		
Per Capita Personal Income (USD)	$25,660	$30,157
Median Household Income (USD)	$40,558	$44,282
Individuals below Poverty Level	13.9%	14.2%

Data: U.S. Census, American Community Survey; U.S. Department of Commerce, Bureau of Economic Analysis

or graduate degrees (national average is 10.0). In 2004 the state's largest industry in terms of employment was retail trade, followed by health care and social assistance. The fastest growing industry was educational services, with 74.4 percent growth from 1998 to 2004. Finance and insurance was the fastest growing major industry, with growth of 31.8 percent from 1998 to 2004.

Tax Profile and Business Climate. In fiscal year 2003–4 Arizona had total tax revenues of $16.5 billion. The largest share was generated from sales and gross receipts taxes, followed by property taxes. The per capita tax burden in Arizona was $2,871 for 2003–4, some $576 below the national average. In terms of business taxes, Arizona ranked thirty-first in a 2006 report by Anderson Economic Group. The state's business climate was ranked fifteenth by Forbes Magazine and twenty-eighth by the Tax Foundation.

Population Projections

	2010	2015	2020	2025
Total Population	6,637,381	7,495,238	8,456,448	9,531,537
Median Age	36.4	37.3	38.2	38.8
Population 18 Years of Age and Older	4,948,917	5,602,941	6,328,068	7,170,395
Population 65 Years of Age and Older	922,010	1,181,358	1,520,622	1,940,356

Data: U.S. Census Bureau

Workforce and Industry Profile

Workforce

	2000	2005
Civilian Labor Force	2,366,372	2,807,298
Labor Force Participation Rate	61.1%	63.9%
Unemployment Rate	4.0%	4.7%
Average Earnings per Job (USD)	$32,610	$34,940
Education Attainment (Population 25 Years and Older)	**(%)**	**(%)**
High School Graduate or Higher	81.0	83.8
Bachelors Degree or Higher	23.5	25.6
Graduate or Professional Degree	8.4	9.3

Data: U.S. Census Bureau, American Community Survey; U.S. Department of Labor, Bureau of Labor Statistics

Industry Overview

	1998	2004
Total Employees	1,763,508	2,044,134
Total Payroll ($1,000)	49,052,246	69,160,754
Total Establishments	110,245	125,693
Establishments with 1–19 Employees	94,264	106,797
Establishments with 20–49 Employees	9,997	11,700
Establishments with 50–249 Employees	5,221	6,278
Establishments with 250–999 Employees	656	805
Establishments with 1,000+ Employees	107	113

Data: U.S. Census Bureau, County Business Patterns

Major Industries (Ranked by 2004 Employment; Payroll in $1,000s)				
Industry	1998 Employment	2004 Employment	1998 Payroll	2004 Payroll
Retail Trade	241,092	295,675	4,734,716	6,827,373
Health Care and Social Assistance	190,110	242,111	5,572,775	9,010,945
Accommodation and Food Services	187,762	222,833	2,091,494	2,962,122
Admin., Support, Waste Mngt., Remediation Services	178,828	194,121	3,566,564	5,183,751
Construction	143,373	184,901	4,191,730	6,610,201
Manufacturing	199,616	167,481	7,565,451	7,492,755
Finance and Insurance	92,132	121,386	3,647,327	5,840,582
Professional, Scientific, Technical Services	98,547	116,458	3,636,335	5,716,255
Wholesale Trade	84,631	91,852	3,175,460	4,101,916
Other Services (except Public Admin.)	73,577	81,437	1,386,582	1,744,751

Data: U.S. Census Bureau, County Business Patterns

Taxes and Business Climate

State and Local Taxes		
Combined Revenues ($1,000)	2001–2	2003–4
Revenue from Property Taxes	4,254,395	4,867,990
Revenue from Sales and Gross Receipts Taxes	7,081,004	7,989,125
Revenue from Individual Income Taxes	2,090,645	2,315,865
Revenue from Corporate Income Taxes	346,280	525,650
Revenue from Other Taxes	647,998	782,544
Total Tax Revenue	14,420,322	16,481,174
Per Capita Taxes		
Property Tax per Capita	829	848
Sales and Gross Receipts Tax per Capita	1,380	1,392
Individual Income Tax per Capita	407	403
Corporate Income Tax per Capita	67	92
Other Taxes per Capita	126	136
Total Taxes per Capita	2,810	2,871

Data: U.S. Census Bureau; Anderson Economic Group, LLC

Business Climate Measures	
Anderson Economic Group: 2006 Business Tax Ranking (1 is Best)	31
Forbes Magazine: 2006 Best States for Business Ranking (1 is Best)	15
Tax Foundation: 2007 Business Tax Climate Ranking (1 is Best)	28
2002–3 Employer Firm Births	14,311
2002–3 Employer Firm Terminations	12,577

Data: Anderson Economic Group; Tax Foundation; Forbes Magazine; U.S. Census, Statistics of U.S. Businesses

Voting Behavior and Elected Officials

Voter Registration and Turnout (%)	1992	1996	2000	2004
Registered Voters Who Voted	75.7	62.6	70.6	76.1
Citizens Age 18+ Who Voted	54.1	44.7	40.7	49.6

Data: Dave Leip's Atlas of U.S. Presidential Elections

Presidential Election Results (Nationwide Winner Listed First)		
2004	**Popular Vote (%)**	**Electoral Votes**
George W. Bush (Republican, Incumbent)	54.8	10
John Kerry (Democrat)	44.4	0
Other	0.8	0
2000		
George W. Bush (Republican)	51.0	8
Albert Gore (Democrat)	44.7	0
Ralph Nader (Green)	3.0	0
Other	1.2	0
1996		
William Clinton (Democrat, Incumbent)	46.5	8
Robert Dole (Republican)	44.3	0
H. Ross Perot (Reformist)	8.0	0
Other	1.2	0
1992		
William Clinton (Democrat)	36.5	0
George H. W. Bush (Republican, Incumbent)	38.5	8
H. Ross Perot (Independent)	23.8	0
Other	1.2	0

Data: Dave Leip's Atlas of U.S. Presidential Elections

Governor and U.S. Congressional Seats				
Governor	**Party**	**Year Term Began**	**Term**	**Max. Consecutive Terms**
Janet Napolitano	D	2003	Second	2
U.S. Senators	**Party**	**Year Elected**	**Term Expires**	
Jon Kyl	R	1994	2013	
John McCain	R	1986	2011	
U.S. Representatives		**Republican**	**Democrat**	**Other**
		4	4	0

Data: National Governors Association, U.S. Senate, U.S. House of Representatives

Business and Economic Agencies

Agency	Website Address
Arizona Chamber of Commerce	www.azchamber.com
Arizona Department of Commerce	www.azcommerce.com
Arizona Small Business Dev. Center	www.maricopa.edu/sbdc
Arizona Secretary of State	www.azsos.gov/business_services

Data: Various Agency Websites

Arkansas

Demographics and Socioeconomics. Arkansas, located in the West South Central region of the United States, has a population of 2.7 million, making it the nineteenth least populous state in 2005. The state's population increased by 28,031 people from 2000 to 2005, and is projected to increase to 3.2 million by 2025. This 0.8 percent projected annual growth rate is slightly below the projected national average of 1.0 percent. The state's 2005 per capita personal income of $26,641 was the fourth lowest in the United States, some $7,854 below the national average. Per capita income in Arkansas grew at an average annual rate of 4.0 percent from 2000 to 2005, compared to 2.9 percent nationally.

Workforce and Industry. In 2004 the state's largest industry in terms of employment was manufacturing, followed by health care and social assistance. Arkansas' fastest growing industry was management of companies and enterprises, which ranked eleventh in terms of 2004 employment, and grew by 61.4 percent from 1998 to 2004. The state's workforce is generally less educated than

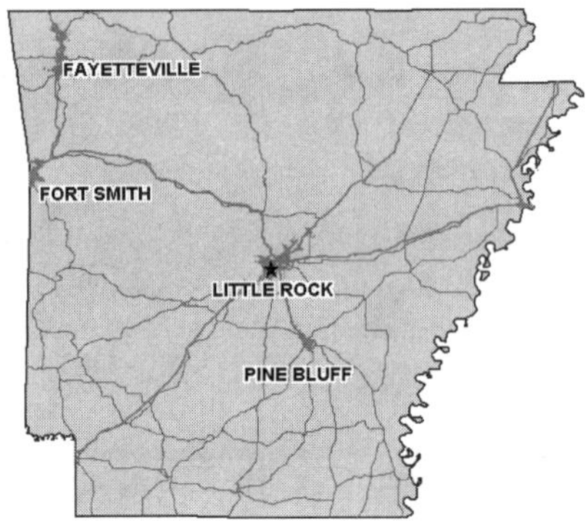

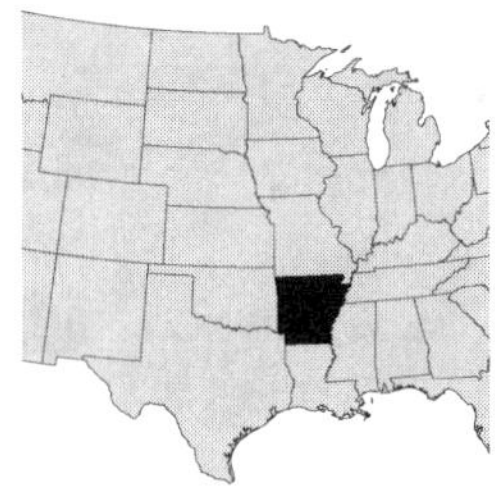

★ State Capitol

Major Urban Area

Major Roadway

Demographic and Socioeconomic Profile

Demographics and Socioeconomic Figures		
Population and Households	**2000**	**2005**
Total Population	2,673,400	2,701,431
Number of Households	1,042,696	1,087,542
Average Household Size	2.5	2.5
Age and Ethnicity		
Median Age	36.0	37.0
Population 18 Years of Age and Older	1,993,342	2,029,097
Population 65 Years of Age and Older	374,729	363,641
Caucasian Population	2,137,166	2,135,069
African-American Population	417,881	414,260
Hispanic Population	85,576	126,932
Asian Population	19,081	25,249
Foreign-Born Population	73,690	101,169
Income		
Per Capita Personal Income (USD)	$21,925	$26,641
Median Household Income (USD)	$32,182	$34,999
Individuals below Poverty Level	15.8%	17.2%

Data: U.S. Census, American Community Survey; U.S. Department of Commerce, Bureau of Economic Analysis

that of other states: 81.0 percent of the state's adult population has graduated from high school, compared to an 84.2 percent national average; 18.9 percent hold a bachelor degree or higher (national average is 27.2 percent); and 6.3 percent hold professional or graduate degrees (national average is 10.0 percent).

Tax Profile and Business Climate. In fiscal year 2003–4 Arkansas had total tax revenues of $7.0 billion. The largest share was generated from sales and gross receipts taxes, followed by other taxes. The per capita tax burden in Arkansas was $2,536 for 2003–4, some $911 below the national average. In terms of business taxes, the state ranked tenth in a 2006 report by Anderson Economic Group. Forbes Magazine and the Tax Foundation ranked the state's business climate twenty-fourth and thirty-fifth, respectively.

Population Projections

	2010	2015	2020	2025
Total Population	2,875,039	2,968,913	3,060,219	3,151,005
Median Age	37.9	38.6	39.4	39.8
Population 18 Years of Age and Older	2,172,383	2,247,849	2,322,453	2,395,591
Population 65 Years of Age and Older	412,152	467,880	531,028	599,028

Data: U.S. Census Bureau

Workforce and Industry Profile

Workforce

	2000	2005
Civilian Labor Force	1,249,546	1,324,066
Labor Force Participation Rate	60.6%	63.1%
Unemployment Rate	4.2%	4.9%
Average Earnings per Job (USD)	$26,317	$29,750
Education Attainment (Population 25 Years and Older)	**(%)**	**(%)**
High School Graduate or Higher	75.3	81.0
Bachelors Degree or Higher	16.6	18.9
Graduate or Professional Degree	5.7	6.3

Data: U.S. Census Bureau, American Community Survey; U.S. Department of Labor, Bureau of Labor Statistics

Industry Overview

	1998	2004
Total Employees	944,935	1,007,512
Total Payroll ($1,000)	21,764,625	28,670,925
Total Establishments	62,353	65,291
Establishments with 1–19 Employees	54,335	56,547
Establishments with 20–49 Employees	4,974	5,546
Establishments with 50–249 Employees	2,547	2,738
Establishments with 250–999 Employees	435	397
Establishments with 1,000+ Employees	62	63

Data: U.S. Census Bureau, County Business Patterns

Major Industries (Ranked by 2004 Employment; Payroll in $1,000s)				
Industry	1998 Employment	2004 Employment	1998 Payroll	2004 Payroll
Manufacturing	232,671	200,533	6,121,981	6,550,654
Health Care and Social Assistance	130,129	149,354	3,187,490	4,711,597
Retail Trade	134,134	141,613	2,072,154	2,627,211
Accommodation and Food Services	73,562	82,711	657,263	827,797
Transportation and Warehousing	39,313	61,131	1,180,877	1,876,896
Admin., Support, Waste Mngt., Remediation Services	51,425	48,566	819,087	910,320
Construction	43,475	48,114	1,097,864	1,419,446
Wholesale Trade	42,470	45,781	1,231,247	1,692,985
Other Services (except Public Admin.)	39,816	45,520	579,680	818,061
Finance and Insurance	32,334	36,146	1,045,075	1,420,151

Data: U.S. Census Bureau, County Business Patterns

Taxes and Business Climate

State and Local Taxes		
Combined Revenues ($1,000)	2001–2	2003–4
Revenue from Property Taxes	1,003,909	1,100,938
Revenue from Sales and Gross Receipts Taxes	3,340,217	3,714,211
Revenue from Individual Income Taxes	1,515,852	1,688,156
Revenue from Corporate Income Taxes	176,874	181,830
Revenue from Other Taxes	374,003	288,030
Total Tax Revenue	6,410,855	6,973,165
Per Capita Taxes		
Property Tax per Capita	376	400
Sales and Gross Receipts Tax per Capita	1,250	1,351
Individual Income Tax per Capita	567	614
Corporate Income Tax per Capita	66	66
Other Taxes per Capita	140	105
Total Taxes per Capita	2,398	2,536

Data: U.S. Census Bureau; Anderson Economic Group, LLC

Business Climate Measures	
Anderson Economic Group: 2006 Business Tax Ranking (1 is Best)	10
Forbes Magazine: 2006 Best States for Business Ranking (1 is Best)	24
Tax Foundation: 2007 Business Tax Climate Ranking (1 is Best)	35
2002–3 Employer Firm Births	6,532
2002–3 Employer Firm Terminations	5,632

Data: Anderson Economic Group; Tax Foundation; Forbes Magazine; U.S. Census, Statistics of U.S. Businesses

Voting Behavior and Elected Officials

Voter Registration and Turnout (%)

	1992	1996	2000	2004
Registered Voters Who Voted	72.1	64.6	59.2	62.6
Citizens Age 18+ Who Voted	53.8	47.2	46.2	51.6

Data: Dave Leip's Atlas of U.S. Presidential Elections

Presidential Election Results (Nationwide Winner Listed First)

2004	Popular Vote (%)	Electoral Votes
George W. Bush (Republican, Incumbent)	54.3	6
John Kerry (Democrat)	44.6	0
Other	1.2	0
2000		
George W. Bush (Republican)	51.3	6
Albert Gore (Democrat)	45.9	0
Ralph Nader (Green)	1.5	0
Other	1.4	0
1996		
William Clinton (Democrat, Incumbent)	53.7	6
Robert Dole (Republican)	36.8	0
H. Ross Perot (Reformist)	7.9	0
Other	1.6	0
1992		
William Clinton (Democrat)	53.2	6
George H. W. Bush (Republican, Incumbent)	35.5	0
H. Ross Perot (Independent)	10.4	0
Other	0.9	0

Data: Dave Leip's Atlas of U.S. Presidential Elections

Governor and U.S. Congressional Seats				
Governor	**Party**	**Year Term Began**	**Term**	**Max. Consecutive Terms**
Mike Beebe	D	2007	First	2
U.S. Senators	**Party**	**Year Elected**	**Term Expires**	
Mark Pryor	D	2002	2009	
Blanche Lincoln	D	1998	2011	
U.S. Representatives		**Republican**	**Democrat**	**Other**
		1	3	0

Data: National Governors Association, U.S. Senate, U.S. House of Representatives

Business and Economic Agencies

Agency	Website Address
Arkansas State Chamber of Commerce	www.statechamber-aia.dina.org
Arkansas Department of Economic Development	www.1800arkansas.com
Arkansas Small Business Dev. Center	www.asbdc.ualr.edu
Arkansas Secretary of State	www.sos.arkansas.gov/corp_ucc.html

Data: Various Agency Websites

California

Demographics and Socioeconomics. California, located in the Pacific region of the United States, has a population of 35.3 million people and was the most populous state in 2005. The state's population increased by 1.4 million people from 2000 to 2005, and is projected to increase to 44.3 million by 2025. This 1.2 percent projected annual growth rate is above the national average of 1.0 percent. In 2005 California had a per capita personal income of $36,890, which was $2,395 above the national average and the twelfth highest in the country. The state's per capita income grew at an average annual rate of 2.6 percent from 2000 to 2005, compared to 2.9 percent nationally.

Workforce and Industry. In terms of the education level of the workforce, 80.1 percent of California's adult population has a high school diploma or the equivalent, compared to the national average of 84.2 percent: 29.5 percent of California's adult population has a bachelor degree or higher (national average is 27.2 percent); and 10.6 percent hold professional or graduate degrees

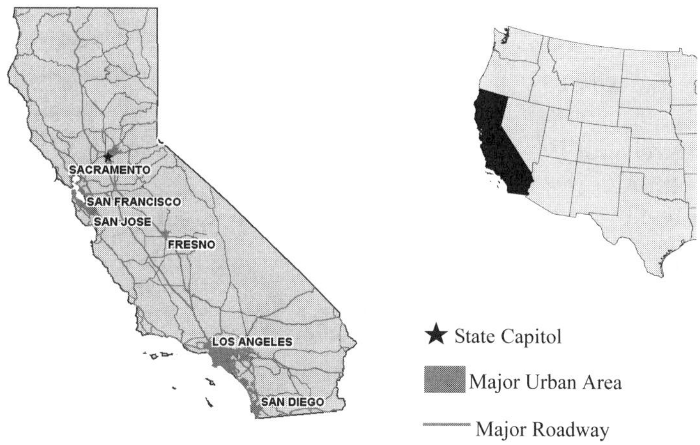

Demographic and Socioeconomic Profile

Demographics and Socioeconomic Figures		
Population and Households	**2000**	**2005**
Total Population	33,871,648	35,278,768
Number of Households	11,502,870	12,097,894
Average Household Size	2.9	2.9
Age and Ethnicity	**2000**	**2005**
Median Age	33.3	34.4
Population 18 Years of Age and Older	24,650,185	25,623,626
Population 65 Years of Age and Older	3,586,794	3,701,104
Caucasian Population	20,122,959	21,491,336
African-American Population	2,219,190	2,163,530
Hispanic Population	10,969,132	12,523,379
Asian Population	3,682,975	4,365,548
Foreign-Born Population	8,864,255	9,611,075
Income	**2000**	**2005**
Per Capita Personal Income (USD)	$32,463	$36,890
Median Household Income (USD)	$47,493	$53,629
Individuals below Poverty Level	14.2%	13.3%

Data: U.S. Census, American Community Survey; U.S. Department of Commerce, Bureau of Economic Analysis

(national average is 10.0 percent). In 2004 the state's largest industry in terms of employment was retail trade, followed by health care and social assistance. The fastest growing industries were construction and professional, scientific, and technical services, both with 34.3 percent growth from 1998 to 2004.

Tax Profile and Business Climate. In fiscal year 2003–4 California had total tax revenues of $134 billion. The largest share was generated from sales and gross receipts taxes, followed by individual taxes. The per capita tax burden in California was $3,736 for 2003–4, some $289 above the national average. In terms of business taxes, California ranked twenty-nineth in a 2006 report by Anderson Economic Group. The state's business climate was ranked thirty-sixth by Forbes Magazine and forty-fifth by the Tax Foundation.

Population Projections

	2010	2015	2020	2025
Total Population	38,067,134	40,123,232	42,206,743	44,305,177
Median Age	34.9	35.2	35.7	36.5
Population 18 Years of Age and Older	28,570,156	30,303,080	31,792,635	33,473,509
Population 65 Years of Age and Older	4,392,708	5,227,964	6,199,126	7,284,978

Data: U.S. Census Bureau

Workforce and Industry Profile

Workforce

	2000	2005
Civilian Labor Force	15,829,202	17,244,650
Labor Force Participation Rate	62.4	64.9
Unemployment Rate	5.0	5.4
Average Earnings per Job (USD)	41,186	42,510
Education Attainment (Population 25 Years and Older)	**(%)**	**(%)**
High School Graduate or Higher	76.8	80.1
Bachelors Degree or Higher	26.6	29.5
Graduate or Professional Degree	9.5	10.6

Data: U.S. Census Bureau, American Community Survey; U.S. Department of Labor, Bureau of Labor Statistics

Industry Overview

	1998	2004
Total Employees	12,026,989	13,264,918
Total Payroll ($1,000)	406,481,070	554,736,012
Total Establishments	773,925	841,774
Establishments with 1–19 Employees	662,920	719,347
Establishments with 20–49 Employees	69,203	76,375
Establishments with 50–249 Employees	36,809	40,554
Establishments with 250–999 Employees	4,372	4,755
Establishments with 1,000+ Employees	621	743

Data: U.S. Census Bureau, County Business Patterns

Major Industries (Ranked by 2004 Employment; Payroll in $1,000s)				
Industry	1998 Employment	2004 Employment	1998 Payroll	2004 Payroll
Retail Trade	1,382,460	1,662,333	29,103,980	41,732,086
Health Care and Social Assistance	1,269,893	1,512,337	39,962,820	59,923,251
Manufacturing	1,827,350	1,476,211	73,353,460	70,372,277
Accommodation and Food Services	1,052,065	1,240,070	13,134,254	18,669,461
Professional, Scientific, Technical Services	923,030	1,239,251	42,291,124	70,228,344
Admin., Support, Waste Mngt., Remediation Services	992,229	981,640	21,527,208	28,448,165
Construction	621,722	834,742	22,673,205	36,014,035
Wholesale Trade	769,617	801,781	32,448,343	44,720,060
Finance and Insurance	599,859	699,086	32,773,849	51,447,628
Other Services (except Public Admin.)	517,331	572,097	10,684,352	14,415,151

Data: U.S. Census Bureau, County Business Patterns

Taxes and Business Climate

State and Local Taxes		
Combined Revenues ($1,000)	2001–2	2003–4
Revenue from Property Taxes	30,242,523	34,499,304
Revenue from Sales and Gross Receipts Taxes	41,559,857	45,193,487
Revenue from Individual Income Taxes	33,046,665	36,398,983
Revenue from Corporate Income Taxes	5,333,036	6,925,916
Revenue from Other Taxes	10,241,985	10,875,934
Total Tax Revenue	120,424,066	133,893,624
Per Capita Taxes		
Property Tax per Capita	893	963
Sales and Gross Receipts Tax per Capita	1,227	1,261
Individual Income Tax per Capita	976	1,016
Corporate Income Tax per Capita	157	193
Other Taxes per Capita	302	303
Total Taxes per Capita	3,555	3,736

Data: U.S. Census Bureau; Anderson Economic Group, LLC

Business Climate Measures	
Anderson Economic Group: 2006 Business Tax Ranking (1 is Best)	29
Forbes Magazine: 2006 Best States for Business Ranking (1 is Best)	36
Tax Foundation: 2007 Business Tax Climate Ranking (1 is Best)	45
2002–3 Employer Firm Births	91,419
2002–3 Employer Firm Terminations	82,346

Data: Anderson Economic Group; Tax Foundation; Forbes Magazine; U.S. Census, Statistics of U.S. Businesses

Voting Behavior and Elected Officials

Voter Registration and Turnout (%)

	1992	1996	2000	2004
Registered Voters Who Voted	73.7	64.0	69.8	75.0
Citizens Age 18+ Who Voted	49.1	43.9	44.5	47.7

Data: Dave Leip's Atlas of U.S. Presidential Elections

Presidential Election Results (Nationwide Winner Listed First)

2004	Popular Vote (%)	Electoral Votes
George W. Bush (Republican, Incumbent)	44.4	0
John Kerry (Democrat)	54.3	55
Other	1.3	0
2000		
George W. Bush (Republican)	41.7	0
Albert Gore (Democrat)	53.5	54
Ralph Nader (Green)	3.8	0
Other	1.1	0
1996		
William Clinton (Democrat, Incumbent)	51.1	54
Robert Dole (Republican)	38.2	0
H. Ross Perot (Reformist)	7.0	0
Other	3.7	0
1992		
William Clinton (Democrat)	46.0	54
George H. W. Bush (Republican, Incumbent)	32.6	0
H. Ross Perot (Independent)	20.6	0
Other	0.8	0

Data: Dave Leip's Atlas of U.S. Presidential Elections

Governor and U.S. Congressional Seats				
Governor	**Party**	**Year Term Began**	**Term**	**Max. Consecutive Terms**
Arnold Schwarzenegger	R	2003	Second	2
U.S. Senators	**Party**	**Year Elected**	**Term Expires**	
Barbara Boxer	D	1992	2011	
Dianne Feinstein	D	1992	2013	
U.S. Representatives		**Republican**	**Democrat**	**Other**
		19	34	0

Data: National Governors Association, U.S. Senate, U.S. House of Representatives

Business and Economic Agencies

Agency	Website Address
California Chamber of Commerce	www.calchamber.com
California Association for Local Economic Development	www.caled.org
California Small Business Dev. Center	sbdc.ucmerced.edu
California Secretary of State	www.ss.ca.gov

Data: Various Agency Websites

Colorado

Demographics and Socioeconomics. With a population of 4.6 people, Colorado was the twenty-second most populous state in 2005. From 2000 to 2005 the state's population increased by 260,983 people, and is projected to increase to 5.5 million by 2025. This 1.0 percent projected annual growth rate is equal to the projected national average. Per capita personal income in Colorado was $37,459 in 2005, ranking eighth highest in the country and $2,964 above the national average. From 2000 to 2005 per capita income in Colorado grew at an average annual rate of 2.3 percent, compared to 2.9 percent nationally.

Workforce and Industry. Colorado's largest industry in terms of 2004 employment was retail trade. The professional, scientific, and technical services industry, which grew by 24.8 percent from 1998 to 2004, had the most growth of major industries during this period. The state's workforce is generally more educated than that of other states: 88.7 percent of the state's adult population has graduated from high school, compared to an 84.2 percent national average; 35.5 percent hold a bachelor degree

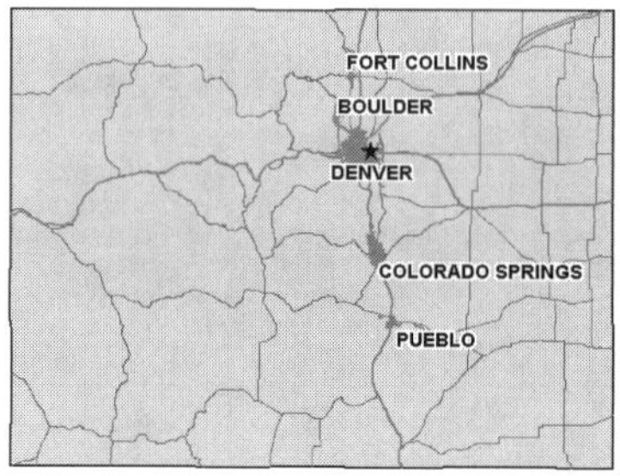

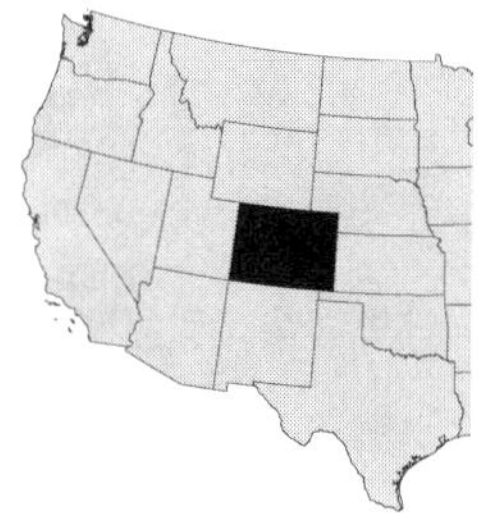

★ State Capitol

Major Urban Area

Major Roadway

Demographic and Socioeconomic Profile

Demographics and Socioeconomic Figures		
Population and Households	**2000**	**2005**
Total Population	4,301,261	4,562,244
Number of Households	1,658,238	1,819,037
Average Household Size	2.5	2.5
Age and Ethnicity		
Median Age	34.3	34.7
Population 18 Years of Age and Older	3,204,471	3,386,081
Population 65 Years of Age and Older	415,782	442,897
Caucasian Population	3,558,579	3,809,054
African-American Population	159,279	165,729
Hispanic Population	735,099	891,614
Asian Population	93,306	117,506
Foreign-Born Population	369,903	460,294
Income		
Per Capita Personal Income (USD)	$33,371	$37,459
Median Household Income (USD)	$47,203	$50,652
Individuals below Poverty Level	9.3%	11.1%

Data: U.S. Census, American Community Survey; U.S. Department of Commerce, Bureau of Economic Analysis

or higher (national average is 27.2 percent); and 12.3 percent hold professional or graduate degrees (national average is 10.0 percent).

Tax Profile and Business Climate. Colorado's total tax revenue was $14.6 billion for fiscal year 2003–4, up from the 2001–2 total revenue of $13.9 billion. The largest share of tax revenue in 2003–4 was generated from sales and gross receipts taxes, followed by property taxes. On a per capita basis, residents of Colorado paid taxes of $3,169, compared to the national average of $3,447 for 2003–4. In terms of business taxes, the state ranked thirteenth in a 2006 report by Anderson Economic Group. Forbes Magazine and the Tax Foundation ranked the state's business climate fifth and fourteenth, respectively.

Population Projections

	2010	2015	2020	2025
Total Population	4,831,554	5,049,493	5,278,867	5,522,803
Median Age	35.7	35.9	36.0	36.0
Population 18 Years of Age and Older	3,642,971	3,793,139	3,951,400	4,128,803
Population 65 Years of Age and Older	517,419	627,408	750,903	869,646

Data: U.S. Census Bureau

Workforce and Industry Profile

Workforce

	2000	2005
Civilian Labor Force	2,304,454	2,487,678
Labor Force Participation Rate	70.1%	71.3%
Unemployment Rate	2.6%	5.0%
Average Earnings per Job (USD)	$37,168	$40,280
Education Attainment (Population 25 Years and Older)	**(%)**	**(%)**
High School Graduate or Higher	86.9	88.7
Bachelors Degree or Higher	32.7	35.5
Graduate or Professional Degree	11.1	12.3

Data: U.S. Census Bureau, American Community Survey; U.S. Department of Labor, Bureau of Labor Statistics

Industry Overview

	1998	2004
Total Employees	1,757,628	1,908,508
Total Payroll ($1,000)	53,790,978	71,579,086
Total Establishments	130,354	147,314
Establishments with 1–19 Employees	114,141	129,662
Establishments with 20–49 Employees	10,144	11,156
Establishments with 50–249 Employees	5,370	5,753
Establishments with 250–999 Employees	602	638
Establishments with 1,000+ Employees	97	105

Data: U.S. Census Bureau, County Business Patterns

Major Industries (Ranked by 2004 Employment; Payroll in $1,000s)				
Industry	1998 Employment	2004 Employment	1998 Payroll	2004 Payroll
Retail Trade	232,581	249,280	4,667,472	6,073,407
Health Care and Social Assistance	180,801	215,712	5,267,467	7,879,482
Accommodation and Food Services	192,632	213,648	2,208,219	2,945,319
Admin., Support, Waste Mngt., Remediation Services	150,768	171,198	3,550,768	5,004,029
Construction	132,921	147,767	4,582,355	6,121,095
Professional, Scientific, Technical Services	117,740	146,891	5,631,574	8,652,745
Manufacturing	173,403	137,726	6,555,826	6,275,219
Finance and Insurance	97,679	103,088	4,292,298	5,972,229
Wholesale Trade	92,992	96,848	3,735,494	5,062,455
Other Services (except Public Admin.)	83,161	94,012	1,666,738	2,222,861

Data: U.S. Census Bureau, County Business Patterns

Taxes and Business Climate

State and Local Taxes		
Combined Revenues ($1,000)	2001–2	2003–4
Revenue from Property Taxes	4,162,161	4,722,286
Revenue from Sales and Gross Receipts Taxes	5,302,034	5,390,069
Revenue from Individual Income Taxes	3,475,760	3,413,891
Revenue from Corporate Income Taxes	205,217	239,591
Revenue from Other Taxes	754,852	815,725
Total Tax Revenue	13,900,024	14,581,562
Per Capita Taxes		
Property Tax per Capita	968	1,026
Sales and Gross Receipts Tax per Capita	1,233	1,171
Individual Income Tax per Capita	808	742
Corporate Income Tax per Capita	48	52
Other Taxes per Capita	176	177
Total Taxes per Capita	3,232	3,169

Data: U.S. Census Bureau; Anderson Economic Group, LLC

Business Climate Measures	
Anderson Economic Group: 2006 Business Tax Ranking (1 is Best)	13
Forbes Magazine: 2006 Best States for Business Ranking (1 is Best)	5
Tax Foundation: 2007 Business Tax Climate Ranking (1 is Best)	14
2002–3 Employer Firm Births	16,693
2002–3 Employer Firm Terminations	14,915

Data: Anderson Economic Group; Tax Foundation; Forbes Magazine; U.S. Census, Statistics of U.S. Businesses

Voting Behavior and Elected Officials

Voter Registration and Turnout (%)

	1992	1996	2000	2004
Registered Voters Who Voted	78.3	66.1	65.9	88.6
Citizens Age 18+ Who Voted	62.7	52.8	54.3	62.7

Data: Dave Leip's Atlas of U.S. Presidential Elections

Presidential Election Results (Nationwide Winner Listed First)

2004	Popular Vote (%)	Electoral Votes
George W. Bush (Republican, Incumbent)	51.7	9
John Kerry (Democrat)	47.0	0
Other	1.3	0
2000		
George W. Bush (Republican)	50.8	8
Albert Gore (Democrat)	42.4	0
Ralph Nader (Green)	5.3	0
Other	1.6	0
1996		
William Clinton (Democrat, Incumbent)	44.4	0
Robert Dole (Republican)	45.8	8
H. Ross Perot (Reformist)	6.6	0
Other	3.2	0
1992		
William Clinton (Democrat)	40.1	8
George H. W. Bush (Republican, Incumbent)	35.9	0
H. Ross Perot (Independent)	23.3	0
Other	0.7	0

Data: Dave Leip's Atlas of U.S. Presidential Elections

Governor and U.S. Congressional Seats				
Governor	**Party**	**Year Term Began**	**Term**	**Max. Consecutive Terms**
Bill Ritter Jr.	D	2007	First	2
U.S. Senators	**Party**	**Year Elected**	**Term Expires**	
Wayne Allard	R	1996	2009	
Ken Salazar	D	2004	2011	
U.S. Representatives		**Republican**	**Democrat**	**Other**
		3	4	0

Data: National Governors Association, U.S. Senate, U.S. House of Representatives

Business and Economic Agencies

Agency	Website Address
Colorado Association of Commerce and Industry	www.cochamber.com
Colorado Office of Economic Development	www.state.co.us/oed
Colorado Small Business Dev. Center	www.coloradosbdc.org
Colorado Secretary of State	www.sos.state.co.us

Data: Various Agency Websites

Connecticut

Demographics and Socioeconomics. Connecticut, located in the New England region of the United States, has a population of 3.4 million people, making it the twenty-second least populous state in 2005. The state's population decreased by 10,814 people from 2000 to 2005, but is projected to increase to 3.7 million by 2025. This 0.4 percent projected annual growth rate is under the projected national average of 1.0 percent. Per capita personal income in Connecticut was $47,519 in 2005, the highest in the country and $13,024 above the national average. From 2000 to 2005 per capita income in Connecticut grew at an average annual rate of 2.8 percent, compared to 2.9 percent nationally.

Workforce and Industry. In 2004 the state's largest industry in terms of employment was health care and social assistance, followed by retail trade. The fastest growing industry was accommodation and food services, with 30 percent growth from 1998 to 2004. The state's workforce is generally more educated than that of other states: 87.9 percent of the state's adult population has graduated

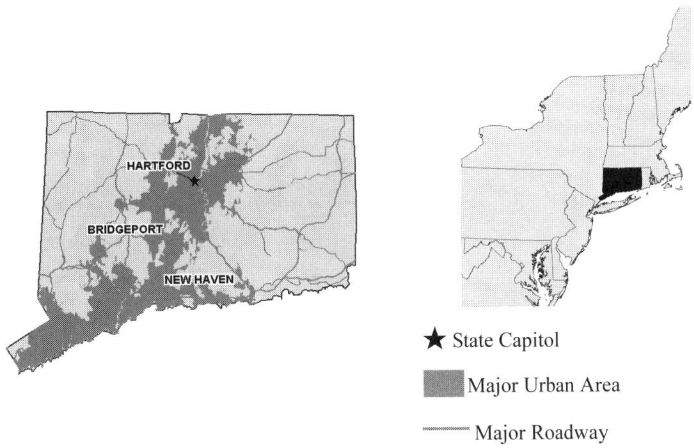

Demographic and Socioeconomic Profile

Demographics and Socioeconomic Figures		
Population and Households	**2000**	**2005**
Total Population	3,405,565	3,394,751
Number of Households	1,301,670	1,323,838
Average Household Size	2.5	2.6
Age and Ethnicity		
Median Age	37.4	39.3
Population 18 Years of Age and Older	2,565,991	2,563,861
Population 65 Years of Age and Older	469,287	442,579
Caucasian Population	2,777,794	2,756,081
African-American Population	305,902	309,769
Hispanic Population	318,947	371,425
Asian Population	82,277	108,644
Foreign-Born Population	369,967	423,254
Income		
Per Capita Personal Income (USD)	$41,489	$47,519
Median Household Income (USD)	$53,935	$60,941
Individuals below Poverty Level	7.9%	8.3%

Data: U.S. Census, American Community Survey; U.S. Department of Commerce, Bureau of Economic Analysis

from high school, compared to an 84.2 percent national average; 34.9 percent hold a bachelor degree or higher (national average is 27.2 percent); and 15.0 percent hold professional or graduate degrees (national average is 10.0 percent).

Tax Profile and Business Climate. In fiscal year 2003–4 Connecticut had total tax revenues of $17.2 billion. The largest share was generated from property taxes. The per capita tax burden in Connecticut was $4,921 for 2003–4, some $1,475 above the national average. In terms of business taxes, the state ranked sixth in a 2006 report by Anderson Economic Group. Forbes Magazine and the Tax Foundation ranked the state's business climate twenty-eighth and thirty-seventh, respectively.

Population Projections

	2010	2015	2020	2025
Total Population	3,577,490	3,635,414	3,675,650	3,691,016
Median Age	39.6	39.6	39.7	40.3
Population 18 Years of Age and Older	2,763,482	2,828,539	2,859,305	2,864,095
Population 65 Years of Age and Older	515,621	577,083	642,541	723,326

Data: U.S. Census Bureau

Workforce and Industry Profile

Workforce

	2000	2005
Civilian Labor Force	1,757,108	1,818,389
Labor Force Participation Rate	66.6%	68.5%
Unemployment Rate	2.4%	4.9%
Average Earnings per Job (USD)	$45,486	$44,860
Education Attainment (Population 25 Years and Older)		
High School Graduate or Higher	84.0%	87.9%
Bachelors Degree or Higher	31.4%	34.9%
Graduate or Professional Degree	13.3%	15.0%

Data: U.S. Census Bureau, American Community Survey; U.S. Department of Labor, Bureau of Labor Statistics

Industry Overview

	1998	2004
Total Employees	1,493,964	1,537,461
Total Payroll ($1,000)	$58,225,763	$72,848,717
Total Establishments	92,362	93,011
Establishments with 1–19 Employees	79,965	79,887
Establishments with 20–49 Employees	7,451	8,035
Establishments with 50–249 Employees	4,315	4,492
Establishments with 250–999 Employees	538	498
Establishments with 1,000+ Employees	93	99

Data: U.S. Census Bureau, County Business Patterns

Major Industries (Ranked by 2004 Employment; Payroll in $1,000s)				
Industry	1998 Employment	2004 Employment	1998 Payroll	2004 Payroll
Health Care and Social Assistance	211,359	237,579	6,617,997	8,967,008
Retail Trade	189,957	197,028	3,989,688	5,024,940
Manufacturing	246,125	188,418	10,779,212	9,578,888
Finance and Insurance	122,463	137,330	9,087,074	14,967,480
Accommodation and Food Services	95,866	124,603	1,208,849	2,284,618
Admin., Support, Waste Mngt., Remediation Services	98,890	105,249	2,434,799	3,073,454
Professional, Scientific, Technical Services	78,060	98,504	4,410,149	6,454,012
Wholesale Trade	73,082	78,892	3,804,026	4,783,036
Construction	60,041	66,752	2,531,796	3,315,374
Other Services (except Public Admin.)	61,578	63,306	1,356,837	1,601,670

Data: U.S. Census Bureau, County Business Patterns

Taxes and Business Climate

State and Local Taxes		
Combined Revenues ($1,000)	2001–2	2003–4
Revenue from Property Taxes	5,995,482	6,801,676
Revenue from Sales and Gross Receipts Taxes	4,516,194	4,900,376
Revenue from Individual Income Taxes	3,685,244	4,319,546
Revenue from Corporate Income Taxes	149,454	379,822
Revenue from Other Taxes	778,554	818,694
Total Tax Revenue	15,124,928	17,220,114
Per Capita Taxes		
Property Tax per Capita	1,760	1,944
Sales and Gross Receipts Tax per Capita	1,326	1,401
Individual Income Tax per Capita	1,082	1,235
Corporate Income Tax per Capita	44	109
Other Taxes per Capita	229	234
Total Taxes per Capita	4,441	4,921

Data: U.S. Census Bureau; Anderson Economic Group, LLC

Business Climate Measures	
Anderson Economic Group: 2006 Business Tax Ranking (1 is Best)	6
Forbes Magazine: 2006 Best States for Business Ranking (1 is Best)	28
Tax Foundation: 2007 Business Tax Climate Ranking (1 is Best)	37
2002–3 Employer Firm Births	7,400
2002–3 Employer Firm Terminations	7,977

Data: Anderson Economic Group; Tax Foundation; Forbes Magazine; U.S. Census, Statistics of U.S. Businesses

Voting Behavior and Elected Officials

Voter Registration and Turnout (%)

	1992	1996	2000	2004
Registered Voters Who Voted	82.4	74.0	76.8	77.2
Citizens Age 18+ Who Voted	63.8	56.2	56.9	59.6

Data: Dave Leip's Atlas of U.S. Presidential Elections

Presidential Election Results (Nationwide Winner Listed First)

2004	Popular Vote (%)	Electoral Votes
George W. Bush (Republican, Incumbent)	44.0	0
John Kerry (Democrat)	54.3	7
Other	1.7	0
2000		
George W. Bush (Republican)	38.4	0
Albert Gore (Democrat)	55.9	8
Ralph Nader (Green)	4.4	0
Other	1.2	0
1996		
William Clinton (Democrat, Incumbent)	52.8	8
Robert Dole (Republican)	34.7	0
H. Ross Perot (Reformist)	10.0	0
Other	2.5	0
1992		
William Clinton (Democrat)	42.2	8
George H. W. Bush (Republican, Incumbent)	35.8	0
H. Ross Perot (Independent)	21.6	0
Other	0.4	0

Data: Dave Leip's Atlas of U.S. Presidential Elections

Governor and U.S. Congressional Seats				
Governor	**Party**	**Year Term Began**	**Term**	**Max. Consecutive Terms**
M. Jodi Rell	R	2004	Second	No limit
U.S. Senators	**Party**	**Year Elected**	**Term Expires**	
Christopher Dodd	D	1980	2011	
Joseph Lieberman	D	1988	2013	
U.S. Representatives		**Republican**	**Democrat**	**Other**
		1	4	0

Data: National Governors Association, U.S. Senate, U.S. House of Representatives

Business and Economic Agencies

Agency	Website Address
Connecticut Business and Industry Association, Inc.	www.cbia.com
Department of Economic and Community Development	www.ct.gov/ecd
Connecticut Small Business Dev. Center	www.sbdc.uconn.edu
Connecticut Secretary of State, Commercial Recording Division	www.sots.ct.gov/CommercialRecording/Crdindex.html

Data: Various Agency Websites

Delaware

Demographics and Socioeconomics. Delaware, located in the New England region of the United States, has a population of 818,587 people, making it the sixth least populous state in 2005. The state's population increased by 34,987 people from 2000 to 2005, and is projected to increase to 990,694 by 2025. This 1.0 percent projected annual growth rate is equal to the projected national average. The state's 2005 per capita personal income of $37,084 was the eleventh highest in the United States and $2,589 above the national average. Per capita income in Delaware grew at an average annual rate of 3.7 percent from 2000 to 2005, compared to 2.9 percent nationally.

Workforce and Industry. In 2004 the state's largest industry in terms of employment was retail trade, followed by health care and social assistance. Of the state's major industries, professional, scientific, and technical services grew the most (55.5 percent) from 1998 to 2004. The state's workforce is generally more educated than that of other states: 85.6 percent of the state's adult population has graduated from

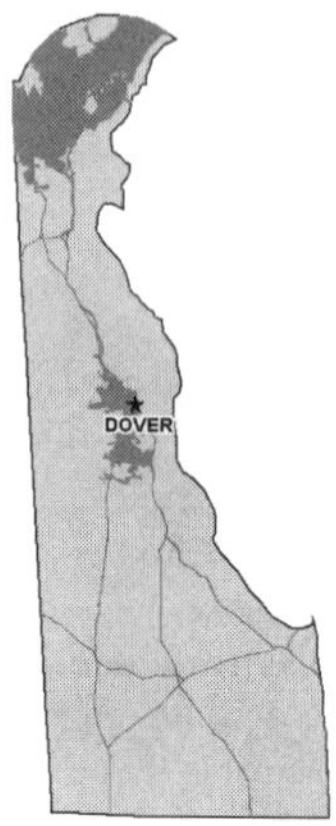

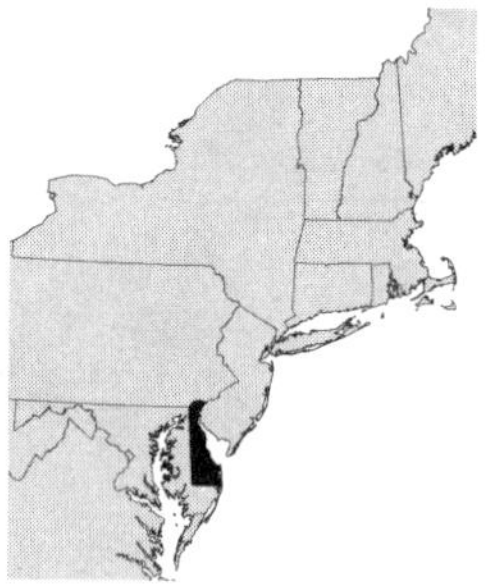

★ State Capitol

Major Urban Area

Major Roadway

Demographic and Socioeconomic Profile

Demographics and Socioeconomic Figures		
Population and Households	**2000**	**2005**
Total Population	783,600	818,587
Number of Households	298,736	317,640
Average Household Size	2.5	2.6
Age and Ethnicity		
Median Age	36.0	37.9
Population 18 Years of Age and Older	589,638	623,124
Population 65 Years of Age and Older	101,670	106,791
Caucasian Population	584,684	602,213
African-American Population	148,823	163,052
Hispanic Population	37,321	50,218
Asian Population	16,053	22,376
Foreign-Born Population	44,898	62,867
Income		
Per Capita Personal Income (USD)	$30,869	$37,084
Median Household Income (USD)	$47,381	$52,499
Individuals below Poverty Level	9.2%	10.4%

Data: U.S. Census, American Community Survey; U.S. Department of Commerce, Bureau of Economic Analysis

high school, compared to an 84.2 percent national average; 27.6 percent hold a bachelor degree or higher (national average is 27.2 percent); and 11.1 percent hold professional or graduate degrees (national average is 10.0 percent).

Tax Profile and Business Climate. In fiscal year 2003–4 Delaware had total tax revenues of $3.0 billion. The largest share was generated from other taxes, followed by individual income taxes. The per capita tax burden in Delaware was $3,608 for 2003–4, some $161 above the national average. In terms of business taxes, Delaware was ranked first in a 2006 report by Anderson Economic Group. Forbes Magazine and the Tax Foundation ranked the state's business climate eighth and nineth, respectively.

Population Projections

	2010	2015	2020	2025
Total Population	884,342	927,400	963,209	990,694
Median Age	39.4	40.5	41.5	42.8
Population 18 Years of Age and Older	682,134	717,862	747,886	772,682
Population 65 Years of Age and Older	124,972	148,682	176,121	208,599

Data: U.S. Census Bureau

Workforce and Industry Profile

Workforce

	2000	2005
Civilian Labor Force	397,360	429,173
Labor Force Participation Rate	65.7%	67.0%
Unemployment Rate	3.3%	4.2%
Average Earnings per Job (USD)	$36,533	$39,190
Education Attainment (Population 25 Years and Older)	**(%)**	**(%)**
High School Graduate or Higher	82.6	85.6
Bachelors Degree or Higher	25.0	27.6
Graduate or Professional Degree	9.4	11.1

Data: U.S. Census Bureau, American Community Survey; U.S. Department of Labor, Bureau of Labor Statistics

Industry Overview

	1998	2004
Total Employees	354,643	391,682
Total Payroll ($1,000)	11,831,134	16,074,764
Total Establishments	22,871	25,391
Establishments with 1–19 Employees	19,941	22,040
Establishments with 20–49 Employees	1,777	2,078
Establishments with 50–249 Employees	985	1,103
Establishments with 250–999 Employees	146	136
Establishments with 1,000+ Employees	22	34

Data: U.S. Census Bureau, County Business Patterns

Major Industries (Ranked by 2004 Employment; Payroll in $1,000s)				
Industry	1998 Employment	2004 Employment	1998 Payroll	2004 Payroll
Retail Trade	47,631	54,748	871,384	1,250,483
Health Care and Social Assistance	41,202	50,355	1,279,822	1,944,029
Finance and Insurance	41,611	40,454	1,909,720	2,629,280
Manufacturing	43,511	35,936	1,632,155	1,644,583
Accommodation and Food Services	25,867	28,794	313,948	420,073
Professional, Scientific, Technical Services	17,043	26,500	824,062	1,814,580
Admin., Support, Waste Mngt., Remediation Services	26,117	26,200	488,195	631,221
Construction	20,367	23,798	676,309	950,101
Mngt. of Companies and Enterprises	20,243	21,633	1,288,596	1,390,991
Wholesale Trade	14,839	20,051	789,212	1,317,847

Data: U.S. Census Bureau, County Business Patterns

Taxes and Business Climate

State and Local Taxes		
Combined Revenues ($1,000)	**2001–2**	**2003–4**
Revenue from Property Taxes	399,939	453,198
Revenue from Sales and Gross Receipts Taxes	326,198	394,434
Revenue from Individual Income Taxes	763,410	827,984
Revenue from Corporate Income Taxes	251,643	217,768
Revenue from Other Taxes	945,908	1,100,944
Total Tax Revenue	2,687,098	2,994,328
Per Capita Taxes		
Property Tax per Capita	510	546
Sales and Gross Receipts Tax per Capita	416	475
Individual Income Tax per Capita	974	998
Corporate Income Tax per Capita	321	262
Other Taxes per Capita	1,207	1,326
Total Taxes per Capita	3,427	3,608

Data: U.S. Census Bureau; Anderson Economic Group, LLC

Business Climate Measures	
Anderson Economic Group: 2006 Business Tax Ranking (1 is Best)	1
Forbes Magazine: 2006 Best States for Business Ranking (1 is Best)	8
Tax Foundation: 2007 Business Tax Climate Ranking (1 is Best)	9
2002–3 Employer Firm Births	2,535
2002–3 Employer Firm Terminations	2,158

Data: Anderson Economic Group; Tax Foundation; Forbes Magazine; U.S. Census, Statistics of U.S. Businesses

Voting Behavior and Elected Officials

Voter Registration and Turnout (%)	1992	1996	2000	2004
Registered Voters Who Voted	84.7	64.2	65.1	67.7
Citizens Age 18+ Who Voted	55.2	49.4	55.6	60.6

Data: Dave Leip's Atlas of U.S. Presidential Elections

Presidential Election Results (Nationwide Winner Listed First)		
2004	**Popular Vote (%)**	**Electoral Votes**
George W. Bush (Republican, Incumbent)	45.8	0
John Kerry (Democrat)	53.4	3
Other	0.9	0
2000		
George W. Bush (Republican)	41.9	0
Albert Gore (Democrat)	55.0	3
Ralph Nader (Green)	2.5	0
Other	0.6	0
1996		
William Clinton (Democrat, Incumbent)	51.8	3
Robert Dole (Republican)	36.6	0
H. Ross Perot (Reformist)	10.6	0
Other	1.0	0
1992		
William Clinton (Democrat)	43.5	3
George H. W. Bush (Republican, Incumbent)	35.3	0
H. Ross Perot (Independent)	20.4	0
Other	0.7	0

Data: Dave Leip's Atlas of U.S. Presidential Elections

Governor and U.S. Congressional Seats				
Governor	**Party**	**Year Term Began**	**Term**	**Max. Consecutive Terms**
Ruth Ann Minner	D	2001	Second	2
U.S. Senators	**Party**	**Year Elected**	**Term Expires**	
Joseph R. Biden Jr.	D	1972	2009	
Thomas Carper	D	2000	2013	
U.S. Representatives		**Republican**	**Democrat**	**Other**
		1	0	0

Data: National Governors Association, U.S. Senate, U.S. House of Representatives

Business and Economic Agencies

Agency	Website Address
Delaware State Chamber of Commerce	www.dscc.com
Delaware Economic Development Office	www.state.de.us/dedo/default.shtml
Delaware Small Business Dev. Center	www.delawaresbdc.org
Delaware Division of Corporations	www.state.de.us/corp

Data: Various Agency Websites

Florida

Demographics and Socioeconomics. With a population of 17.4 million people, Florida was the fourth most populous state in the United States in 2005. From 2000 to 2005 the state's population increased by 1.4 million people, and is projected to increase to 25.9 million by 2025. This 2.0 percent projected annual growth rate is double the projected national average. In 2005 Florida had a per capita personal income of $34,099, which was $396 below the national average and the twentieth highest in the country. The state's per capita income grew at an average annual rate of 3.6 percent from 2000 to 2005, compared to 2.9 percent nationally.

Workforce and Industry. In 2004 Florida's largest industry in terms of employment was administrative and support and waste management and remediation services. This was also their fastest growing industry, with 63.9 percent growth from 1998 to 2004. In terms of the education level of the workforce, 84.6 percent of Florida's adult population has a high school diploma or the equivalent, compared to the national average of

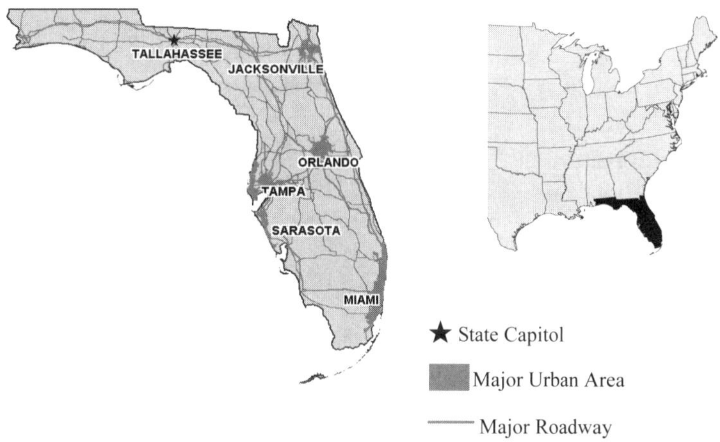

Demographic and Socioeconomic Profile

Demographics and Socioeconomic Figures		
Population and Households	**2000**	**2005**
Total Population	15,982,378	17,382,511
Number of Households	6,337,929	7,048,800
Average Household Size	2.5	2.5
Age and Ethnicity		
Median Age	38.7	39.5
Population 18 Years of Age and Older	12,347,806	13,335,661
Population 65 Years of Age and Older	2,806,137	2,881,213
Caucasian Population	12,463,302	13,341,532
African-American Population	2,312,105	2,613,628
Hispanic Population	2,680,314	3,414,414
Asian Population	264,377	371,385
Foreign-Born Population	2,670,828	3,212,955
Income		
Per Capita Personal Income (USD)	$28,509	$34,099
Median Household Income (USD)	$38,819	$42,433
Individuals below Poverty Level	12.5%	12.8%

Data: U.S. Census, American Community Survey; U.S. Department of Commerce, Bureau of Economic Analysis

84.2 percent; 25.1 percent of Florida's adult population has a bachelor degree or higher (national average is 27.2 percent); and 8.8 percent hold professional or graduate degrees (national average is 10.0 percent).

Tax Profile and Business Climate. Florida's total tax revenue was $53.8 billion for fiscal year 2003–4. The largest share of tax revenue in 2003–4 was generated from sales and gross receipts taxes, followed by property taxes. The state does not have an individual income tax. In terms of business taxes, the state ranked thirty-eighth in a 2006 report by Anderson Economic Group. Forbes Magazine and the Tax Foundation ranked the state's business climate nineth and fifth, respectively.

Population Projections

	2010	2015	2020	2025
Total Population	19,251,691	21,204,132	23,406,525	25,912,458
Median Age	41.9	43.2	44.1	44.8
Population 18 Years of Age and Older	15,165,568	16,749,420	18,518,914	20,611,286
Population 65 Years of Age and Older	3,418,697	4,133,945	5,106,857	6,387,843

Data: U.S. Census Bureau

Workforce and Industry Profile

Workforce

	2000	2005
Civilian Labor Force	7,407,458	8,426,125
Labor Force Participation Rate	58.6%	61.4%
Unemployment Rate	3.8%	3.8%
Average Earnings per Job (USD)	$30,560	$34,420
Education Attainment (Population 25 Years and Older)	**(%)**	**(%)**
High School Graduate or Higher	79.9	84.6
Bachelors Degree or Higher	22.3	25.1
Graduate or Professional Degree	8.1	8.8

Data: U.S. Census Bureau, American Community Survey; U.S. Department of Labor, Bureau of Labor Statistics

Industry Overview

	1998	2004
Total Employees	5,756,353	6,864,987
Total Payroll ($1,000)	149,936,849	219,794,114
Total Establishments	420,638	484,938
Establishments with 1–19 Employees	371,384	429,069
Establishments with 20–49 Employees	29,930	33,891
Establishments with 50–249 Employees	17,086	19,351
Establishments with 250–999 Employees	1,890	2,242
Establishments with 1,000+ Employees	348	385

Data: U.S. Census Bureau, County Business Patterns

Major Industries (Ranked by 2004 Employment; Payroll in $1,000s)				
Industry	**1998 Employment**	**2004 Employment**	**1998 Payroll**	**2004 Payroll**
Admin., Support, Waste Mngt., Remediation Services	705,898	1,157,253	13,287,683	30,801,536
Retail Trade	872,391	960,282	15,636,653	21,259,324
Health Care and Social Assistance	740,828	857,299	21,829,102	31,327,156
Accommodation and Food Services	596,481	699,500	6,994,893	9,565,922
Construction	341,673	437,383	9,674,731	15,410,686
Professional, Scientific, Technical Services	318,814	414,127	13,047,144	20,068,990
Finance and Insurance	302,704	372,380	12,522,788	19,079,507
Manufacturing	428,642	371,713	13,514,960	14,635,459
Other Services (except Public Admin.)	288,705	309,894	5,192,259	6,392,631
Wholesale Trade	298,551	307,833	10,388,706	13,028,463

Data: U.S. Census Bureau, County Business Patterns

Taxes and Business Climate

State and Local Taxes		
Combined Revenues ($1,000)	**2001–2**	**2003–4**
Revenue from Property Taxes	15,799,202	18,500,291
Revenue from Sales and Gross Receipts Taxes	22,936,417	27,407,756
Revenue from Individual Income Taxes	0	0
Revenue from Corporate Income Taxes	1,218,864	1,441,338
Revenue from Other Taxes	4,930,954	6,440,069
Total Tax Revenue	44,885,437	53,789,454
Per Capita Taxes		
Property Tax per Capita	989	1,064
Sales and Gross Receipts Tax per Capita	1,435	1,577
Individual Income Tax per Capita	0	0
Corporate Income Tax per Capita	76	83
Other Taxes per Capita	309	370
Total Taxes per Capita	2,808	3,094

Data: U.S. Census Bureau; Anderson Economic Group, LLC

Business Climate Measures	
Anderson Economic Group: 2006 Business Tax Ranking (1 is Best)	38
Forbes Magazine: 2006 Best States for Business Ranking (1 is Best)	9
Tax Foundation: 2007 Business Tax Climate Ranking (1 is Best)	5
2002–3 Employer Firm Births	58,956
2002–3 Employer Firm Terminations	48,340

Data: Anderson Economic Group; Tax Foundation; Forbes Magazine; U.S. Census, Statistics of U.S. Businesses

Voting Behavior and Elected Officials

Voter Registration and Turnout (%)

	1992	1996	2000	2004
Registered Voters Who Voted	81.2	65.7	68.1	73.9
Citizens Age 18+ Who Voted	50.2	48.0	48.3	58.1

Data: Dave Leip's Atlas of U.S. Presidential Elections

Presidential Election Results (Nationwide Winner Listed First)

2004	Popular Vote (%)	Electoral Votes
George W. Bush (Republican, Incumbent)	52.1	27
John Kerry (Democrat)	47.1	0
Other	0.8	0
2000		
George W. Bush (Republican)	48.9	25
Albert Gore (Democrat)	48.8	0
Ralph Nader (Green)	1.6	0
Other	0.7	0
1996		
William Clinton (Democrat, Incumbent)	48.0	25
Robert Dole (Republican)	42.3	0
H. Ross Perot (Reformist)	9.1	0
Other	0.5	0
1992		
William Clinton (Democrat)	39.0	0
George H. W. Bush (Republican, Incumbent)	40.9	25
H. Ross Perot (Independent)	19.8	0
Other	0.3	0

Data: Dave Leip's Atlas of U.S. Presidential Elections

Governor and U.S. Congressional Seats				
Governor	**Party**	**Year Term Began**	**Term**	**Max. Consecutive Terms**
Charlie Crist	R	2007	First	2
U.S. Senators	**Party**	**Year Elected**	**Term Expires**	
Mel Martinez	R	2004	2011	
Bill Nelson	D	2000	2013	
U.S. Representatives		**Republican**	**Democrat**	**Other**
		16	9	0

Data: National Governors Association, U.S. Senate, U.S. House of Representatives

Business and Economic Agencies

Agency	Website Address
Florida Chamber of Commerce	www.flchamber.com
Governor's Office of Trade, Tourism, and Economic Development	www.flgov.com/otted_home
Florida Small Business Dev. Center	www.floridasbdc.com
Florida Department of State, Division of Corporations	www.sunbiz.org

Data: Various Agency Websites

Georgia

Demographics and Socio-economics. Georgia is located in the South Atlantic region of the United States and has a population of 8.8 million people, making it the nineth most populous state in 2005. The state's population increased by 634,689 people from 2000 to 2005, and is projected to increase to 11.4 million by 2025. This 1.3 percent projected annual growth rate is above the national average of 1.0 percent. Per capita personal income in Georgia was $31,191 in 2005, ranking eighteenth lowest in the country and $3,304 below the national average. Per capita income in Georgia grew at an average annual rate of 2.2 percent from 2000 to 2005, compared to 2.9 percent nationally.

Workforce and Industry. The state's workforce is generally less educated than that of other states: 82.8 percent of the state's adult population has graduated from high school, compared to an 84.2 percent national average; 27.1 percent hold a bachelor degree or higher (national average is 27.2 percent); and 9.5 percent hold professional or graduate degrees (national average is 10.0). In 2004 the state's largest industry in

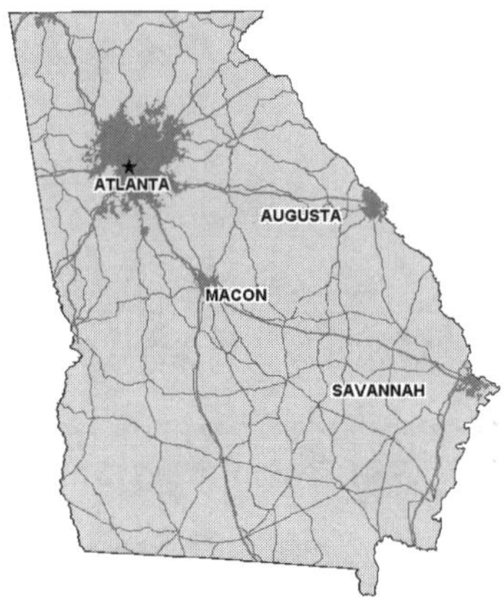

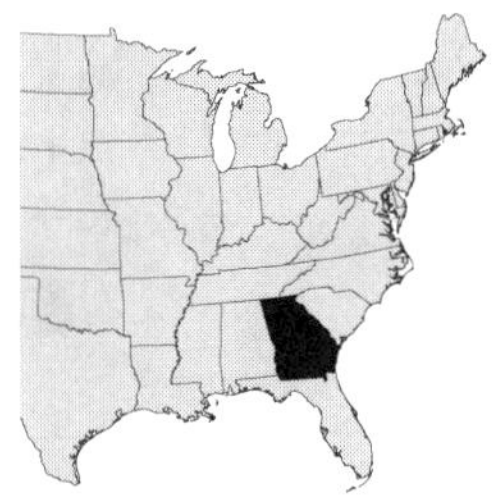

★ State Capitol

Major Urban Area

Major Roadway

Demographic and Socioeconomic Profile

Demographics and Socioeconomic Figures		
Population and Households	**2000**	**2005**
Total Population	8,186,453	8,821,142
Number of Households	3,006,369	3,320,278
Average Household Size	2.6	2.7
Age and Ethnicity		
Median Age	33.4	34.3
Population 18 Years of Age and Older	6,020,679	6,468,467
Population 65 Years of Age and Older	787,906	811,503
Caucasian Population	5,327,175	5,516,920
African-American Population	2,342,110	2,571,396
Hispanic Population	429,976	625,028
Asian Population	171,463	240,832
Foreign-Born Population	577,273	795,419
Income		
Per Capita Personal Income (USD)	$27,989	$31,191
Median Household Income (USD)	$42,433	$45,604
Individuals below Poverty Level	13.0%	14.4%

Data: U.S. Census, American Community Survey; U.S. Department of Commerce, Bureau of Economic Analysis

terms of employment was retail trade, followed by manufacturing. Transportation and warehousing, which ranked eleventh in terms of 2004 employment, grew the most (27.8 percent) from 1998 to 2004.

Tax Profile and Business Climate. In fiscal year 2003–4 Georgia had total tax revenues of $25.6 billion. The largest share was generated from sales and gross receipts taxes, followed by property taxes. The per capita tax burden in Georgia was $2,877 for 2003–4, some $570 below the national average. In terms of business taxes, Georgia ranked twelfth in a 2006 report by Anderson Economic Group. The state's business climate was ranked tenth by Forbes Magazine and nineteenth by the Tax Foundation.

Population Projections

	2010	2015	2020	2025
Total Population	9,589,080	10,230,578	10,843,753	11,438,622
Median Age	34.7	35.1	35.4	35.5
Population 18 Years of Age and Older	7,086,694	7,551,789	8,006,490	8,453,077
Population 65 Years of Age and Older	980,824	1,187,576	1,409,923	1,659,679

Data: U.S. Census Bureau

Workforce and Industry Profile

Workforce

	2000	2005
Civilian Labor Force	4,062,808	4,518,717
Labor Force Participation Rate	66.1%	67.7%
Unemployment Rate	3.5%	5.3%
Average Earnings per Job (USD)	$34,214	$36,290
Education Attainment (Population 25 Years and Older)	**(%)**	**(%)**
High School Graduate or Higher	78.6	82.8
Bachelors Degree or Higher	24.3	27.1
Graduate or Professional Degree	8.3	9.5

Data: U.S. Census Bureau, American Community Survey; U.S. Department of Labor, Bureau of Labor Statistics

Industry Overview

	1998	2004
Total Employees	3,198,950	3,452,451
Total Payroll ($1,000)	94,687,270	121,341,653
Total Establishments	194,213	214,714
Establishments with 1–19 Employees	166,186	183,593
Establishments with 20–49 Employees	17,122	19,120
Establishments with 50–249 Employees	9,306	10,399
Establishments with 250–999 Employees	1,403	1,395
Establishments with 1,000+ Employees	196	207

Data: U.S. Census Bureau, County Business Patterns

Major Industries (Ranked by 2004 Employment; Payroll in $1,000s)				
Industry	1998 Employment	2004 Employment	1998 Payroll	2004 Payroll
Retail Trade	431,806	474,034	7,798,334	9,777,623
Manufacturing	535,051	432,512	16,722,306	15,894,086
Health Care and Social Assistance	331,889	401,707	9,810,907	14,334,688
Accommodation and Food Services	273,389	329,704	3,035,725	4,126,423
Admin., Support, Waste Mngt., Remediation Services	261,555	298,726	5,596,097	7,939,574
Professional, Scientific, Technical Services	166,535	200,213	7,679,090	10,873,282
Wholesale Trade	193,112	199,327	8,167,514	9,775,655
Construction	174,774	198,234	5,527,052	7,293,307
Finance and Insurance	154,798	175,183	6,662,088	9,876,761
Other Services (except Public Admin.)	135,530	153,123	2,539,172	3,256,915

Data: U.S. Census Bureau, County Business Patterns

Taxes and Business Climate

State and Local Taxes		
Combined Revenues ($1,000)	2001–2	2003–4
Revenue from Property Taxes	6,640,041	7,844,826
Revenue from Sales and Gross Receipts Taxes	9,395,052	9,422,758
Revenue from Individual Income Taxes	6,487,638	6,830,486
Revenue from Corporate Income Taxes	568,080	494,701
Revenue from Other Taxes	967,569	1,061,989
Total Tax Revenue	24,058,380	25,654,760
Per Capita Taxes		
Property Tax per Capita	811	880
Sales and Gross Receipts Tax per Capita	1,148	1,057
Individual Income Tax per Capita	793	766
Corporate Income Tax per Capita	69	55
Other Taxes per Capita	118	119
Total Taxes per Capita	2,939	2,877

Data: U.S. Census Bureau; Anderson Economic Group, LLC

Business Climate Measures

Anderson Economic Group: 2006 Business Tax Ranking (1 is Best)	12
Forbes Magazine: 2006 Best States for Business Ranking (1 is Best)	10
Tax Foundation: 2007 Business Tax Climate Ranking (1 is Best)	19
2002–3 Employer Firm Births	23,958
2002–3 Employer Firm Terminations	20,975

Data: Anderson Economic Group; Tax Foundation; Forbes Magazine; U.S. Census, Statistics of U.S. Businesses

Voting Behavior and Elected Officials

Voter Registration and Turnout (%)

	1992	1996	2000	2004
Registered Voters Who Voted	73.1	60.3	67.3	79.4
Citizens Age 18+ Who Voted	46.9	42.4	43.1	51.7

Data: Dave Leip's Atlas of U.S. Presidential Elections

Presidential Election Results (Nationwide Winner Listed First)

2004	Popular Vote (%)	Electoral Votes
George W. Bush (Republican, Incumbent)	58.0	15
John Kerry (Democrat)	41.4	0
Other	0.7	0
2000		
George W. Bush (Republican)	54.7	13
Albert Gore (Democrat)	43.0	0
Ralph Nader (Green)	0.5	0
Other	1.8	0
1996		
William Clinton (Democrat, Incumbent)	45.8	0
Robert Dole (Republican)	47.0	13
H. Ross Perot (Reformist)	6.4	0
Other	0.8	0
1992		
William Clinton (Democrat)	43.5	13
George H. W. Bush (Republican, Incumbent)	42.9	0
H. Ross Perot (Independent)	13.3	0
Other	0.3	0

Data: Dave Leip's Atlas of U.S. Presidential Elections

Governor and U.S. Congressional Seats				
Governor	**Party**	**Year Term Began**	**Term**	**Max. Consecutive Terms**
Sonny Perdue	R	2003	Second	2
U.S. Senators	**Party**	**Year Elected**	**Term Expires**	
Saxby Chambliss	R	2002	2009	
Johnny Isakson	R	2005	2011	
U.S. Representatives		**Republican**	**Democrat**	**Other**
		7	6	0

Data: National Governors Association, U.S. Senate, U.S. House of Representatives

Business and Economic Agencies

Agency	Website Address
Georgia Chamber of Commerce	www.gachamber.com
Georgia Department of Economic Development	www.georgia.org
Georgia Small Business Dev. Center	www.sbdc.uga.edu
Georgia Secretary of State, Corporations Division	www.sos.state.ga.us/corporations

Data: Various Agency Websites

Hawaii

Demographics and Socioeconomics. Hawaii is located in the Pacific Southwest and is one of only two states that is not a part of the continental United States. Hawaii has a population of 1.2 million people, making it the nineth least populous state in 2005. The state's population increased by 26,621 people from 2000 to 2005, and is projected to increase to 1.4 million by 2025. This 0.8 percent projected annual growth rate is slightly below the national average of 1.0 percent. Per capita personal income in Hawaii was $34,468 in 2005, ranking nineteenth highest in the country. This compares to the national average of $34,495. From 2000 to 2005 per capita income in Hawaii grew at an average annual rate of 3.9 percent, compared to 2.9 percent nationally.

Workforce and Industry. The state's workforce is generally more educated than that of other states: 88.1 percent of the state's adult population has graduated from high school, compared to an 84.2 percent national average; 27.9 percent hold a bachelor degree or higher (national average is 27.2 percent); and 9.1 percent hold professional

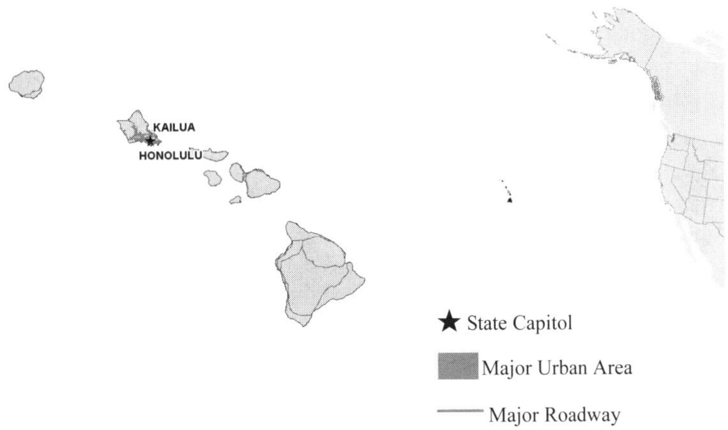

Demographic and Socioeconomic Profile

Demographics and Socioeconomic Figures		
Population and Households	**2000**	**2005**
Total Population	1,211,537	1,238,158
Number of Households	403,240	430,007
Average Household Size	2.9	2.9
Age and Ethnicity		
Median Age	36.2	38.5
Population 18 Years of Age and Older	917,212	939,587
Population 65 Years of Age and Older	161,141	168,895
Caucasian Population	292,457	308,912
African-American Population	20,945	24,239
Hispanic Population	87,582	98,699
Asian Population	503,950	520,564
Foreign-Born Population	212,229	212,404
Income		
Per Capita Personal Income (USD)	$28,422	$34,468
Median Household Income (USD)	$49,820	$58,112
Individuals below Poverty Level	10.7%	9.8%

Data: U.S. Census, American Community Survey; U.S. Department of Commerce, Bureau of Economic Analysis

or graduate degrees (national average is 10.0). In 2004 the state's largest industry in terms of employment was accommodation and food services, followed by retail trade. The fastest growing industry, with 38.6 percent growth from 1998 to 2004, was educational services, which also ranked eleventh in terms of 2004 employment. The state's professional, scientific, and technical services industry saw a similar growth rate of 38.5 percent over the 1998 to 2004 period.

Tax Profile and Business Climate. In fiscal year 2003–4 Hawaii had total tax revenues of $4.8 billion. The largest share was generated from sales and gross receipts taxes, followed by individual income taxes. The per capita tax burden in Hawaii was $3,813 for 2003–4, some $366 above the national average. In terms of business taxes, Hawaii ranked forty-second in a 2006 report by Anderson Economic Group. The state's business climate was ranked forty-second by Forbes Magazine and twenty-fourth by the Tax Foundation.

Population Projections

	2010	2015	2020	2025
Total Population	1,340,674	1,385,952	1,412,373	1,438,720
Median Age	37.4	37.3	37.5	38.1
Population 18 Years of Age and Older	1,024,411	1,055,684	1,073,236	1,105,783
Population 65 Years of Age and Older	191,065	226,189	264,527	300,743

Data: U.S. Census Bureau

Workforce and Industry Profile

Workforce

	2000	2005
Civilian Labor Force	573,795	609,666
Labor Force Participation Rate	64.5%	65.0%
Unemployment Rate	4.0%	2.8%
Average Earnings per Job (USD)	$30,628	$37,050
Education Attainment (Population 25 Years and Older)	**(%)**	**(%)**
High School Graduate or Higher	84.6	88.1
Bachelors Degree or Higher	26.2	27.9
Graduate or Professional Degree	8.4	9.1

Data: U.S. Census Bureau, American Community Survey; U.S. Department of Labor, Bureau of Labor Statistics

Industry Overview

	1998	2004
Total Employees	416,571	473,500
Total Payroll ($1,000)	11,291,978	15,074,629
Total Establishments	29,603	31,605
Establishments with 1–19 Employees	25,653	27,142
Establishments with 20–49 Employees	2,498	2,766
Establishments with 50–249 Employees	1,287	1,491
Establishments with 250–999 Employees	142	179
Establishments with 1,000+ Employees	23	27

Data: U.S. Census Bureau, County Business Patterns

Major Industries (Ranked by 2004 Employment; Payroll in $1,000s)				
Industry	1998 Employment	2004 Employment	1998 Payroll	2004 Payroll
Accommodation and Food Services	83,261	95,337	1,519,689	2,028,382
Retail Trade	60,620	66,584	1,179,640	1,563,190
Health Care and Social Assistance	47,389	59,349	1,670,402	2,211,263
Admin., Support, Waste Mngt., Remediation Services	31,342	36,958	649,096	876,279
Construction	21,265	27,020	862,290	1,361,382
Transportation and Warehousing	23,635	24,578	773,653	891,219
Other Services (except Public Admin.)	22,790	24,096	456,924	556,078
Professional, Scientific, Technical Services	17,140	23,738	690,001	1,086,591
Wholesale Trade	18,442	19,986	602,585	746,536
Finance and Insurance	20,050	19,256	807,310	1,099,212

Data: U.S. Census Bureau, County Business Patterns

Taxes and Business Climate

State and Local Taxes		
Combined Revenues ($1,000)	2001–2	2003–4
Revenue from Property Taxes	614,930	720,798
Revenue from Sales and Gross Receipts Taxes	2,244,245	2,605,694
Revenue from Individual Income Taxes	1,111,590	1,169,205
Revenue from Corporate Income Taxes	52,640	58,119
Revenue from Other Taxes	216,152	258,240
Total Tax Revenue	4,239,557	4,812,056
Per Capita Taxes		
Property Tax per Capita	507	571
Sales and Gross Receipts Tax per Capita	1,852	2,065
Individual Income Tax per Capita	917	926
Corporate Income Tax per Capita	43	46
Other Taxes per Capita	178	205
Total Taxes per Capita	3,498	3,813

Data: U.S. Census Bureau; Anderson Economic Group, LLC

Business Climate Measures	
Anderson Economic Group: 2006 Business Tax Ranking (1 is Best)	42
Forbes Magazine: 2006 Best States for Business Ranking (1 is Best)	42
Tax Foundation: 2007 Business Tax Climate Ranking (1 is Best)	24
2002–3 Employer Firm Births	2,927
2002–3 Employer Firm Terminations	2,461

Data: Anderson Economic Group; Tax Foundation; Forbes Magazine; U.S. Census, Statistics of U.S. Businesses

Voting Behavior and Elected Officials

Voter Registration and Turnout (%)	1992	1996	2000	2004
Registered Voters Who Voted	80.3	66.1	57.7	66.3
Citizens Age 18+ Who Voted	41.9	40.5	40.1	44.7

Data: Dave Leip's Atlas of U.S. Presidential Elections

Presidential Election Results (Nationwide Winner Listed First)		
2004	**Popular Vote (%)**	**Electoral Votes**
George W. Bush (Republican, Incumbent)	45.3	0
John Kerry (Democrat)	54.0	4
Other	0.7	0
2000		
George W. Bush (Republican)	37.5	0
Albert Gore (Democrat)	55.8	4
Ralph Nader (Green)	5.9	0
Other	0.9	0
1996		
William Clinton (Democrat, Incumbent)	56.9	4
Robert Dole (Republican)	31.6	0
H. Ross Perot (Reformist)	7.6	0
Other	3.8	0
1992		
William Clinton (Democrat)	48.1	4
George H. W. Bush (Republican, Incumbent)	36.7	0
H. Ross Perot (Independent)	14.2	0
Other	1.0	0

Data: Dave Leip's Atlas of U.S. Presidential Elections

Governor and U.S. Congressional Seats				
Governor	**Party**	**Year Term Began**	**Term**	**Max. Consecutive Terms**
Linda Lingle	R	2002	Second	2
U.S. Senators	**Party**	**Year Elected**	**Term Expires**	
Daniel K. Akaka	D	1990	2013	
Daniel K. Inouye	D	1962	2011	
U.S. Representatives		**Republican**	**Democrat**	**Other**
		0	2	0

Data: National Governors Association, U.S. Senate, U.S. House of Representatives

Business and Economic Agencies

Agency	Website Address
Chamber of Commerce of Hawaii	www.cochawaii.com
Department of Business, Economic Development and Tourism	www.hawaii.gov/dbedt
Hawaii Small Business Dev. Center	www.hawaii-sbdc.org
Department of Commerce and Consumer Affairs	www.hawaii.gov/dcca

Data: Various Agency Websites

Idaho

Demographics and Socioeconomics. Idaho, located in the Mountain region of the United States, has a population of 1.4 million people, making it the twelfth least populous state in 2005. The state's population increased by 101,681 people from 2000 to 2005, and is projected to increase to 1.9 million by 2025. This 1.4 percent projected annual growth rate is above the projected national average of 1.0 percent. In 2005 Idaho had a per capita personal income of $28,938, which was $6,097 below the national average and the nineth lowest in the country. The state's per capita income grew at an average annual rate of 3.4 percent from 2000 to 2005, compared to 2.9 percent nationally.

Workforce and Industry. In 2004 the state's largest industry in terms of employment was retail trade, followed by health care and social assistance. The fastest growing industry was administrative and support and waste management and remediation services, with 60.5 percent growth from 1998 to 2004. In terms of the education level of the workforce, 86.7 percent of Idaho's adult population has a high school

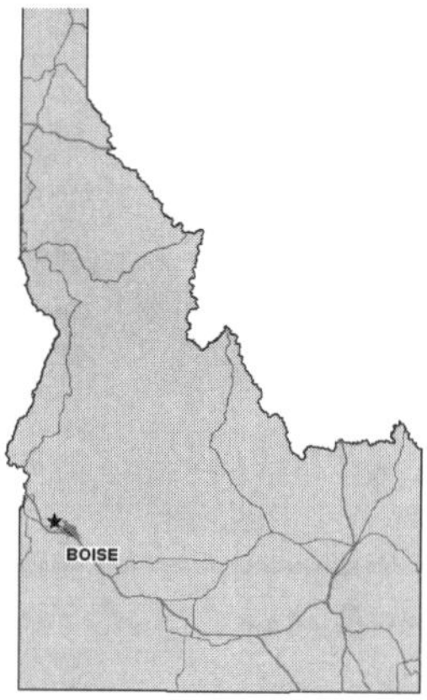

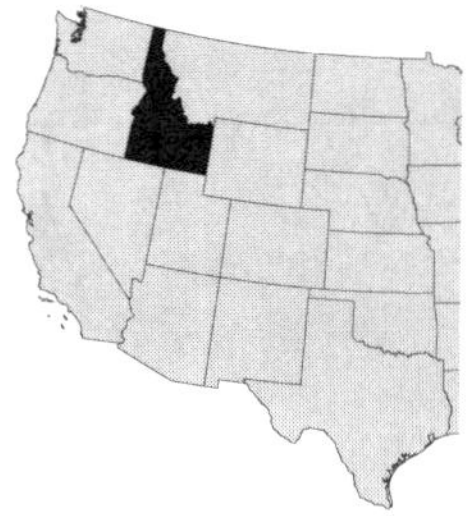

★ State Capitol

Major Urban Area

Major Roadway

Demographic and Socioeconomic Profile

Demographics and Socioeconomic Figures		
Population and Households	**2000**	**2005**
Total Population	1,293,953	1,395,634
Number of Households	469,645	532,135
Average Household Size	2.7	2.6
Age and Ethnicity		
Median Age	33.2	34.6
Population 18 Years of Age and Older	925,822	1,022,698
Population 65 Years of Age and Older	145,945	156,720
Caucasian Population	1,176,568	1,281,279
African-American Population	5,244	5,931
Hispanic Population	101,594	126,785
Asian Population	11,321	15,117
Foreign-Born Population	64,080	76,377
Income		
Per Capita Personal Income (USD)	$24,075	$28,398
Median Household Income (USD)	$37,572	$41,443
Individuals below Poverty Level	11.8%	13.9%

Data: U.S. Census, American Community Survey; U.S. Department of Commerce, Bureau of Economic Analysis

diploma or the equivalent, compared to the national average of 84.2 percent. 23.3 percent of Idaho's adult population has a bachelor degree or higher (national average is 27.2 percent); and 7.4 percent hold professional or graduate degrees (national average is 10.0 percent).

Tax Profile and Business Climate. In fiscal year 2003–4 Idaho had total tax revenues of $3.8 billion. The largest share was generated from sales and gross receipts taxes, followed by property taxes. The per capita tax burden in Idaho was $2,728 for 2003–4, some $719 below the national average. In terms of business taxes, the state ranked fortieth in a 2006 report by Anderson Economic Group. Forbes Magazine and the Tax Foundation ranked the state's business climate sixth and thirty-second, respectively.

Population Projections

	2010	2015	2020	2025
Total Population	1,517,291	1,630,045	1,741,333	1,852,627
Median Age	34.8	35.9	37.5	38.6
Population 18 Years of Age and Older	1,117,054	1,202,945	1,292,913	1,385,569
Population 65 Years of Age and Older	181,416	220,113	269,439	320,205

Data: U.S. Census Bureau

Workforce and Industry Profile

Workforce

	2000	2005
Civilian Labor Force	636,237	712,586
Labor Force Participation Rate	66.1%	67.2%
Unemployment Rate	4.6%	3.8%
Average Earnings per Job (USD)	$27,701	$33,050
Education Attainment (Population 25 Years and Older)		
High School Graduate or Higher	84.7%	86.7%
Bachelors Degree or Higher	21.7%	23.3%
Graduate or Professional Degree	6.8%	7.4%

Data: U.S. Census Bureau, American Community Survey; U.S. Department of Labor, Bureau of Labor Statistics

Industry Overview

	1998	2004
Total Employees	423,615	488,676
Total Payroll ($1,000)	10,595,285	14,207,992
Total Establishments	35,961	41,336
Establishments with 1–19 Employees	32,152	36,960
Establishments with 20–49 Employees	2,562	2,923
Establishments with 50–249 Employees	1,105	1,280
Establishments with 250–999 Employees	125	152
Establishments with 1,000+ Employees	17	21

Data: U.S. Census Bureau, County Business Patterns

Major Industries (Ranked by 2004 Employment; Payroll in $1,000s)				
Industry	1998 Employment	2004 Employment	1998 Payroll	2004 Payroll
Retail Trade	65,665	72,840	1,173,071	1,545,466
Health Care and Social Assistance	50,674	66,383	1,285,725	2,072,613
Manufacturing	66,719	60,102	2,214,164	2,415,085
Accommodation and Food Services	44,106	49,916	389,942	548,785
Admin., Support, Waste Mngt., Remediation Services	25,398	40,631	452,844	847,172
Construction	35,446	39,034	1,064,026	1,347,556
Professional, Scientific, Technical Services	22,338	31,256	902,270	1,241,562
Wholesale Trade	23,488	23,094	699,924	838,572
Finance and Insurance	16,285	20,604	531,207	806,172
Other Services (except Public Admin.)	16,899	18,170	249,420	339,108

Data: U.S. Census Bureau, County Business Patterns

Taxes and Business Climate

State and Local Taxes		
Combined Revenues ($1,000)	2001–2	2003–4
Revenue from Property Taxes	958,763	1,084,470
Revenue from Sales and Gross Receipts Taxes	1,135,452	1,426,827
Revenue from Individual Income Taxes	842,375	907,795
Revenue from Corporate Income Taxes	76,769	103,784
Revenue from Other Taxes	277,736	282,951
Total Tax Revenue	3,291,095	3,805,827
Per Capita Taxes		
Property Tax per Capita	741	777
Sales and Gross Receipts Tax per Capita	877	1,023
Individual Income Tax per Capita	651	651
Corporate Income Tax per Capita	59	74
Other Taxes per Capita	215	203
Total Taxes per Capita	2,543	2,728

Data: U.S. Census Bureau; Anderson Economic Group, LLC

Business Climate Measures	
Anderson Economic Group: 2006 Business Tax Ranking (1 is Best)	40
Forbes Magazine: 2006 Best States for Business Ranking (1 is Best)	6
Tax Foundation: 2007 Business Tax Climate Ranking (1 is Best)	32
2002–3 Employer Firm Births	4,627
2002–3 Employer Firm Terminations	3,616

Data: Anderson Economic Group; Tax Foundation; Forbes Magazine; U.S. Census, Statistics of U.S. Businesses

Voting Behavior and Elected Officials

Voter Registration and Turnout (%)

	1992	1996	2000	2004
Registered Voters Who Voted	78.9	70.2	68.9	75.0
Citizens Age 18+ Who Voted	65.2	57.3	54.2	60.2

Data: Dave Leip's Atlas of U.S. Presidential Elections

Presidential Election Results (Nationwide Winner Listed First)

2004	Popular Vote (%)	Electoral Votes
George W. Bush (Republican, Incumbent)	68.4	4
John Kerry (Democrat)	30.3	0
Other	1.4	0
2000		
George W. Bush (Republican)	67.2	4
Albert Gore (Democrat)	27.6	0
Ralph Nader (Green)	2.5	0
Other	2.7	0
1996		
William Clinton (Democrat, Incumbent)	33.7	0
Robert Dole (Republican)	52.2	4
H. Ross Perot (Reformist)	12.7	0
Other	1.5	0
1992		
William Clinton (Democrat)	28.4	0
George H. W. Bush (Republican, Incumbent)	42.0	4
H. Ross Perot (Independent)	27.0	0
Other	2.5	0

Data: Dave Leip's Atlas of U.S. Presidential Elections

Governor and U.S. Congressional Seats				
Governor	Party	Year Term Began	Term	Max. Consecutive Terms
C. L. "Butch" Otter	R	2007	First	2
U.S. Senators	Party	Year Elected	Term Expires	
Larry E. Craig	R	1990	2009	
Michael Crapo	R	1998	2011	
U.S. Representatives		Republican	Democrat	Other
		2	0	0

Data: National Governors Association, U.S. Senate, U.S. House of Representatives

Business and Economic Agencies

Agency	Website Address
Boise Metro Chamber of Commerce	www.boisechamber.org
Idaho Department of Commerce and Labor	www.cl.idaho.gov
Idaho Small Business Dev. Center	www.idahosbdc.org
Idaho Secretary of State	www.idsos.state.id.us

Data: Various Agency Websites

Illinois

Demographics and Socioeconomics. With a population of 12.4 million people, Illinois was the fifth most populous state in the United States in 2005. From 2000 to 2005 the state's population increased by 21,058 people, and is projected to increase to 13.3 million by 2025. This 0.4 percent projected annual growth rate compares to the projected national average of 1.0 percent. The state's 2005 per capita personal income of $36,264 was the thirteenth highest in the United States, some $1,769 above the national average. Per capita income in Illinois grew at an average annual rate of 2.4 percent from 2000 to 2005, compared to 2.9 percent nationally.

Workforce and Industry. Illinois' largest industry in terms of 2004 employment was manufacturing. The fastest growing major industry was construction, with 14.5 percent growth from 1998 to 2004. The state's workforce is generally more educated than that of other states: 85.7 percent of the state's adult population has graduated from high school, compared to an 84.2 percent national average; 29.2 percent hold a bachelor degree or higher

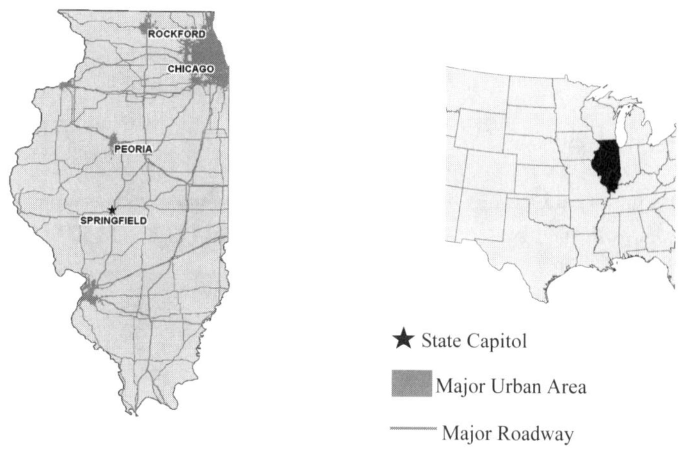

Demographic and Socioeconomic Profile

Demographics and Socioeconomic Figures		
Population and Households	**2000**	**2005**
Total Population	12,419,293	12,440,351
Number of Households	4,591,779	4,691,020
Average Household Size	2.6	2.7
Age and Ethnicity		
Median Age	34.7	35.6
Population 18 Years of Age and Older	9,180,064	9,208,765
Population 65 Years of Age and Older	1,498,929	1,436,153
Caucasian Population	9,123,564	8,986,032
African-American Population	1,864,619	1,803,613
Hispanic Population	1,529,141	1,804,619
Asian Population	423,440	507,687
Foreign-Born Population	1,529,058	1,695,289
Income		
Per Capita Personal Income (USD)	$32,185	$36,264
Median Household Income (USD)	$46,590	$50,260
Individuals below Poverty Level	10.7%	12.0%

Data: U.S. Census, American Community Survey; U.S. Department of Commerce, Bureau of Economic Analysis

(national average is 27.2 percent); and 10.9 percent hold professional or graduate degrees (national average is 10.0 percent).

Tax Profile and Business Climate. Illinois' total tax revenue was $45.1 billion for fiscal year 2003–4. The largest share was generated from property taxes, followed by sales and gross receipts taxes. Total Taxes per Capita in Illinois were $3,555, compared to the national average of $3,447 for 2003–4. In terms of business taxes, the state ranked twenty-eighth in a 2006 report by Anderson Economic Group. Forbes Magazine and the Tax Foundation ranked the state's business climate forty-fourth and twenty-fifth, respectively.

Population Projections

	2010	2015	2020	2025
Total Population	12,916,894	13,097,218	13,236,720	13,340,507
Median Age	36.0	36.3	37.0	37.4
Population 18 Years of Age and Older	9,719,988	9,882,541	9,980,950	10,075,188
Population 65 Years of Age and Older	1,600,863	1,777,487	1,988,764	2,226,431

Data: U.S. Census Bureau

Workforce and Industry Profile

Workforce

	2000	2005
Civilian Labor Force	6,208,597	6,459,240
Labor Force Participation Rate	65.4%	67.6%
Unemployment Rate	4.5%	5.7%
Average Earnings per Job (USD)	$38,044	$39,290
Education Attainment (Population 25 Years and Older)		
High School Graduate or Higher	81.4	85.7
Bachelors Degree or Higher	26.1	29.2
Graduate or Professional Degree	9.5	10.9

Data: U.S. Census Bureau, American Community Survey; U.S. Department of Labor, Bureau of Labor Statistics

Industry Overview

	1998	2004
Total Employees	5,221,782	5,217,160
Total Payroll ($1,000)	175,703,556	207,884,485
Total Establishments	304,533	315,854
Establishments with 1–19 Employees	259,572	269,744
Establishments with 20–49 Employees	26,877	27,849
Establishments with 50–249 Employees	15,634	15,901
Establishments with 250–999 Employees	2,124	2,031
Establishments with 1,000+ Employees	326	329

Data: U.S. Census Bureau, County Business Patterns

Major Industries (Ranked by 2004 Employment; Payroll in $1,000s)				
Industry	1998 Employment	2004 Employment	1998 Payroll	2004 Payroll
Manufacturing	883,472	685,368	33,319,088	29,466,846
Health Care and Social Assistance	612,855	673,842	17,914,037	23,957,897
Retail Trade	632,626	625,829	11,503,179	13,720,959
Accommodation and Food Services	395,322	438,895	4,554,156	5,904,182
Admin., Support, Waste Mngt., Remediation Services	407,556	415,654	9,080,901	10,768,908
Finance and Insurance	338,042	354,651	17,736,564	23,874,461
Professional, Scientific, Technical Services	311,731	343,894	16,023,793	21,160,060
Wholesale Trade	330,787	323,273	15,093,685	17,305,932
Other Services (except Public Admin.)	247,420	263,191	5,247,616	6,407,783
Construction	225,301	258,041	10,004,410	13,026,332

Data: U.S. Census Bureau, County Business Patterns

Taxes and Business Climate

State and Local Taxes		
Combined Revenues ($1,000)	2001–2	2003–4
Revenue from Property Taxes	15,872,667	17,888,828
Revenue from Sales and Gross Receipts Taxes	13,958,336	15,344,201
Revenue from Individual Income Taxes	7,471,385	7,218,428
Revenue from Corporate Income Taxes	1,383,823	1,278,538
Revenue from Other Taxes	2,966,030	3,460,734
Total Tax Revenue	41,652,241	45,190,729
Per Capita Taxes		
Property Tax per Capita	1,278	1,407
Sales and Gross Receipts Tax per Capita	1,124	1,207
Individual Income Tax per Capita	602	568
Corporate Income Tax per Capita	111	101
Other Taxes per Capita	239	272
Total Taxes per Capita	3,354	3,555

Data: U.S. Census Bureau; Anderson Economic Group, LLC

Business Climate Measures

Anderson Economic Group: 2006 Business Tax Ranking (1 is Best)	28
Forbes Magazine: 2006 Best States for Business Ranking (1 is Best)	44
Tax Foundation: 2007 Business Tax Climate Ranking (1 is Best)	25
2002–3 Employer Firm Births	28,426
2002–3 Employer Firm Terminations	26,661

Data: Anderson Economic Group; Tax Foundation; Forbes Magazine; U.S. Census, Statistics of U.S. Businesses

Voting Behavior and Elected Officials

Voter Registration and Turnout (%)

	1992	1996	2000	2004
Registered Voters Who Voted	76.5	64.7	66.5	70.3
Citizens Age 18+ Who Voted	58.9	49.3	51.7	56.0

Data: Dave Leip's Atlas of U.S. Presidential Elections

Presidential Election Results (Nationwide Winner Listed First)

2004	Popular Vote (%)	Electoral Votes
George W. Bush (Republican, Incumbent)	44.5	0
John Kerry (Democrat)	54.8	21
Other	0.7	0
2000		
George W. Bush (Republican)	42.6	0
Albert Gore (Democrat)	54.6	22
Ralph Nader (Green)	2.2	0
Other	0.6	0
1996		
William Clinton (Democrat, Incumbent)	54.3	22
Robert Dole (Republican)	36.8	0
H. Ross Perot (Reformist)	8.0	0
Other	0.8	0
1992		
William Clinton (Democrat)	48.6	22
George H. W. Bush (Republican, Incumbent)	34.3	0
H. Ross Perot (Independent)	16.6	0
Other	0.4	0

Data: Dave Leip's Atlas of U.S. Presidential Elections

Governor and U.S. Congressional Seats				
Governor	**Party**	**Year Term Began**	**Term**	**Max. Consecutive Terms**
Rod Blagojevich	D	2003	Second	No limit
U.S. Senators	**Party**	**Year Elected**	**Term Expires**	
Richard Durbin	D	1996	2009	
Barack Obama	D	2004	2011	
U.S. Representatives		**Republican**	**Democrat**	**Other**
		9	10	0

Data: National Governors Association, U.S. Senate, U.S. House of Representatives

Business and Economic Agencies

Agency	Website Address
Illinois State Chamber of Commerce	www.ilchamber.org
Department of Commerce and Economic Opportunity	www.commerce.state.il.us/dceo
Illinois Small Business Dev. Center	www.ilsbdc.biz
Illinois Secretary of State	www.sos.state.il.us

Data: Various Agency Websites

Indiana

Demographics and Socioeconomics. Indiana, located in the East North Central region of the United States, has a population of 6.1 million people, making it the fifteenth most populous state in 2005. The state's population increased by 12,887 people from 2000 to 2005, and is projected to increase to 6.7 million by 2025. This 0.5 percent projected annual growth rate compares to the projected national average of 1.0 percent. Per capita personal income in Indiana was $31,150 in 2005, ranking seventeenth lowest in the country and $3,345 below the national average. From 2000 to 2005 per capita income in Indiana grew at an average annual rate of 2.8 percent, compared to 2.9 percent nationally.

Workforce and Industry. In 2004 the state's largest industry in terms of employment was manufacturing, followed by health care and social assistance. The fastest growing industry was transportation and warehousing, with 28.1 percent growth from 1998 to 2004. In terms of the education level of the workforce, 85.3 percent of Indiana's adult population has a high school diploma or the

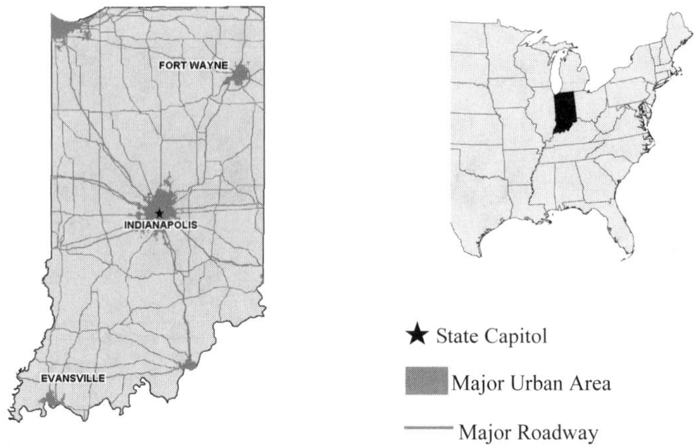

Demographic and Socioeconomic Profile

Demographics and Socioeconomic Figures		
Population and Households	**2000**	**2005**
Total Population	6,080,485	6,093,372
Number of Households	2,336,306	2,443,010
Average Household Size	2.5	2.5
Age and Ethnicity		
Median Age	35.2	36.1
Population 18 Years of Age and Older	4,507,679	4,500,356
Population 65 Years of Age and Older	752,885	727,171
Caucasian Population	5,317,334	5,247,604
African-American Population	504,449	522,377
Hispanic Population	210,538	277,558
Asian Population	57,193	72,494
Foreign-Born Population	186,534	242,281
Income		
Per Capita Personal Income (USD)	$27,132	$31,150
Median Household Income (USD)	$41,567	$43,993
Individuals below Poverty Level	9.5%	12.2%

Data: U.S. Census, American Community Survey; U.S. Department of Commerce, Bureau of Economic Analysis

equivalent, compared to the national average of 84.2 percent; 21.3 percent of the state's adult population has a bachelor degree or higher (national average is 27.2 percent); and 7.7 percent hold professional or graduate degrees (national average is 10.0 percent).

Tax Profile and Business Climate. In fiscal year 2003–4 Indiana had total tax revenues of $18.7 billion. The largest share was generated from sales and gross receipts taxes, followed by individual income taxes. The per capita tax burden in Indiana was $2,999 for 2003–4, some $448 bclow the national average. In terms of business taxes, the state ranked twenty-second in a 2006 report by Anderson Economic Group. Forbes Magazine and the Tax Foundation ranked the state's business climate thirty-second and twelfth, respectively.

Population Projections

	2010	2015	2020	2025
Total Population	6,392,139	6,517,631	6,627,008	6,721,322
Median Age	36.5	36.8	37.4	37.5
Population 18 Years of Age and Older	4,795,954	4,903,401	4,992,020	5,055,039
Population 65 Years of Age and Older	811,290	906,361	1,019,707	1,140,690

Data: U.S. Census Bureau

Workforce and Industry Profile

Workforce

	2000	2005
Civilian Labor Force	3,117,897	3,135,875
Labor Force Participation Rate	66.6%	67.2%
Unemployment Rate	2.9%	5.4%
Average Earnings per Job (USD)	$31,017	$34,080
Education Attainment (Population 25 Years and Older)	**(%)**	**(%)**
High School Graduate or Higher	82.1	85.3
Bachelors Degree or Higher	19.4	21.3
Graduate or Professional Degree	7.2	7.7

Data: U.S. Census Bureau, American Community Survey; U.S. Department of Labor, Bureau of Labor Statistics

Industry Overview

	1998	2004
Total Employees	2,540,866	2,586,799
Total Payroll ($1,000)	71,435,864	85,098,401
Total Establishments	146,197	149,381
Establishments with 1–19 Employees	123,653	126,069
Establishments with 20–49 Employees	13,836	14,306
Establishments with 50–249 Employees	7,559	7,817
Establishments with 250–999 Employees	987	1,014
Establishments with 1,000+ Employees	162	175

Data: U.S. Census Bureau, County Business Patterns

Major Industries (Ranked by 2004 Employment; Payroll in $1,000s)				
Industry	1998 Employment	2004 Employment	1998 Payroll	2004 Payroll
Manufacturing	635,658	544,310	23,729,035	23,739,029
Health Care and Social Assistance	313,865	354,380	8,403,195	11,756,625
Retail Trade	344,444	352,149	5,719,109	6,783,081
Accommodation and Food Services	216,578	243,887	2,066,860	2,849,446
Admin., Support, Waste Mngt., Remediation Services	136,135	149,017	2,782,884	3,820,550
Construction	138,326	140,808	4,770,384	5,629,849
Other Services (except Public Admin.)	124,828	135,509	2,097,725	2,709,168
Wholesale Trade	115,519	114,962	4,082,819	4,925,987
Finance and Insurance	110,993	112,304	4,202,678	5,273,565
Transportation and Warehousing	81,360	104,191	2,510,293	3,480,579

Data: U.S. Census Bureau, County Business Patterns

Taxes and Business Climate

State and Local Taxes		
Combined Revenues ($1,000)	2001–2	2003–4
Revenue from Property Taxes	5,976,203	6,073,538
Revenue from Sales and Gross Receipts Taxes	5,522,432	6,992,455
Revenue from Individual Income Taxes	4,121,231	4,231,727
Revenue from Corporate Income Taxes	709,412	644,787
Revenue from Other Taxes	657,359	732,517
Total Tax Revenue	16,986,637	18,675,024
Per Capita Taxes		
Property Tax per Capita	983	975
Sales and Gross Receipts Tax per Capita	908	1,123
Individual Income Tax per Capita	678	680
Corporate Income Tax per Capita	117	104
Other Taxes per Capita	108	118
Total Taxes per Capita	2,794	2,999

Data: U.S. Census Bureau; Anderson Economic Group, LLC

Business Climate Measures	
Anderson Economic Group: 2006 Business Tax Ranking (1 is Best)	22
Forbes Magazine: 2006 Best States for Business Ranking (1 is Best)	32
Tax Foundation: 2007 Business Tax Climate Ranking (1 is Best)	12
2002–3 Employer Firm Births	12,958
2002–3 Employer Firm Terminations	12,405

Data: Anderson Economic Group; Tax Foundation; Forbes Magazine; U.S. Census, Statistics of U.S. Businesses

Voting Behavior and Elected Officials

Voter Registration and Turnout (%)

	1992	1996	2000	2004
Registered Voters Who Voted	72.5	61.2	55.1	57.4
Citizens Age 18+ Who Voted	55.2	48.8	48.8	53.7

Data: Dave Leip's Atlas of U.S. Presidential Elections

Presidential Election Results (Nationwide Winner Listed First)

2004	Popular Vote (%)	Electoral Votes
George W. Bush (Republican, Incumbent)	59.9	11
John Kerry (Democrat)	39.3	0
Other	0.8	0
2000		
George W. Bush (Republican)	56.7	12
Albert Gore (Democrat)	41.0	0
Ralph Nader (Green)	0.8	0
Other	1.5	0
1996		
William Clinton (Democrat, Incumbent)	41.6	0
Robert Dole (Republican)	47.1	12
H. Ross Perot (Reformist)	10.5	0
Other	0.8	0
1992		
William Clinton (Democrat)	36.8	0
George H. W. Bush (Republican, Incumbent)	42.9	12
H. Ross Perot (Independent)	19.8	0
Other	0.5	0

Data: Dave Leip's Atlas of U.S. Presidential Elections

Governor and U.S. Congressional Seats				
Governor	**Party**	**Year Term Began**	**Term**	**Max. Consecutive Terms**
Mitch Daniels	R	2005	First	2
U.S. Senators	**Party**	**Year Elected**	**Term Expires**	
Evan Bayh	D	1998	2011	
Richard G. Lugar	R	1976	2013	
U.S. Representatives		**Republican**	**Democrat**	**Other**
		4	5	0

Data: National Governors Association, U.S. Senate, U.S. House of Representatives

Business and Economic Agencies

Agency	Website Address
Indiana Chamber of Commerce	www.indianachamber.com
Indiana Economic Development Corporation	www.in.gov/iedc
Indiana Small Business Dev. Center	www.isbdc.org
Indiana Secretary of State	www.state.in.us/sos/business

Data: Various Agency Websites

Iowa

Demographics and Socioeconomics. With a 2005 population of 2.9 million people, Iowa was the twenty-first least populous state. From 2000 to 2005 the state's population decreased by 63,783 people, but is projected to increase to nearly 3.0 million by 2025. This 0.2 percent projected annual growth rate compares to the projected national average of 1.0 percent. The state's 2005 per capita personal income of $31,795 was the twenty-first lowest in the United States and $2,700 below the national average. Per capita income in Iowa grew at an average annual rate of 3.7 percent from 2000 to 2005, compared to 2.9 percent nationally.

Workforce and Industry. The state's largest industry in terms of 2004 employment was manufacturing. The fastest growing industry was transportation and warehousing, with 31.2 percent growth from 1998 to 2004. In terms of the education level of the workforce, 89.6 percent of Iowa's adult population has a high school diploma or the equivalent, compared to the national average of 84.2 percent; 23.8 percent of Iowa's

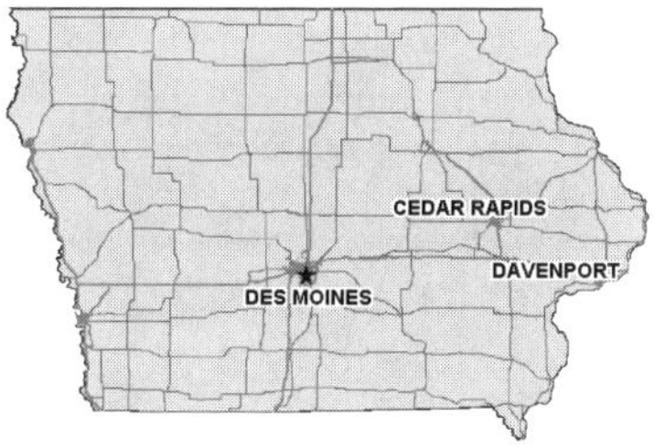

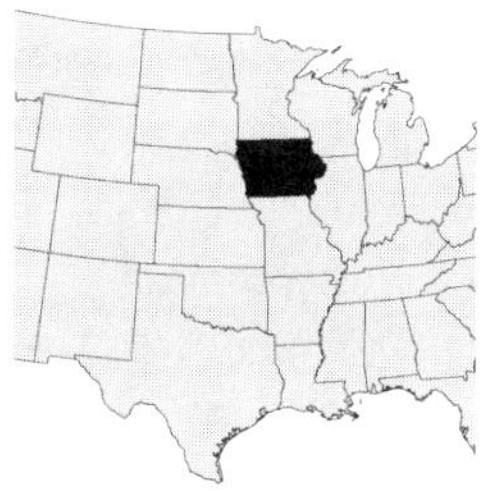

★ State Capitol

Major Urban Area

Major Roadway

Demographic and Socioeconomic Profile

Demographics and Socioeconomic Figures		
Population and Households	**2000**	**2005**
Total Population	2,926,324	2,862,541
Number of Households	1,149,276	1,200,833
Average Household Size	2.5	2.4
Age and Ethnicity		
Median Age	36.6	38.6
Population 18 Years of Age and Older	2,193,990	2,194,615
Population 65 Years of Age and Older	436,377	402,167
Caucasian Population	2,749,737	2,675,878
African-American Population	59,758	62,827
Hispanic Population	81,501	106,052
Asian Population	35,023	41,510
Foreign-Born Population	91,085	103,143
Income		
Per Capita Personal Income (USD)	$26,554	$31,795
Median Household Income (USD)	$39,469	$43,609
Individuals below Poverty Level	9.1%	10.9%

Data: U.S. Census, American Community Survey; U.S. Department of Commerce, Bureau of Economic Analysis

adult population has a bachelor degree or higher (national average is 27.2 percent); and 7.3 percent hold professional or graduate degrees (national average is 10.0 percent).

Tax Profile and Business Climate. Iowa's total tax revenue was $9.0 billion for fiscal year 2003–4. The largest share of this revenue was generated from property taxes, followed by sales and gross receipts taxes. Total Taxes per Capita for Iowa were $3,054, compared to the national average of $3,447 for 2003–4. In terms of business taxes, the state ranked twenty-fifth in a 2006 report by Anderson Economic Group. Forbes Magazine and the Tax Foundation ranked the state's business climate twenty-fifth and forty-third, respectively.

Population Projections

	2010	2015	2020	2025
Total Population	3,009,907	3,026,380	3,020,496	2,993,222
Median Age	38.3	38.9	40.1	41.3
Population 18 Years of Age and Older	2,298,851	2,319,340	2,323,127	2,311,474
Population 65 Years of Age and Older	449,887	494,565	556,540	619,227

Data: U.S. Census Bureau

Workforce and Industry Profile

Workforce

	2000	2005
Civilian Labor Force	1,554,722	1,588,632
Labor Force Participation Rate	68.2%	69.9%
Unemployment Rate	2.7%	4.6%
Average Earnings per Job (USD)	$27,929	$32,340
Education Attainment (Population 25 Years and Older)	**(%)**	**(%)**
High School Graduate or Higher	86.1	89.6
Bachelors Degree or Higher	21.2	23.8
Graduate or Professional Degree	6.5	7.3

Data: U.S. Census Bureau, American Community Survey; U.S. Department of Labor, Bureau of Labor Statistics

Industry Overview

	1998	2004
Total Employees	1,213,285	1,241,864
Total Payroll ($1,000)	30,409,574	37,643,817
Total Establishments	80,838	81,565
Establishments with 1–19 Employees	70,187	70,485
Establishments with 20–49 Employees	6,524	6,839
Establishments with 50–249 Employees	3,598	3,674
Establishments with 250–999 Employees	462	491
Establishments with 1,000+ Employees	67	76

Data: U.S. Census Bureau, County Business Patterns

Major Industries (Ranked by 2004 Employment; Payroll in $1,000s)				
Industry	1998 Employment	2004 Employment	1998 Payroll	2004 Payroll
Manufacturing	245,282	219,188	8,193,004	8,643,842
Health Care and Social Assistance	172,793	185,688	4,111,821	5,726,027
Retail Trade	177,723	178,251	2,846,480	3,400,874
Accommodation and Food Services	103,641	107,271	907,513	1,091,163
Finance and Insurance	73,746	92,053	2,715,795	4,175,815
Wholesale Trade	64,101	61,423	1,991,922	2,375,518
Construction	58,557	61,166	1,947,744	2,408,617
Admin., Support, Waste Mngt., Remediation Services	58,306	59,810	993,597	1,282,876
Other Services (except Public Admin.)	52,875	54,106	790,560	976,726
Transportation and Warehousing	37,379	49,028	1,050,574	1,595,112

Data: U.S. Census Bureau, County Business Patterns

Taxes and Business Climate

State and Local Taxes		
Combined Revenues ($1,000)	**2001–2**	**2003–4**
Revenue from Property Taxes	2,877,921	3,188,869
Revenue from Sales and Gross Receipts Taxes	2,886,338	3,011,578
Revenue from Individual Income Taxes	1,814,488	2,010,610
Revenue from Corporate Income Taxes	88,310	89,826
Revenue from Other Taxes	663,357	717,865
Total Tax Revenue	8,330,414	9,018,748
Per Capita Taxes		
Property Tax per Capita	984	1,080
Sales and Gross Receipts Tax per Capita	986	1,020
Individual Income Tax per Capita	620	681
Corporate Income Tax per Capita	30	30
Other Taxes per Capita	227	243
Total Taxes per Capita	2,847	3,054

Data: U.S. Census Bureau; Anderson Economic Group, LLC

Business Climate Measures	
Anderson Economic Group: 2006 Business Tax Ranking (1 is Best)	25
Forbes Magazine: 2006 Best States for Business Ranking (1 is Best)	25
Tax Foundation: 2007 Business Tax Climate Ranking (1 is Best)	43
2002–3 Employer Firm Births	6,815
2002–3 Employer Firm Terminations	6,485

Data: Anderson Economic Group; Tax Foundation; Forbes Magazine; U.S. Census, Statistics of U.S. Businesses

Voting Behavior and Elected Officials

Voter Registration and Turnout (%)

	1992	1996	2000	2004
Registered Voters Who Voted	79.5	69.5	71.4	75.9
Citizens Age 18+ Who Voted	65.3	57.7	60.0	66.9

Data: Dave Leip's Atlas of U.S. Presidential Elections

Presidential Election Results (Nationwide Winner Listed First)

2004	Popular Vote (%)	Electoral Votes
George W. Bush (Republican, Incumbent)	49.9	7
John Kerry (Democrat)	49.2	0
Other	0.9	0
2000		
George W. Bush (Republican)	48.2	0
Albert Gore (Democrat)	48.5	7
Ralph Nader (Green)	2.2	0
Other	1.0	0
1996		
William Clinton (Democrat, Incumbent)	50.3	7
Robert Dole (Republican)	39.9	0
H. Ross Perot (Reformist)	8.5	0
Other	1.3	0
1992		
William Clinton (Democrat)	43.3	7
George H. W. Bush (Republican, Incumbent)	37.3	0
H. Ross Perot (Independent)	18.7	0
Other	0.7	0

Data: Dave Leip's Atlas of U.S. Presidential Elections

Governor and U.S. Congressional Seats				
Governor	**Party**	**Year Term Began**	**Term**	**Max. Consecutive Terms**
Chet Culver	D	2007	First	No limit
U.S. Senators	**Party**	**Year Elected**	**Term Expires**	
Chuck Grassley	R	1980	2011	
Tom Harkin	D	1984	2009	
U.S. Representatives		**Republican**	**Democrat**	**Other**
		2	3	0

Data: National Governors Association, U.S. Senate, U.S. House of Representatives

Business and Economic Agencies

Agency	Website Address
Iowa Chamber Alliance	www.iowachamberalliance.org
Iowa Department of Economic Development	www.iowalifechanging.com
Iowa Small Business Dev. Center	www.iowasbdc.org
Iowa Secretary of State	www.sos.state.ia.us

Data: Various Agency Websites

Kansas

Demographics and Socioeconomics. With a population of 2.7 million people, Kansas was the eighteenth least populous state in the United States in 2005. From 2000 to 2005 the state's population decreased by 25,802 people, but is projected to increase to 2.9 million by 2025. This 0.5 percent projected annual growth rate compares to the projected national average of 1.0 percent. In 2005 Kansas had a per capita personal income of $32,948, which was $1,547 below the national average and the twenty-third highest in the country. The state's per capita income grew at an average annual rate of 3.5 percent from 2000 to 2005, compared to 2.9 percent nationally.

Workforce and Industry. The state's largest industry in terms of 2004 employment was manufacturing. The industry with the fastest growth in employment was information, with 37.9 percent growth from 1998 to 2004. The information industry ranked eleventh in terms of 2004 employment. The state's workforce is generally more educated than that of other states: 88.7 percent of the state's adult population has graduated from high

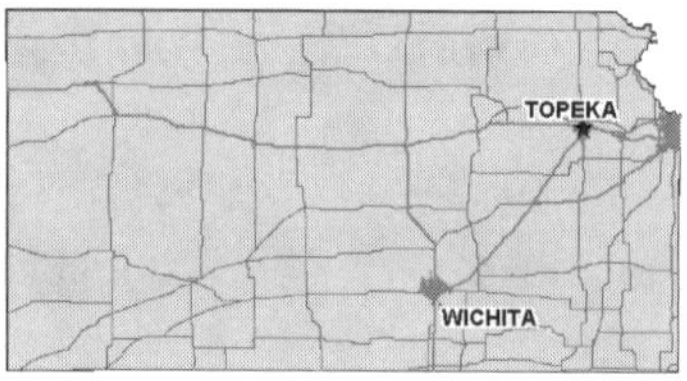

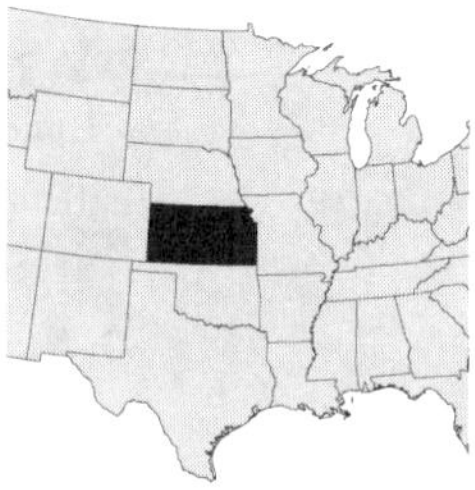

★ State Capitol

Major Urban Area

Major Roadway

Demographic and Socioeconomic Profile

Demographics and Socioeconomic Figures		
Population and Households	**2000**	**2005**
Total Population	2,688,418	2,662,616
Number of Households	1,037,891	1,071,938
Average Household Size	2.5	2.5
Age and Ethnicity		
Median Age	35.2	36.1
Population 18 Years of Age and Older	1,977,198	1,991,169
Population 65 Years of Age and Older	355,681	330,128
Caucasian Population	2,312,119	2,269,482
African-American Population	150,584	147,455
Hispanic Population	186,299	224,152
Asian Population	44,772	53,129
Foreign-Born Population	134,735	153,535
Income		
Per Capita Personal Income (USD)	$27,694	$32,948
Median Household Income (USD)	$40,624	$42,920
Individuals below Poverty Level	9.9%	11.7%

Data: U.S. Census, American Community Survey; U.S. Department of Commerce, Bureau of Economic Analysis

school, compared to an 84.2 percent national average; 28.2 percent hold a bachelor degree or higher (national average is 27.2 percent); and 9.6 percent hold professional or graduate degrees (national average is 10.0 percent).

Tax Profile and Business Climate. Kansas' total tax revenue was $9.4 billion for fiscal year 2003–4. The largest share was generated from sales and gross receipts taxes, followed by property taxes. Taxes per capita in Kansas were $3,380, compared to the national average of $3,447 for 2003–4. In terms of business taxes, the state ranked forty-first in a 2006 report by Anderson Economic Group. Forbes Magazine and the Tax Foundation ranked the state's business climate twenty-first and thirty-first, respectively.

Population Projections

	2010	2015	2020	2025
Total Population	2,805,470	2,852,690	2,890,566	2,919,002
Median Age	36.4	36.9	37.8	38.5
Population 18 Years of Age and Older	2,106,474	2,144,722	2,176,667	2,205,455
Population 65 Years of Age and Older	375,315	419,748	479,919	544,756

Data: U.S. Census Bureau

Workforce and Industry Profile

Workforce

	2000	2005
Civilian Labor Force	1,374,698	1,435,160
Labor Force Participation Rate	67.5%	69.9%
Unemployment Rate	3.7%	5.1%
Average Earnings per Job (USD)	$29,360	$33,960
Education Attainment (Population 25 Years and Older)	**(%)**	**(%)**
High School Graduate or Higher	86.0	88.7
Bachelors Degree or Higher	25.8	28.2
Graduate or Professional Degree	8.7	9.6

Data: U.S. Census Bureau, American Community Survey; U.S. Department of Labor, Bureau of Labor Statistics

Industry Overview

	1998	2004
Total Employees	1,081,941	1,116,277
Total Payroll ($1,000)	28,747,577	35,725,813
Total Establishments	74,019	75,827
Establishments with 1–19 Employees	64,030	65,554
Establishments with 20–49 Employees	6,304	6,499
Establishments with 50–249 Employees	3,263	3,325
Establishments with 250–999 Employees	373	402
Establishments with 1,000+ Employees	49	47

Data: U.S. Census Bureau, County Business Patterns

Major Industries (Ranked by 2004 Employment; Payroll in $1,000s)				
Industry	1998 Employment	2004 Employment	1998 Payroll	2004 Payroll
Manufacturing	196,519	173,236	6,666,326	6,985,656
Health Care and Social Assistance	154,002	166,906	3,801,133	5,232,394
Retail Trade	149,270	149,777	2,476,930	2,847,826
Accommodation and Food Services	90,431	98,511	842,346	1,046,901
Construction	60,896	62,899	1,947,778	2,302,854
Wholesale Trade	63,953	62,274	2,370,432	2,663,196
Admin., Support, Waste Mngt., Remediation Services	54,086	60,729	1,076,557	1,544,442
Professional, Scientific, Technical Services	49,417	60,378	1,762,448	2,531,457
Finance and Insurance	52,839	58,767	1,875,213	2,676,910
Other Services (except Public Admin.)	51,825	52,109	870,742	970,383

Data: U.S. Census Bureau, County Business Patterns

Taxes and Business Climate

State and Local Taxes		
Combined Revenues ($1,000)	2001–2	2003–4
Revenue from Property Taxes	2,524,888	3,246,616
Revenue from Sales and Gross Receipts Taxes	3,066,260	3,427,052
Revenue from Individual Income Taxes	1,854,848	1,915,530
Revenue from Corporate Income Taxes	121,931	166,609
Revenue from Other Taxes	407,048	486,166
Total Tax Revenue	7,974,975	9,241,973
Per Capita Taxes		
Property Tax per Capita	939	1,187
Sales and Gross Receipts Tax per Capita	1,141	1,253
Individual Income Tax per Capita	690	701
Corporate Income Tax per Capita	45	61
Other Taxes per Capita	151	178
Total Taxes per Capita	2,967	3,380

Data: U.S. Census Bureau; Anderson Economic Group, LLC

Business Climate Measures	
Anderson Economic Group: 2006 Business Tax Ranking (1 is Best)	41
Forbes Magazine: 2006 Best States for Business Ranking (1 is Best)	21
Tax Foundation: 2007 Business Tax Climate Ranking (1 is Best)	31
2002–3 Employer Firm Births	6,895
2002–3 Employer Firm Terminations	6,569

Data: Anderson Economic Group; Tax Foundation; Forbes Magazine; U.S. Census, Statistics of U.S. Businesses

Voting Behavior and Elected Officials

Voter Registration and Turnout (%)

	1992	1996	2000	2004
Registered Voters Who Voted	84.7	74.6	66.0	70.1
Citizens Age 18+ Who Voted	63.0	56.6	54.2	58.6

Data: Dave Leip's Atlas of U.S. Presidential Elections

Presidential Election Results (Nationwide Winner Listed First)

2004	Popular Vote (%)	Electoral Votes
George W. Bush (Republican, Incumbent)	62.0	6
John Kerry (Democrat)	36.6	0
Other	1.4	0
2000		
George W. Bush (Republican)	58.0	6
Albert Gore (Democrat)	37.2	0
Ralph Nader (Green)	3.4	0
Other	1.4	0
1996		
William Clinton (Democrat, Incumbent)	36.1	0
Robert Dole (Republican)	54.3	6
H. Ross Perot (Reformist)	8.6	0
Other	1.0	0
1992		
William Clinton (Democrat)	33.7	0
George H. W. Bush (Republican, Incumbent)	38.9	6
H. Ross Perot (Independent)	27.0	0
Other	0.4	0

Data: Dave Leip's Atlas of U.S. Presidential Elections

Governor and U.S. Congressional Seats				
Governor	**Party**	**Year Term Began**	**Term**	**Max. Consecutive Terms**
Kathleen Sebelius	D	2003	Second	2
U.S. Senators	**Party**	**Year Elected**	**Term Expires**	
Sam Brownback	R	1996	2011	
Pat Roberts	R	1996	2009	
U.S. Representatives		**Republican**	**Democrat**	**Other**
		2	2	0

Data: National Governors Association, U.S. Senate, U.S. House of Representatives

Business and Economic Agencies

Agency	Website Address
Kansas Chamber of Commerce and Industry	www.kansaschamber.org
Kansas Department of Commerce	www.kansascommerce.com
Kansas Small Business Dev. Center	www.fhsu.edu/ksbdc
Kansas Secretary of State, Business Services	www.kssos.org/business/business.html

Data: Various Agency Websites

Kentucky

Demographics and Socioeconomics. Kentucky is located in the East South Central region of the United States and has a population of 4.1 million people, making it the twenty-sixth most populous state in 2005. The state's population increased by 16,864 people from 2000 to 2005, and is projected to grow to 4.5 million by 2025. This 0.5 percent projected annual growth rate is below the national average of 1.0 percent. Per capita personal income in Kentucky was $28,317 in 2005, ranking eighth lowest in the country and $6,178 below the national average. From 2000 to 2005 per capita income in Kentucky grew at an average annual rate of 3.0 percent, compared to 2.9 percent nationally.

Workforce and Industry. The state's workforce is generally less educated than that of other states: 79.0 percent of the State's adult population has graduated from high school, compared to an 84.2 percent national average; 19.3 percent hold a bachelor degree or higher (national average is 27.2 percent); and 7.8 percent hold professional or graduate degrees (national average is

★ State Capitol

Major Urban Area

Major Roadway

Demographic and Socioeconomic Profile

Demographics and Socioeconomic Figures		
Population and Households	**2000**	**2005**
Total Population	4,041,769	4,058,633
Number of Households	1,590,647	1,653,898
Average Household Size	2.5	2.5
Age and Ethnicity		
Median Age	35.9	37.5
Population 18 Years of Age and Older	3,047,928	3,082,522
Population 65 Years of Age and Older	503,668	495,885
Caucasian Population	3,639,168	3,646,690
African-American Population	293,915	292,012
Hispanic Population	56,414	69,702
Asian Population	28,994	35,561
Foreign-Born Population	80,271	98,798
Income		
Per Capita Personal Income (USD)	$24,412	$28,317
Median Household Income (USD)	$33,672	$37,369
Individuals below Poverty Level	15.8%	16.8%

Data: U.S. Census, American Community Survey; U.S. Department of Commerce, Bureau of Economic Analysis

10.0). In 2004 the state's largest industry in terms of employment was manufacturing, followed by retail trade. The fastest growing industry was transportation and warehousing, with 26.3 percent growth from 1998 to 2004.

Tax Profile and Business Climate. In fiscal year 2003–4 Kentucky had total tax revenues of $11.5 billion. The largest share was generated from sales and gross receipts taxes, followed by individual income taxes. The per capita tax burden in Kentucky was $2,767 for 2003–4, some $680 below the national average. In terms of business taxes, Kentucky ranked nineteenth in a 2006 report by Anderson Economic Group. The state's business climate was ranked thirty-third by Forbes Magazine and thirty-nineth by the Tax Foundation.

Population Projections

	2010	2015	2020	2025
Total Population	4,265,117	4,351,188	4,424,431	4,489,662
Median Age	38.0	38.6	39.4	39.8
Population 18 Years of Age and Older	3,262,810	3,344,209	3,417,155	3,480,547
Population 65 Years of Age and Older	557,471	637,351	729,741	826,659

Data: U.S. Census Bureau

Workforce and Industry Profile

Workforce

	2000	2005
Civilian Labor Force	1,907,614	1,964,060
Labor Force Participation Rate	60.9%	61.8%
Unemployment Rate	4.2%	6.1%
Average Earnings per Job (USD)	$28,801	$32,550
Education Attainment (Population 25 Years and Older)	**(%)**	**(%)**
High School Graduate or Higher	74.1	79.0
Bachelors Degree or Higher	17.1	19.3
Graduate or Professional Degree	6.9	7.8

Data: U.S. Census Bureau, American Community Survey; U.S. Department of Labor, Bureau of Labor Statistics

Industry Overview

	1998	2004
Total Employees	1,443,015	1,489,497
Total Payroll ($1,000)	36,889,001	46,163,189
Total Establishments	89,593	91,797
Establishments with 1–19 Employees	76,564	78,015
Establishments with 20–49 Employees	8,100	8,581
Establishments with 50–249 Employees	4,227	4,513
Establishments with 250–999 Employees	638	621
Establishments with 1,000+ Employees	64	67

Data: U.S. Census Bureau, County Business Patterns

Major Industries (Ranked by 2004 Employment; Payroll in $1,000s)				
Industry	1998 Employment	2004 Employment	1998 Payroll	2004 Payroll
Manufacturing	290,665	258,090	9,829,745	10,715,919
Retail Trade	221,580	223,304	3,385,861	4,227,111
Health Care and Social Assistance	194,305	221,193	5,052,060	7,200,869
Accommodation and Food Services	127,561	143,457	1,245,296	1,612,947
Construction	77,191	81,444	2,263,487	2,803,071
Transportation and Warehousing	60,183	76,014	2,054,206	2,894,238
Admin., Support, Waste Mngt., Remediation Services	70,020	72,783	1,103,006	1,561,552
Wholesale Trade	69,862	68,653	2,214,967	2,739,250
Other Services (except Public Admin.)	62,968	68,398	1,042,453	1,345,108
Finance and Insurance	61,079	67,090	1,989,927	2,732,244

Data: U.S. Census Bureau, County Business Patterns

Taxes and Business Climate

State and Local Taxes		
Combined Revenues ($1,000)	**2001–2**	**2003–4**
Revenue from Property Taxes	1,977,011	2,136,455
Revenue from Sales and Gross Receipts Taxes	3,942,387	4,313,337
Revenue from Individual Income Taxes	3,496,353	3,629,392
Revenue from Corporate Income Taxes	302,129	381,538
Revenue from Other Taxes	1,062,877	999,772
Total Tax Revenue	10,780,757	11,460,494
Per Capita Taxes		
Property Tax per Capita	489	516
Sales and Gross Receipts Tax per Capita	975	1,041
Individual Income Tax per Capita	865	876
Corporate Income Tax per Capita	75	92
Other Taxes per Capita	263	241
Total Taxes per Capita	2,667	2,767

Data: U.S. Census Bureau; Anderson Economic Group, LLC

Business Climate Measures	
Anderson Economic Group: 2006 Business Tax Ranking (1 is Best)	19
Forbes Magazine: 2006 Best States for Business Ranking (1 is Best)	33
Tax Foundation: 2007 Business Tax Climate Ranking (1 is Best)	39
2002–3 Employer Firm Births	8,036
2002–3 Employer Firm Terminations	7,730

Data: Anderson Economic Group; Tax Foundation; Forbes Magazine; U.S. Census, Statistics of U.S. Businesses

Voting Behavior and Elected Officials

Voter Registration and Turnout (%)

	1992	1996	2000	2004
Registered Voters Who Voted	71.9	58.1	60.4	64.3
Citizens Age 18+ Who Voted	53.7	47.4	50.7	57.5

Data: Dave Leip's Atlas of U.S. Presidential Elections

Presidential Election Results (Nationwide Winner Listed First)

2004	Popular Vote (%)	Electoral Votes
George W. Bush (Republican, Incumbent)	59.6	8
John Kerry (Democrat)	39.7	0
Other	0.8	0
2000		
George W. Bush (Republican)	56.5	8
Albert Gore (Democrat)	41.4	0
Ralph Nader (Green)	1.5	0
Other	0.6	0
1996		
William Clinton (Democrat, Incumbent)	45.8	8
Robert Dole (Republican)	44.9	0
H. Ross Perot (Reformist)	8.7	0
Other	0.6	0
1992		
William Clinton (Democrat)	44.6	8
George H. W. Bush (Republican, Incumbent)	41.3	0
H. Ross Perot (Independent)	13.7	0
Other	0.5	0

Data: Dave Leip's Atlas of U.S. Presidential Elections

Governor and U.S. Congressional Scats				
Governor	**Party**	**Year Term Began**	**Term**	**Max. Consecutive Terms**
Ernie Fletcher	R	2003	First	2
U.S. Senators	**Party**	**Year Elected**	**Term Expires**	
Mitch McConnell	R	1984	2009	
Jim Bunning	R	1998	2011	
U.S. Representatives		**Republican**	**Democrat**	**Other**
		4	2	0

Data: National Governors Association, U.S. Senate, U.S. House of Representatives

Business and Economic Agencies

Agency	Website Address
Kentucky Chamber of Commerce	www.kychamber.com
Kentucky Cabinet for Economic Development	www.thinkkentucky.com
Kentucky Small Business Dev. Center	www.ksbdc.org
Kentucky Secretary of State, Business Services	www.sos.ky.gov/business

Data: Various Agency Websites

Louisiana

Demographics and Socioeconomics. Louisiana, located in the West South Central region of the United States, has a population of 4.4 million people, making it the twenty-fourth most populous state in 2005. The state's population decreased by 79,229 people from 2000 to 2005, but is projected to increase to 4.8 million by 2025. This 0.4 percent projected annual growth rate compares to the projected national average of 1.0 percent. The state's 2005 per capita personal income of $24,582 was the lowest in the United States and $9,913 below the national average. Per capita income in Louisiana grew at an average annual rate of 1.3 percent from 2000 to 2005, compared to 2.9 percent nationally.

Workforce and Industry. In 2004 the state's largest industry in terms of employment was health care and social assistance, followed by retail trade. The fastest growing major industry in Louisiana was administrative and support and waste management and remediation services, which saw 16.3 percent growth from 1998 to 2004. The state's workforce is generally less educated than that of other states: 80.5 percent

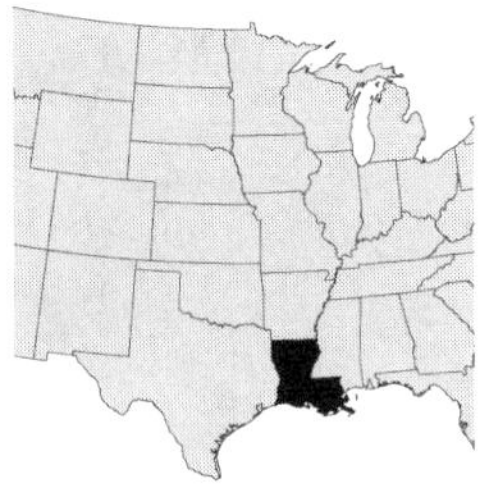

★ State Capitol

Major Urban Area

Major Roadway

Demographic and Socioeconomic Profile

Demographics and Socioeconomic Figures		
Population and Households	**2000**	**2005**
Total Population	4,468,976	4,389,747
Number of Households	1,656,053	1,676,599
Average Household Size	2.6	2.6
Age and Ethnicity		
Median Age	34.0	35.4
Population 18 Years of Age and Older	3,250,523	3,249,119
Population 65 Years of Age and Older	518,097	498,883
Caucasian Population	2,855,964	2,795,263
African-American Population	1,444,566	1,425,685
Hispanic Population	107,854	123,066
Asian Population	55,492	58,392
Foreign-Born Population	115,885	121,590
Income		
Per Capita Personal Income (USD)	$23,078	$24,582
Median Household Income (USD)	$32,566	$36,729
Individuals below Poverty Level	19.6%	19.8%

Data: U.S. Census, American Community Survey; U.S. Department of Commerce, Bureau of Economic Analysis

of the state's adult population has graduated from high school, compared to an 84.2 percent national average; 20.6 percent hold a bachelor degree or higher (national average is 27.2 percent); and 7.1 percent hold professional or graduate degrees (national average is 10.0 percent).

Tax Profile and Business Climate. In fiscal year 2003–4 Louisiana had total tax revenues of $13.1 billion. The largest share was generated from sales and gross receipts taxes, followed by property taxes. The per capita tax burden in Louisiana was $2,899 for 2003–4, some $548 below the national average and. In terms of business taxes, the state ranked fifteenth in a 2006 report by Anderson Economic Group. Forbes Magazine and the Tax Foundation ranked the state's business climate fiftieth and thirtieth, respectively.

Population Projections

	2010	2015	2020	2025
Total Population	4,612,679	4,673,721	4,719,160	4,762,398
Median Age	35.7	36.4	37.5	38.3
Population 18 Years of Age and Older	3,441,177	3,497,533	3,546,384	3,609,162
Population 65 Years of Age and Older	582,340	663,788	763,468	868,502

Data: U.S. Census Bureau

Workforce and Industry Profile

Workforce

	2000	2005
Civilian Labor Force	1,997,995	2,104,456
Labor Force Participation Rate	59.4%	62.7%
Unemployment Rate	5.0%	7.1%
Average Earnings per Job (USD)	$27,889	$31,430
Education Attainment (Population 25 Years and Older)	**(%)**	**(%)**
High School Graduate or Higher	74.8	80.5
Bachelors Degree or Higher	18.7	20.6
Graduate or Professional Degree	6.5	7.1

Data: U.S. Census Bureau, American Community Survey; U.S. Department of Labor, Bureau of Labor Statistics

Industry Overview

	1998	2004
Total Employees	1,577,220	1,623,680
Total Payroll ($1,000)	40,802,387	49,047,249
Total Establishments	100,667	103,067
Establishments with 1–19 Employees	85,803	87,549
Establishments with 20–49 Employees	9,421	9,841
Establishments with 50–249 Employees	4,775	5,032
Establishments with 250–999 Employees	580	549
Establishments with 1,000+ Employees	88	96

Data: U.S. Census Bureau, County Business Patterns

Major Industries (Ranked by 2004 Employment; Payroll in $1,000s)				
Industry	1998 Employment	2004 Employment	1998 Payroll	2004 Payroll
Health Care and Social Assistance	234,869	259,988	5,910,937	7,852,111
Retail Trade	226,586	231,777	3,610,877	4,423,008
Accommodation and Food Services	157,120	177,247	1,724,134	2,191,434
Manufacturing	171,549	148,750	6,373,959	6,979,560
Construction	124,838	122,875	3,622,058	3,983,070
Admin., Support, Waste Mngt., Remediation Services	90,251	104,943	1,688,891	2,351,492
Professional, Scientific, Technical Services	74,826	81,969	2,580,019	3,316,325
Other Services (except Public Admin.)	78,090	79,245	1,330,511	1,509,482
Wholesale Trade	79,877	73,609	2,592,307	2,856,525
Finance and Insurance	68,110	70,389	2,391,798	2,913,427

Data: U.S. Census Bureau, County Business Patterns

Taxes and Business Climate

State and Local Taxes		
Combined Revenues ($1,000)	2001–2	2003–4
Revenue from Property Taxes	1,940,420	2,263,204
Revenue from Sales and Gross Receipts Taxes	6,948,740	7,239,436
Revenue from Individual Income Taxes	1,788,922	2,192,038
Revenue from Corporate Income Taxes	264,419	236,745
Revenue from Other Taxes	1,239,564	1,134,007
Total Tax Revenue	12,182,065	13,065,430
Per Capita Taxes		
Property Tax per Capita	434	502
Sales and Gross Receipts Tax per Capita	1,555	1,606
Individual Income Tax per Capita	400	486
Corporate Income Tax per Capita	59	53
Other Taxes per Capita	277	252
Total Taxes per Capita	2,726	2,899

Data: U.S. Census Bureau; Anderson Economic Group, LLC

Business Climate Measures	
Anderson Economic Group: 2006 Business Tax Ranking (1 is Best)	15
Forbes Magazine: 2006 Best States for Business Ranking (1 is Best)	50
Tax Foundation: 2007 Business Tax Climate Ranking (1 is Best)	30
2002–3 Employer Firm Births	9,372
2002–3 Employer Firm Terminations	8,751

Data: Anderson Economic Group; Tax Foundation; Forbes Magazine; U.S. Census, Statistics of U.S. Businesses

Voting Behavior and Elected Officials

Voter Registration and Turnout (%)	1992	1996	2000	2004
Registered Voters Who Voted	78.1	69.7	63.1	66.5
Citizens Age 18+ Who Voted	59.8	57.0	54.3	58.5

Data: Dave Leip's Atlas of U.S. Presidential Elections

Presidential Election Results (Nationwide Winner Listed First)		
2004	**Popular Vote (%)**	**Electoral Votes**
George W. Bush (Republican, Incumbent)	56.7	9
John Kerry (Democrat)	42.2	0
Other	1.1	0
2000		
George W. Bush (Republican)	52.6	9
Albert Gore (Democrat)	44.9	0
Ralph Nader (Green)	1.2	0
Other	1.4	0
1996		
William Clinton (Democrat, Incumbent)	52.0	9
Robert Dole (Republican)	39.9	0
H. Ross Perot (Reformist)	6.9	0
Other	1.1	0
1992		
William Clinton (Democrat)	45.6	9
George H. W. Bush (Republican, Incumbent)	41.0	0
H. Ross Perot (Independent)	11.8	0
Other	1.6	0

Data: Dave Leip's Atlas of U.S. Presidential Elections

Governor and U.S. Congressional Seats				
Governor	**Party**	**Year Term Began**	**Term**	**Max. Consecutive Terms**
Kathleen Babineaux Blanco	D	2004	First	2
U.S. Senators	**Party**	**Year Elected**	**Term Expires**	
Mary L. Landrieu	D	1996	2009	
David Vitter	R	2004	2011	
U.S. Representatives		**Republican**	**Democrat**	**Other**
		5	2	0

Data: National Governors Association, U.S. Senate, U.S. House of Representatives

Business and Economic Agencies

Agency	Website Address
Louisiana Association of Business and Industry	www.labi.org
Louisiana Economic Development	www.lded.state.la.us
Louisiana Small Business Dev. Center	www.lsbdc.org
Louisiana Secretary of State, Commercial Division	www.sec.state.la.us/comm/comm-index.htm

Data: Various Agency Websites

Maine

Demographics and Socioeconomics. Maine, located in the New England region of the United States, has a population of 1.3 million people, making it the eleventh least populous state in 2005. The state's population increased by 8,750 people from 2000 to 2005, and is projected to reach 1.4 million by 2025. This 0.5 percent projected annual growth rate compares to the projected national average of 1.0 percent. Per capita personal income in Maine was $30,808 in 2005, ranking the fourteenth lowest in the country and $3,687 below the national average. Per capita income in Maine grew at an average annual rate of 3.5 percent from 2000 to 2005, compared to 2.9 percent nationally.

Workforce and Industry. In 2004 the state's largest industry in terms of employment was health care and social assistance, followed by retail trade. The fastest growing major industry from 1998 to 2004 was construction, which saw total growth of 25.3 percent. In terms of the education level of the workforce, 89.0 percent of Maine's adult population has a high school diploma or the equivalent,

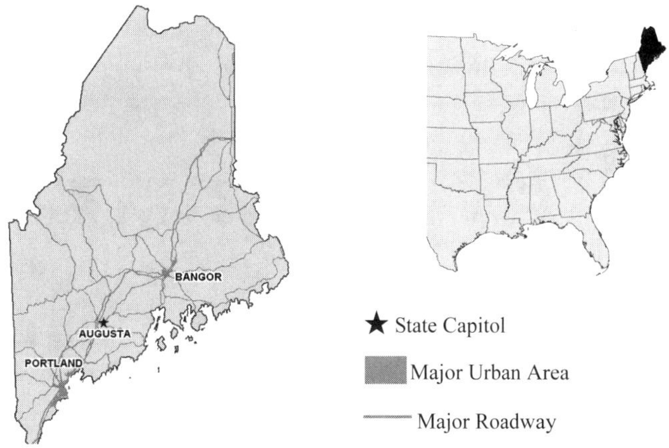

Demographic and Socioeconomic Profile

Demographics and Socioeconomic Figures		
Population and Households	**2000**	**2005**
Total Population	1,274,923	1,283,673
Number of Households	518,200	542,158
Average Household Size	2.4	2.4
Age and Ethnicity		
Median Age	38.6	41.2
Population 18 Years of Age and Older	973,945	1,007,454
Population 65 Years of Age and Older	183,642	181,315
Caucasian Population	1,236,422	1,239,525
African-American Population	6,047	8,788
Hispanic Population	9,226	12,059
Asian Population	8,259	10,907
Foreign-Born Population	36,691	38,727
Income		
Per Capita Personal Income (USD)	$25,969	$30,808
Median Household Income (USD)	$37,240	$42,801
Individuals below Poverty Level	10.9%	12.6%

Data: U.S. Census, American Community Survey; U.S. Department of Commerce, Bureau of Economic Analysis

compared to the national average of 84.2 percent; 25.6 percent of Maine's adult population has a bachelor degree or higher (national average is 27.2 percent); and 8.6 percent hold professional or graduate degrees (national average is 10.0 percent).

Tax Profile and Business Climate. In fiscal year 2003–4 Maine had total tax revenues of $5.0 billion. The largest share was generated from property taxes, followed by sales and gross receipts taxes. The per capita tax burden in Maine was $3,789 for 2003–4, some $342 above the national average. In terms of business taxes, the state ranked forty-nineth in a 2006 report by Anderson Economic Group. Forbes Magazine and the Tax Foundation ranked the state's business climate forty-sixth and forty-second, respectively.

Population Projections

	2010	2015	2020	2025
Total Population	1,357,134	1,388,878	1,408,665	1,414,402
Median Age	42.2	43.4	44.1	45.3
Population 18 Years of Age and Older	1,087,902	1,120,280	1,140,230	1,149,909
Population 65 Years of Age and Older	212,278	250,195	293,990	339,038

Data: U.S. Census Bureau

Workforce and Industry Profile

Workforce

	2000	2005
Civilian Labor Force	655,176	694,704
Labor Force Participation Rate	65.3%	66.9%
Unemployment Rate	3.4%	4.8%
Average Earnings per Job (USD)	$27,664	$33,920
Education Attainment (Population 25 Years and Older)	**(%)**	**(%)**
High School Graduate or Higher	85.4	89.0
Bachelors Degree or Higher	22.9	25.6
Graduate or Professional Degree	7.9	8.6

Data: U.S. Census Bureau, American Community Survey; U.S. Department of Labor, Bureau of Labor Statistics

Industry Overview

	1998	2004
Total Employees	456,715	494,256
Total Payroll ($1,000)	11,559,136	15,439,092
Total Establishments	38,334	41,269
Establishments with 1–19 Employees	34,326	36,717
Establishments with 20–49 Employees	2,516	2,955
Establishments with 50–249 Employees	1,312	1,404
Establishments with 250–999 Employees	162	173
Establishments with 1,000+ Employees	18	20

Data: U.S. Census Bureau, County Business Patterns

Major Industries (Ranked by 2004 Employment; Payroll in $1,000s)				
Industry	1998 Employment	2004 Employment	1998 Payroll	2004 Payroll
Health Care and Social Assistance	79,828	96,894	2,029,109	3,113,137
Retail Trade	74,220	82,234	1,263,051	1,780,053
Manufacturing	80,640	62,738	2,630,781	2,526,271
Accommodation and Food Services	41,273	44,769	512,859	693,324
Construction	23,766	27,950	729,676	1,024,278
Finance and Insurance	21,374	27,384	839,098	1,297,860
Admin., Support, Waste Mngt., Remediation Services	23,318	25,170	445,008	669,102
Professional, Scientific, Technical Services	16,708	22,540	584,864	975,155
Other Services (except Public Admin.)	17,445	19,439	294,070	400,098
Wholesale Trade	20,932	18,796	658,579	770,707

Data: U.S. Census Bureau, County Business Patterns

Taxes and Business Climate

State and Local Taxes		
Combined Revenues ($1,000)	**2001–2**	**2003–4**
Revenue from Property Taxes	1,912,158	2,099,394
Revenue from Sales and Gross Receipts Taxes	1,241,788	1,336,680
Revenue from Individual Income Taxes	1,072,861	1,160,389
Revenue from Corporate Income Taxes	77,366	111,616
Revenue from Other Taxes	236,973	274,462
Total Tax Revenue	4,541,146	4,982,541
Per Capita Taxes		
Property Tax per Capita	1,500	1,596
Sales and Gross Receipts Tax per Capita	974	1,016
Individual Income Tax per Capita	841	882
Corporate Income Tax per Capita	61	85
Other Taxes per Capita	186	209
Total Taxes per Capita	3,562	3,789

Data: U.S. Census Bureau; Anderson Economic Group, LLC

Business Climate Measures	
Anderson Economic Group: 2006 Business Tax Ranking (1 is Best)	49
Forbes Magazine: 2006 Best States for Business Ranking (1 is Best)	46
Tax Foundation: 2007 Business Tax Climate Ranking (1 is Best)	42
2002–3 Employer Firm Births	3,626
2002–3 Employer Firm Terminations	3,256

Data: Anderson Economic Group; Tax Foundation; Forbes Magazine; U.S. Census, Statistics of U.S. Businesses

Voting Behavior and Elected Officials

Voter Registration and Turnout (%)				
	1992	1996	2000	2004
Registered Voters Who Voted	69.7	60.5	68.8	72.3
Citizens Age 18+ Who Voted	72.0	64.1	66.9	72.7

Data: Dave Leip's Atlas of U.S. Presidential Elections

Presidential Election Results (Nationwide Winner Listed First)		
2004	Popular Vote (%)	Electoral Votes
George W. Bush (Republican, Incumbent)	44.6	0
John Kerry (Democrat)	53.6	4
Other	1.9	0
2000		
George W. Bush (Republican)	44.0	0
Albert Gore (Democrat)	49.1	4
Ralph Nader (Green)	5.7	0
Other	1.2	0
1996		
William Clinton (Democrat, Incumbent)	51.6	4
Robert Dole (Republican)	30.8	0
H. Ross Perot (Reformist)	14.2	0
Other	3.4	0
1992		
William Clinton (Democrat)	38.8	4
George H. W. Bush (Republican, Incumbent)	30.4	0
H. Ross Perot (Independent)	30.4	0
Other	0.4	0

Data: Dave Leip's Atlas of U.S. Presidential Elections

Governor and U.S. Congressional Seats				
Governor	**Party**	**Year Term Began**	**Term**	**Max. Consecutive Terms**
John Baldacci	D	2003	Second	2
U.S. Senators	**Party**	**Year Elected**	**Term Expires**	
Susan M. Collins	R	1996	2009	
Olympia J. Snowe	R	1994	2013	
U.S. Representatives		**Republican**	**Democrat**	**Other**
		0	2	0

Data: National Governors Association, U.S. Senate, U.S. House of Representatives

Business and Economic Agencies

Agency	Website Address
Maine State Chamber of Commerce	www.mainechamber.org
The Maine Department of Economic and Community Development	www.econdevmaine.com
Maine Small Business Dev. Center	www.mainesbdc.org
Maine Bureau of Corporations	www.state.me.us/sos/cec/index.html

Data: Various Agency Websites

Maryland

Demographics and Socioeconomics. With a population of 5.5 million people, Maryland was the nineteenth most populous state in 2005. From 2000 to 2005 the state's population increased by 164,832 people, and is projected to increase to 6.8 million by 2025. This 1.1 percent projected annual growth rate is slightly above the projected national average of 1.0 percent. In 2005 Maryland had a per capita personal income of $41,996, which was $7,501 above the national average and the fourth highest in the country. The state's per capita income grew at an average annual rate of 4.2 percent from 2000 to 2005, compared to 2.9 percent nationally.

Workforce and Industry. In 2004 Maryland's largest industry in terms of employment was retail trade. The fastest growing major industry was construction, with 25.3 percent growth from 1998 to 2004. The state's workforce is generally more educated than that of other states: 87.0 percent of the state's adult population has graduated from high school, compared to an 84.2 percent national average; 34.5 percent hold a bachelor degree or higher (national average is

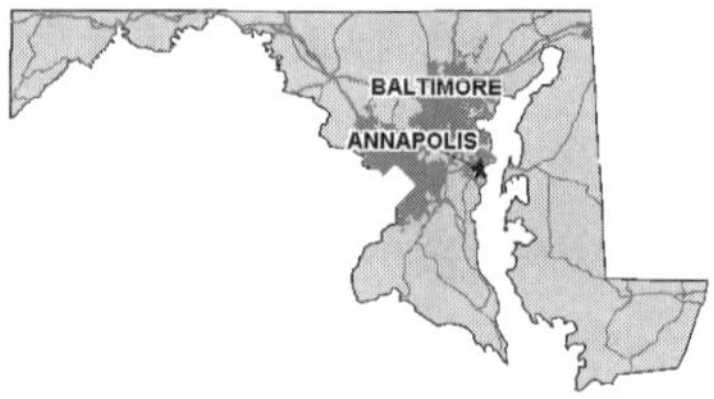

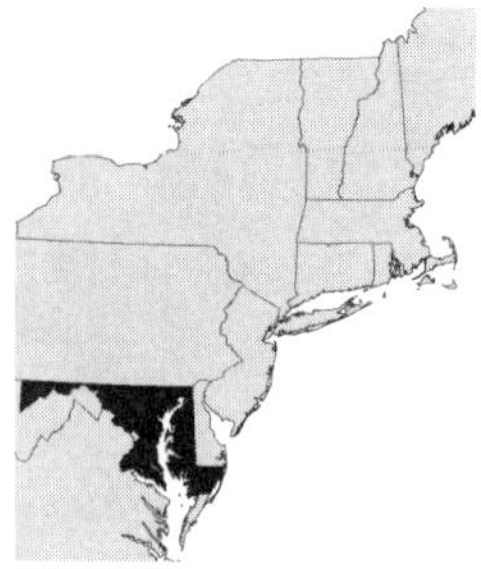

★ State Capitol

Major Urban Area

Major Roadway

Demographic and Socioeconomic Profile

Demographics and Socioeconomic Figures		
Population and Households	**2000**	**2005**
Total Population	5,296,486	5,461,318
Number of Households	1,980,859	2,085,647
Average Household Size	2.6	2.6
Age and Ethnicity		
Median Age	36.0	37.1
Population 18 Years of Age and Older	3,943,067	4,063,655
Population 65 Years of Age and Older	598,004	609,450
Caucasian Population	3,391,021	3,356,489
African-American Population	1,468,243	1,564,914
Hispanic Population	227,105	316,257
Asian Population	209,713	258,529
Foreign-Born Population	518,315	641,373
Income		
Per Capita Personal Income (USD)	$34,257	$41,996
Median Household Income (USD)	$52,868	$61,592
Individuals below Poverty Level	8.5%	8.2%

Data: U.S. Census, American Community Survey; U.S. Department of Commerce, Bureau of Economic Analysis

27.2 percent); and 15.2 percent hold professional or graduate degrees (national average is 10.0 percent).

Tax Profile and Business Climate. Maryland's total tax revenue was $22.3 billion for fiscal year 2003–4. The largest share of tax revenue in 2003–4 was generated from individual income taxes, followed by property taxes. On a per capita basis Maryland had taxes of $4,016, compared to the national average of $3,447 for 2003–4. In terms of business taxes, the state ranked twenty-first in a 2006 report by Anderson Economic Group. Forbes Magazine and the Tax Foundation ranked the state's business climate eleventh and twenty-nineth, respectively.

Population Projections

	2010	2015	2020	2025
Total Population	5,904,970	6,208,392	6,497,626	6,762,732
Median Age	36.8	36.1	36.4	36.9
Population 18 Years of Age and Older	4,498,676	4,721,718	4,911,565	5,098,221
Population 65 Years of Age and Older	717,987	837,124	962,160	1,104,757

Data: U.S. Census Bureau

Workforce and Industry Profile

Workforce

	2000	2005
Civilian Labor Force	2,737,359	2,927,143
Labor Force Participation Rate	67.8%	69.8%
Unemployment Rate	3.6%	4.1%
Average Earnings per Job (USD)	$36,395	$42,080
Education Attainment (Population 25 Years and Older)	**(%)**	**(%)**
High School Graduate or Higher	83.8	87.0
Bachelors Degree or Higher	31.4	34.5
Graduate or Professional Degree	13.4	15.2

Data: U.S. Census Bureau, American Community Survey; U.S. Department of Labor, Bureau of Labor Statistics

Industry Overview

	1998	2004
Total Employees	1,938,727	2,151,474
Total Payroll ($1,000)	59,817,673	84,346,365
Total Establishments	126,577	136,062
Establishments with 1–19 Employees	108,830	115,881
Establishments with 20–49 Employees	10,961	12,322
Establishments with 50–249 Employees	5,980	6,980
Establishments with 250–999 Employees	702	770
Establishments with 1,000+ Employees	104	109

Data: U.S. Census Bureau, County Business Patterns

Major Industries (Ranked by 2004 Employment; Payroll in $1,000s)				
Industry	1998 Employment	2004 Employment	1998 Payroll	2004 Payroll
Retail Trade	273,016	299,177	5,245,293	6,886,730
Health Care and Social Assistance	258,901	296,856	7,607,050	11,190,993
Professional, Scientific, Technical Services	172,671	215,303	8,145,127	12,722,352
Accommodation and Food Services	160,294	184,041	1,838,370	2,573,589
Construction	142,650	178,787	4,851,310	7,660,016
Admin., Support, Waste Mngt., Remediation Services	160,362	157,969	3,665,695	4,623,857
Manufacturing	163,123	140,803	6,191,401	6,747,194
Finance and Insurance	104,336	124,803	4,556,298	7,512,802
Other Services (except Public Admin.)	105,452	112,584	2,288,378	2,952,909
Wholesale Trade	91,987	95,065	3,925,037	4,848,172

Data: U.S. Census Bureau, County Business Patterns

Taxes and Business Climate

State and Local Taxes		
Combined Revenues ($1,000)	2001–2	2003–4
Revenue from Property Taxes	5,412,209	6,018,629
Revenue from Sales and Gross Receipts Taxes	4,973,619	5,455,744
Revenue from Individual Income Taxes	7,644,183	8,286,551
Revenue from Corporate Income Taxes	359,420	569,700
Revenue from Other Taxes	1,484,850	2,000,503
Total Tax Revenue	19,874,281	22,331,127
Per Capita Taxes		
Property Tax per Capita	1,022	1,082
Sales and Gross Receipts Tax per Capita	939	981
Individual Income Tax per Capita	1,443	1,490
Corporate Income Tax per Capita	68	102
Other Taxes per Capita	280	360
Total Taxes per Capita	3,753	4,016

Data: U.S. Census Bureau; Anderson Economic Group, LLC

Business Climate Measures

Anderson Economic Group: 2006 Business Tax Ranking (1 is Best)	21
Forbes Magazine: 2006 Best States for Business Ranking (1 is Best)	11
Tax Foundation: 2007 Business Tax Climate Ranking (1 is Best)	29
2002–3 Employer Firm Births	12,979
2002–3 Employer Firm Terminations	11,294

Data: Anderson Economic Group; Tax Foundation; Forbes Magazine; U.S. Census, Statistics of U.S. Businesses

Voting Behavior and Elected Officials

Voter Registration and Turnout (%)

	1992	1996	2000	2004
Registered Voters Who Voted	80.6	69.1	74.5	77.7
Citizens Age 18+ Who Voted	53.4	46.6	51.4	57.8

Data: Dave Leip's Atlas of U.S. Presidential Elections

Presidential Election Results (Nationwide Winner Listed First)

2004	Popular Vote (%)	Electoral Votes
George W. Bush (Republican, Incumbent)	42.9	0
John Kerry (Democrat)	55.9	10
Other	1.2	0
2000		
George W. Bush (Republican)	40.2	0
Albert Gore (Democrat)	56.6	10
Ralph Nader (Green)	2.7	0
Other	0.6	0
1996		
William Clinton (Democrat, Incumbent)	54.3	10
Robert Dole (Republican)	38.3	0
H. Ross Perot (Reformist)	6.5	0
Other	1.0	0
1992		
William Clinton (Democrat)	49.8	10
George H. W. Bush (Republican, Incumbent)	35.6	0
H. Ross Perot (Independent)	14.2	0
Other	0.4	0

Data: Dave Leip's Atlas of U.S. Presidential Elections

Governor and U.S. Congressional Seats				
Governor	**Party**	**Year Term Began**	**Term**	**Max. Consecutive Terms**
Martin O'Malley	D	2007	First	2
U.S. Senators	**Party**	**Year Elected**	**Term Expires**	
Barbara A. Mikulski	D	1986	2011	
Ben Cardin	D	2006	2013	
U.S. Representatives		**Republican**	**Democrat**	**Other**
		2	6	0

Data: National Governors Association, U.S. Senate, U.S. House of Representatives

Business and Economic Agencies

Agency	Website Address
Maryland Chamber of Commerce	www.mdchamber.org
Maryland Department of Business and Economic Development	www.dbed.state.md.us
Maryland Small Business Dev. Center	www.mdsbdc.umd.edu
Maryland Department of Assessments and Taxation	www.dat.state.md.us/sdatweb/charter.html

Data: Various Agency Websites

Massachusetts

Demographics and Socioeconomics. Massachusetts is located in the New England region of the United States and has a population of 6.2 million people, making it the thirteenth most populous state in 2005. The state's population decreased by 166,237 people from 2000 to 2005, but is projected to increase to 6.9 million by 2025. This 0.6 percent projected annual growth rate is below the national average of 1.0 percent. Per capita personal income in Massachusetts was $43,702 in 2005, ranking the third highest in the country and $9,207 above the national average. From 2000 to 2005 per capita income in the state grew at an average annual rate of 3.0 percent, compared to 2.9 percent nationally.

Workforce and Industry. The state's workforce is generally more educated than that of other states: 88.0 percent of the state's adult population has graduated from high school, compared to an 84.2 percent national average; 36.9 percent hold a bachelor degree or higher (national average is 27.2 percent); and 15.7 percent hold professional or graduate degrees (national average is 10.0). In

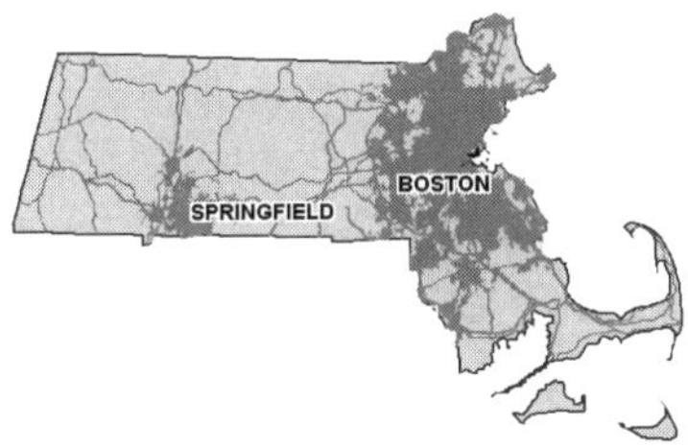

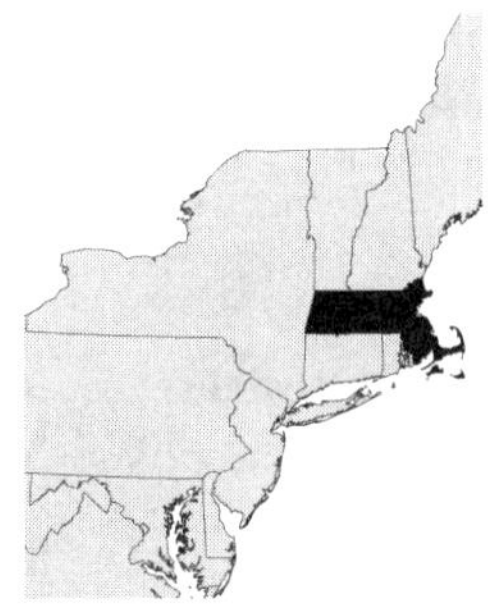

★ State Capitol

Major Urban Area

Major Roadway

Demographic and Socioeconomic Profile

Demographics and Socioeconomic Figures		
Population and Households	**2000**	**2005**
Total Population	6,349,097	6,182,860
Number of Households	2,443,580	2,448,032
Average Household Size	2.5	2.5
Age and Ethnicity		
Median Age	36.5	38.2
Population 18 Years of Age and Older	4,853,130	4,732,189
Population 65 Years of Age and Older	859,601	796,788
Caucasian Population	5,365,139	5,156,426
African-American Population	337,157	363,095
Hispanic Population	427,340	490,839
Asian Population	238,246	292,537
Foreign-Born Population	772,983	891,184
Income		
Per Capita Personal Income (USD)	$37,756	$43,702
Median Household Income (USD)	$50,502	$57,184
Individuals below Poverty Level	9.3%	10.3%

Data: U.S. Census, American Community Survey; U.S. Department of Commerce, Bureau of Economic Analysis

2004 the state's largest industry in terms of employment was health care and social assistance, followed by retail trade. The major industry with the fastest employment growth from 1998 to 2004 was construction, which grew 22.1 percent.

Tax Profile and Business Climate. In fiscal year 2003–4 Massachusetts had total tax revenues of $27.0 billion. The largest share was generated from property taxes, followed by individual income taxes. The per capita tax burden in Massachusetts was $4,217 for 2003–4, some $770 above the national average. In terms of business taxes, Massachusetts ranked sixteenth in a 2006 report by Anderson Economic Group. The state's business climate was ranked thirty-seventh by Forbes Magazine and thirty-sixth by the Tax Foundation.

Population Projections

	2010	2015	2020	2025
Total Population	6,649,441	6,758,580	6,855,546	6,938,636
Median Age	38.8	39.2	39.5	39.7
Population 18 Years of Age and Older	5,165,588	5,284,629	5,362,379	5,419,996
Population 65 Years of Age and Older	908,565	1,025,448	1,159,817	1,317,940

Data: U.S. Census Bureau

Workforce and Industry Profile

Workforce

	2000	2005
Civilian Labor Force	3,312,039	3,331,806
Labor Force Participation Rate	66.2%	68.1%
Unemployment Rate	2.7%	4.8%
Average Earnings per Job (USD)	$44,329	$45,970
Education Attainment (Population 25 Years and Older)	**(%)**	**(%)**
High School Graduate or Higher	84.8	88.0
Bachelors Degree or Higher	33.2	36.9
Graduate or Professional Degree	13.7	15.7

Data: U.S. Census Bureau, American Community Survey; U.S. Department of Labor, Bureau of Labor Statistics

Industry Overview

	1998	2004
Total Employees	2,924,913	2,979,690
Total Payroll ($1,000)	105,871,311	135,244,829
Total Establishments	167,929	175,933
Establishments with 1–19 Employees	143,459	150,563
Establishments with 20–49 Employees	14,454	15,276
Establishments with 50–249 Employees	8,658	8,851
Establishments with 250–999 Employees	1,148	1,043
Establishments with 1,000+ Employees	210	200

Data: U.S. Census Bureau, County Business Patterns

Major Industries (Ranked by 2004 Employment; Payroll in $1,000s)				
Industry	1998 Employment	2004 Employment	1998 Payroll	2004 Payroll
Health Care and Social Assistance	452,465	483,615	13,494,246	18,156,092
Retail Trade	340,548	369,537	6,558,993	8,704,974
Manufacturing	409,938	294,278	17,170,367	15,590,341
Accommodation and Food Services	232,603	245,121	2,994,758	3,978,333
Professional, Scientific, Technical Services	201,084	236,527	11,773,454	17,983,939
Finance and Insurance	214,807	213,848	13,055,694	19,225,574
Educational Services	152,797	182,586	4,016,307	5,630,596
Admin., Support, Waste Mngt., Remediation Services	179,590	180,387	4,639,257	6,023,870
Wholesale Trade	147,661	143,292	7,145,803	8,664,702
Construction	106,184	129,607	4,591,611	6,870,271

Data: U.S. Census Bureau, County Business Patterns

Taxes and Business Climate

State and Local Taxes		
Combined Revenues ($1,000)	**2001–2**	**2003–4**
Revenue from Property Taxes	8,721,832	9,814,315
Revenue from Sales and Gross Receipts Taxes	5,363,254	5,740,153
Revenue from Individual Income Taxes	7,912,934	8,830,334
Revenue from Corporate Income Taxes	812,257	1,301,076
Revenue from Other Taxes	1,085,159	1,329,269
Total Tax Revenue	23,895,436	27,015,147
Per Capita Taxes		
Property Tax per Capita	1,374	1,532
Sales and Gross Receipts Tax per Capita	845	896
Individual Income Tax per Capita	1,246	1,378
Corporate Income Tax per Capita	128	203
Other Taxes per Capita	171	207
Total Taxes per Capita	3,764	4,217

Data: U.S. Census Bureau; Anderson Economic Group, LLC

Business Climate Measures	
Anderson Economic Group: 2006 Business Tax Ranking (1 is Best)	16
Forbes Magazine: 2006 Best States for Business Ranking (1 is Best)	37
Tax Foundation: 2007 Business Tax Climate Ranking (1 is Best)	36
2002–3 Employer Firm Births	16,906
2002–3 Employer Firm Terminations	14,825

Data: Anderson Economic Group; Tax Foundation; Forbes Magazine; U.S. Census, Statistics of U.S. Businesses

Voting Behavior and Elected Officials

Voter Registration and Turnout (%)	1992	1996	2000	2004
Registered Voters Who Voted	82.7	73.8	67.4	71.1
Citizens Age 18+ Who Voted	60.2	55.0	55.7	58.9

Data: Dave Leip's Atlas of U.S. Presidential Elections

Presidential Election Results (Nationwide Winner Listed First)		
2004	**Popular Vote (%)**	**Electoral Votes**
George W. Bush (Republican, Incumbent)	36.8	0
John Kerry (Democrat)	61.9	12
Other	1.3	0
2000		
George W. Bush (Republican)	32.5	0
Albert Gore (Democrat)	59.8	12
Ralph Nader (Green)	6.4	0
Other	1.3	0
1996		
William Clinton (Democrat, Incumbent)	61.5	12
Robert Dole (Republican)	28.1	0
H. Ross Perot (Reformist)	8.9	0
Other	1.6	0
1992		
William Clinton (Democrat)	47.5	12
George H. W. Bush (Republican, Incumbent)	29.0	0
H. Ross Perot (Independent)	22.7	0
Other	0.7	0

Data: Dave Leip's Atlas of U.S. Presidential Elections

Governor and U.S. Congressional Seats				
Governor	**Party**	**Year Term Began**	**Term**	**Max. Consecutive Terms**
Deveal Patrick	D	2007	First	No limit
U.S. Senators	**Party**	**Year Elected**	**Term Expires**	
John Kerry	D	1984	2009	
Edward Kennedy	D	1962	2013	
U.S. Representatives		**Republican**	**Democrat**	**Other**
		0	10	0

Data: National Governors Association, U.S. Senate, U.S. House of Representatives

Business and Economic Agencies

Agency	Website Address
Massachusetts Economic Development	www.mass.gov/?pageID=econhomepage&L=1&L0=Home&sid=Eecon
Massachusetts Small Business Dev. Center	www.msbdc.org
Massachusetts Corporations Division	www.sec.state.ma.us/cor/coridx.htm

Data: Various Agency Websites

Michigan

Demographics and Socio-economics. Michigan, located in the East North Central region of the United States, has a population of 9.9 million people, making it the eighth most populous state in 2005. The state's population decreased by 72,861 people from 2000 to 2005, but is projected to increase to 10.7 million by 2025. This 0.4 percent projected annual growth rate is below the national average of 1.0 percent. In 2005 the state's per capita personal income of $32,735 was the twenty-fourth highest in the United States, but $1,760 below the national average. Per capita income in Michigan grew at an average annual rate of 2.1 percent from 2000 to 2005, compared to 2.9 percent nationally.

Workforce and Industry. In terms of the education level of the workforce, 87.0 percent of Michigan's adult population has a high school diploma or the equivalent, compared to the national average of 84.2 percent; 24.7 percent of Michigan's adult population has a bachelor degree or higher (national average is 27.2 percent); and 9.5 percent hold professional or graduate degrees (national average is 10.0 percent). In

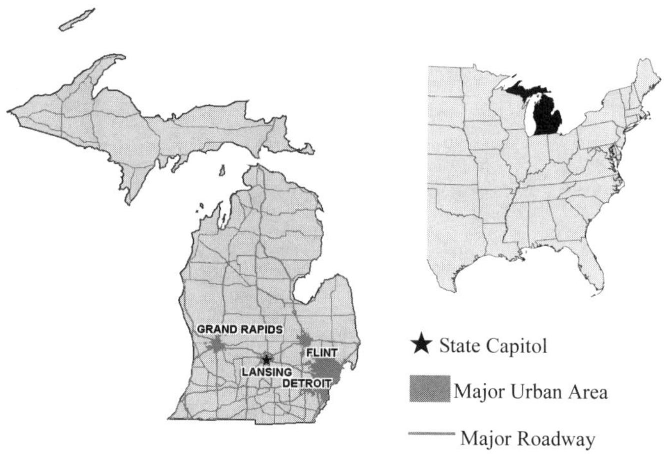

Demographic and Socioeconomic Profile

Demographics and Socioeconomic Figures		
Population and Households	**2000**	**2005**
Total Population	9,938,444	9,865,583
Number of Households	3,785,661	3,887,994
Average Household Size	2.6	2.5
Age and Ethnicity		
Median Age	35.5	36.9
Population 18 Years of Age and Older	7,345,849	7,352,920
Population 65 Years of Age and Older	1,219,232	1,194,502
Caucasian Population	7,960,342	7,890,608
African-American Population	1,401,723	1,379,010
Hispanic Population	322,160	371,627
Asian Population	174,824	227,585
Foreign-Born Population	523,589	605,656
Income		
Per Capita Personal Income (USD)	$29,552	$32,735
Median Household Income (USD)	$44,667	$46,039
Individuals below Poverty Level	10.5%	13.2%

Data: U.S. Census, American Community Survey; U.S. Department of Commerce, Bureau of Economic Analysis

2004 the state's largest industry in terms of employment was manufacturing, followed by health care and social assistance. The fastest growing industry was professional, scientific, and technical services, with 53.1 percent growth from 1998 to 2004.

Tax Profile and Business Climate. In fiscal year 2003–4 Michigan had total tax revenues of $33.5 billion. The largest share was generated from property taxes, followed by sales and gross receipts taxes. The per capita tax burden in Michigan was $3,313 for 2003–4, some $133 below the national average. In terms of business taxes, Michigan ranked twenty-seventh in a 2006 report by Anderson Economic Group. The state's business climate was ranked forty-fifth by Forbes Magazine and twenty-seventh by the Tax Foundation.

Population Projections

	2010	2015	2020	2025
Total Population	10,428,683	10,599,122	10,695,993	10,713,730
Median Age	37.4	37.8	38.6	39.4
Population 18 Years of Age and Older	7,941,625	8,120,199	8,216,729	8,241,856
Population 65 Years of Age and Older	1,334,491	1,506,856	1,711,476	1,926,396

Data: U.S. Census Bureau

Workforce and Industry Profile

Workforce

	2000	2005
Civilian Labor Force	2,304,452	4,981,647
Labor Force Participation Rate	58.4%	65.2%
Unemployment Rate	3.7%	6.7%
Average Earnings per Job (USD)	$37,011	$40,040
Education Attainment (Population 25 Years and Older)	**(%)**	**(%)**
High School Graduate or Higher	83.4	87.0
Bachelors Degree or Higher	21.8	24.7
Graduate or Professional Degree	8.1	9.5

Data: U.S. Census Bureau, American Community Survey; U.S. Department of Labor, Bureau of Labor Statistics

Industry Overview

	1998	2004
Total Employees	3,919,567	3,895,914
Total Payroll ($1,000)	128,649,484	147,721,534
Total Establishments	235,403	237,984
Establishments with 1–19 Employees	201,308	203,298
Establishments with 20–49 Employees	21,230	21,638
Establishments with 50–249 Employees	11,163	11,417
Establishments with 250–999 Employees	1,456	1,405
Establishments with 1,000+ Employees	246	226

Data: U.S. Census Bureau, County Business Patterns

Major Industries (Ranked by 2004 Employment; Payroll in $1,000s)				
Industry	1998 Employment	2004 Employment	1998 Payroll	2004 Payroll
Manufacturing	828,751	661,699	35,615,528	32,391,363
Health Care and Social Assistance	486,987	537,404	14,340,634	18,822,785
Retail Trade	537,895	523,056	9,629,527	10,529,856
Accommodation and Food Services	320,768	335,036	3,167,701	3,774,935
Admin., Support, Waste Mngt., Remediation Services	271,928	317,073	6,276,011	9,358,717
Professional, Scientific, Technical Services	192,200	294,303	8,926,124	18,041,765
Other Services (except Public Admin.)	178,300	179,298	3,419,688	3,858,577
Wholesale Trade	191,469	172,962	8,163,387	8,920,325
Construction	179,122	172,163	7,147,499	7,523,856
Finance and Insurance	164,990	170,576	6,929,849	8,545,863

Data: U.S. Census Bureau, County Business Patterns

Taxes and Business Climate

State and Local Taxes		
Combined Revenues ($1,000)	**2001–2**	**2003–4**
Revenue from Property Taxes	9,814,422	11,978,654
Revenue from Sales and Gross Receipts Taxes	10,237,929	11,065,649
Revenue from Individual Income Taxes	6,621,875	6,361,981
Revenue from Corporate Income Taxes	2,065,241	1,841,010
Revenue from Other Taxes	1,952,663	2,230,888
Total Tax Revenue	30,692,130	33,478,182
Per Capita Taxes		
Property Tax per Capita	988	1,186
Sales and Gross Receipts Tax per Capita	1,030	1,095
Individual Income Tax per Capita	666	630
Corporate Income Tax per Capita	208	182
Other Taxes per Capita	196	221
Total Taxes per Capita	3,088	3,313

Data: U.S. Census Bureau; Anderson Economic Group, LLC

Business Climate Measures	
Anderson Economic Group: 2006 Business Tax Ranking (1 is Best)	27
Forbes Magazine: 2006 Best States for Business Ranking (1 is Best)	45
Tax Foundation: 2007 Business Tax Climate Ranking (1 is Best)	27
2002–3 Employer Firm Births	21,185
2002–3 Employer Firm Terminations	20,876

Data: Anderson Economic Group; Tax Foundation; Forbes Magazine; U.S. Census, Statistics of U.S. Businesses

Voting Behavior and Elected Officials

Voter Registration and Turnout (%)

	1992	1996	2000	2004
Registered Voters Who Voted	69.5	57.6	61.7	67.5
Citizens Age 18+ Who Voted	61.7	54.4	57.6	64.2

Data: Dave Leip's Atlas of U.S. Presidential Elections

Presidential Election Results (Nationwide Winner Listed First)

2004	Popular Vote (%)	Electoral Votes
George W. Bush (Republican, Incumbent)	47.8	0
John Kerry (Democrat)	51.2	17
Other	1.0	0
2000		
George W. Bush (Republican)	46.1	0
Albert Gore (Democrat)	51.3	18
Ralph Nader (Green)	2.0	0
Other	0.6	0
1996		
William Clinton (Democrat, Incumbent)	51.7	18
Robert Dole (Republican)	38.5	0
H. Ross Perot (Reformist)	8.8	0
Other	1.1	0
1992		
William Clinton (Democrat)	43.8	18
George H. W. Bush (Republican, Incumbent)	36.4	0
H. Ross Perot (Independent)	19.3	0
Other	0.6	0

Data: Dave Leip's Atlas of U.S. Presidential Elections

Governor and U.S. Congressional Seats				
Governor	**Party**	**Year Term Began**	**Term**	**Max. Consecutive Terms**
Jennifer Granholm	D	2003	Second	2
U.S. Senators	**Party**	**Year Elected**	**Term Expires**	
Carl Levin	D	1978	2009	
Debbie Stabenow	D	2000	2013	
U.S. Representatives		**Republican**	**Democrat**	**Other**
		9	6	0

Data: National Governors Association, U.S. Senate, U.S. House of Representatives

Business and Economic Agencies

Agency	Website Address
Michigan Chamber of Commerce	www.michamber.com
Michigan Economic Development Corporation	www.michigan.org/medc/keywordsearch/?txtSearchString=MEDC&qsearch=fs
Michigan Small Business and Tech Dev. Center	www.misbtdc.org
Michigan Department of Labor and Economic Growth	www.michigan.gov/cis/0,1607,7-154-35299_35413---,00.html

Data: Various Agency Websites

Minnesota

Demographics and Socioeconomics. With a population of 5.0 million people, Minnesota was the twenty-first most populous state in the United States in 2005. From 2000 to 2005 the state's population increased by 70,369 people, and is projected to increase to 6.1 million by 2025. This 1.0 percent projected annual growth rate is equal to the projected national average. The state's 2005 per capita personal income of $37,322 was the nineth highest in the United States and $2,827 above the national average. Per capita income in Minnesota grew at an average annual rate of 3.1 percent from 2000 to 2005, compared to 2.9 percent nationally.

Workforce and Industry. The state's largest industry in terms of 2004 employment was health care and social assistance. The fastest growing major industry was construction, with 23.8 percent growth from 1998 to 2004. The state's workforce is generally more educated than that of other states: 90.9 percent of the state's adult population has graduated from high school, compared to an 84.2 percent national average;

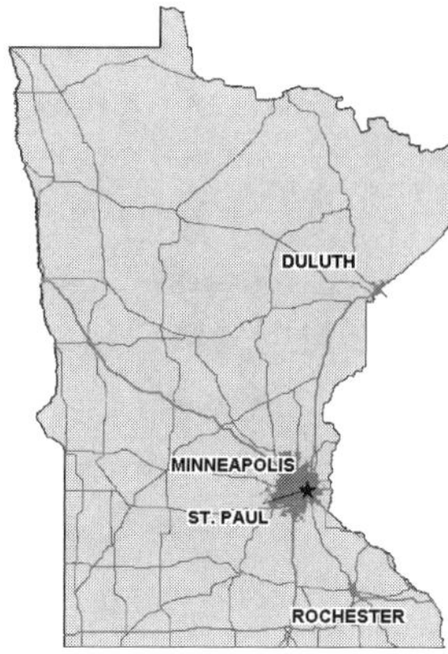

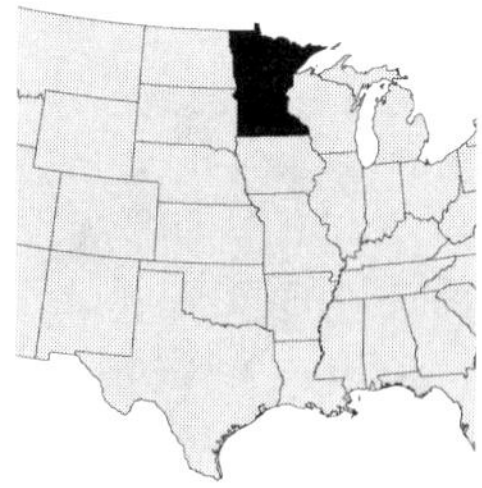

★ State Capitol
Major Urban Area
Major Roadway

Demographic and Socioeconomic Profile

Demographics and Socioeconomic Figures		
Population and Households	**2000**	**2005**
Total Population	4,919,479	4,989,848
Number of Households	1,895,127	2,020,144
Average Household Size	2.5	2.5
Age and Ethnicity		
Median Age	35.4	36.7
Population 18 Years of Age and Older	3,632,940	3,763,129
Population 65 Years of Age and Older	593,415	577,318
Caucasian Population	4,402,124	4,390,040
African-American Population	167,857	205,160
Hispanic Population	141,786	181,959
Asian Population	139,245	177,645
Foreign-Born Population	260,463	316,716
Income		
Per Capita Personal Income (USD)	$32,017	$37,322
Median Household Income (USD)	$47,111	$52,024
Individuals below Poverty Level	7.9%	9.2%

Data: U.S. Census, American Community Survey; U.S. Department of Commerce, Bureau of Economic Analysis

30.7 percent hold a bachelor degree or higher (national average is 27.2 percent); and 9.7 percent hold professional or graduate degrees (national average is 10.0 percent).

Tax Profile and Business Climate. Minnesota's total tax revenue was $19.4 billion for fiscal year 2003–4. The largest share of this was generated from sales and gross receipts taxes, followed by individual income taxes. On a per capita basis, taxes in Minnesota were $3,811, compared to the national average of $3,447 for 2003–4. In terms of business taxes, the state ranked second in a 2006 report by Anderson Economic Group. Forbes Magazine and the Tax Foundation ranked the state's business climate fourteenth and forty-first, respectively.

Population Projections

	2010	2015	2020	2025
Total Population	5,420,636	5,668,211	5,900,769	6,108,787
Median Age	36.5	36.7	37.5	38.4
Population 18 Years of Age and Older	4,130,673	4,318,787	4,484,545	4,636,987
Population 65 Years of Age and Older	670,429	774,390	909,950	1,063,116

Data: U.S. Census Bureau

Workforce and Industry Profile

Workforce

	2000	2005
Civilian Labor Force	2,689,115	2,818,655
Labor Force Participation Rate	71.2%	72.2%
Unemployment Rate	3.2%	4.0%
Average Earnings per Job (USD)	$35,413	$40,340
Education Attainment (Population 25 Years and Older)	**(%)**	**(%)**
High School Graduate or Higher	87.9	90.9
Bachelors Degree or Higher	27.4	30.7
Graduate or Professional Degree	8.3	9.7

Data: U.S. Census Bureau, American Community Survey; U.S. Department of Labor, Bureau of Labor Statistics

Industry Overview

	1998	2004
Total Employees	2,271,671	2,393,126
Total Payroll ($1,000)	70,094,975	92,395,099
Total Establishments	134,981	148,626
Establishments with 1–19 Employees	115,369	127,350
Establishments with 20–49 Employees	11,910	13,050
Establishments with 50–249 Employees	6,637	7,144
Establishments with 250–999 Employees	918	935
Establishments with 1,000+ Employees	147	147

Data: U.S. Census Bureau, County Business Patterns

Major Industries (Ranked by 2004 Employment; Payroll in $1,000s)				
Industry	1998 Employment	2004 Employment	1998 Payroll	2004 Payroll
Health Care and Social Assistance	304,550	367,753	8,290,432	12,600,060
Manufacturing	378,392	332,501	13,760,626	15,026,254
Retail Trade	295,669	312,319	5,089,588	6,840,470
Accommodation and Food Services	181,104	207,157	1,923,350	2,649,857
Finance and Insurance	129,833	151,970	6,191,235	9,753,722
Admin., Support, Waste Mngt., Remediation Services	140,086	136,635	2,847,993	3,861,536
Wholesale Trade	133,590	136,382	5,616,725	7,674,158
Professional, Scientific, Technical Services	110,695	124,194	4,944,905	6,833,019
Construction	98,539	122,029	4,227,371	6,215,908
Other Services (except Public Admin.)	115,687	116,611	2,015,766	2,411,189

Data: U.S. Census Bureau, County Business Patterns

Taxes and Business Climate

State and Local Taxes		
Combined Revenues ($1,000)	2001–2	2003–4
Revenue from Property Taxes	5,214,735	4,920,174
Revenue from Sales and Gross Receipts Taxes	5,917,693	6,564,330
Revenue from Individual Income Taxes	5,443,355	5,709,584
Revenue from Corporate Income Taxes	533,901	637,183
Revenue from Other Taxes	1,346,725	1,592,366
Total Tax Revenue	18,456,409	19,423,637
Per Capita Taxes		
Property Tax per Capita	1,060	965
Sales and Gross Receipts Tax per Capita	1,203	1,288
Individual Income Tax per Capita	1,107	1,120
Corporate Income Tax per Capita	109	125
Other Taxes per Capita	274	312
Total Taxes per Capita	3,752	3,811

Data: U.S. Census Bureau; Anderson Economic Group, LLC

Business Climate Measures	
Anderson Economic Group: 2006 Business Tax Ranking (1 is Best)	2
Forbes Magazine: 2006 Best States for Business Ranking (1 is Best)	14
Tax Foundation: 2007 Business Tax Climate Ranking (1 is Best)	41
2002–3 Employer Firm Births	13,864
2002–3 Employer Firm Terminations	12,018

Data: Anderson Economic Group; Tax Foundation; Forbes Magazine; U.S. Census, Statistics of U.S. Businesses

Voting Behavior and Elected Officials

Voter Registration and Turnout (%)

	1992	1996	2000	2004
Registered Voters Who Voted	74.8	71.5	74.7	79.5
Citizens Age 18+ Who Voted	71.6	64.3	67.1	74.2

Data: Dave Leip's Atlas of U.S. Presidential Elections

Presidential Election Results (Nationwide Winner Listed First)

2004	Popular Vote (%)	Electoral Votes
George W. Bush (Republican, Incumbent)	47.6	0
John Kerry (Democrat)	51.1	9
Other	1.3	0
2000		
George W. Bush (Republican)	45.5	0
Albert Gore (Democrat)	47.9	10
Ralph Nader (Green)	5.2	0
Other	1.4	0
1996		
William Clinton (Democrat, Incumbent)	51.1	10
Robert Dole (Republican)	35.0	0
H. Ross Perot (Reformist)	11.8	0
Other	2.2	0
1992		
William Clinton (Democrat)	43.5	10
George H. W. Bush (Republican, Incumbent)	31.9	0
H. Ross Perot (Independent)	24.0	0
Other	0.7	0

Data: Dave Leip's Atlas of U.S. Presidential Elections

Governor and U.S. Congressional Seats				
Governor	**Party**	**Year Term Began**	**Term**	**Max. Consecutive Terms**
Tim Pawlenty	R	2003	Second	No limit
U.S. Senators	**Party**	**Year Elected**	**Term Expires**	
Norm Coleman	R	2002	2009	
Amy Klobuchar	D	2007	2013	
U.S. Representatives		**Republican**	**Democrat**	**Other**
		3	5	0

Data: National Governors Association, U.S. Senate, U.S. House of Representatives

Business and Economic Agencies

Agency	Website Address
Minnesota Chamber of Commerce	www.mnchamber.com
Minnesota Department of Commerce	www.state.mn.us/portal/mn/jsp/home.do?agency=Commerce
Minnesota Small Business Dev. Center	www.mnsbdc.com
Minnesota Secretary of State	www.sos.state.mn.us/home/index.asp?page=3

Data: Various Agency Websites

Mississippi

Demographics and Socioeconomics. With a population of 2.8 million people, Mississippi was the twentieth least populous state in the United States in 2005. The state's population decreased by 20,502 people from 2000 to 2005, but is projected to increase to 3.1 million by 2025. This 0.4 percent projected annual growth rate compares to the projected national average of 1.0 percent. In 2005 Mississippi had a per capita personal income of $24,925, which was $9,570 below the national average and the second lowest in the country. The state's per capita income grew at an average annual rate of 3.5 percent from 2000 to 2005, compared to 2.9 percent nationally.

Workforce and Industry. In 2004, Mississippi's largest industry in terms of employment was manufacturing. The fastest growing industry was transportation and warehousing, with 29.1 percent growth from 1998 to 2004. The state's workforce is generally less educated than that of other states: 78.5 percent of the state's adult population has graduated from high school, compared to an 84.2 percent national average; 18.7 percent hold a bachelor

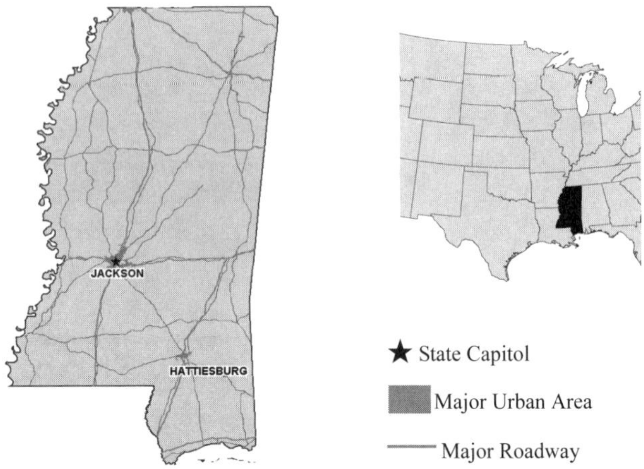

Demographic and Socioeconomic Profile

Demographics and Socioeconomic Figures		
Population and Households	**2000**	**2005**
Total Population	2,844,658	2,824,156
Number of Households	1,046,434	1,084,034
Average Household Size	2.6	2.6
Age and Ethnicity		
Median Age	33.8	35.5
Population 18 Years of Age and Older	2,070,254	2,080,210
Population 65 Years of Age and Older	344,288	337,462
Caucasian Population	1,745,353	1,716,444
African-American Population	1,033,437	1,030,075
Hispanic Population	37,790	43,275
Asian Population	17,709	21,523
Foreign-Born Population	39,908	43,336
Income		
Per Capita Personal Income (USD)	$21,005	$24,925
Median Household Income (USD)	$31,330	$32,938
Individuals below Poverty Level	19.9%	21.3%

Data: U.S. Census, American Community Survey; U.S. Department of Commerce, Bureau of Economic Analysis

degree or higher (national average is 27.2 percent); and 6.5 percent hold professional or graduate degrees (national average is 10.0 percent).

Tax Profile and Business Climate. Mississippi's total tax revenue was $7.1 billion for fiscal year 2003–4. The largest share of tax revenue was generated from sales and gross receipts taxes, followed by property taxes. Total Taxes per Capita in Mississippi were $2,444, compared to the national average of $3,447 for 2003–4. In terms of business taxes, the state ranked forty-fifth in a 2006 report by Anderson Economic Group. Forbes Magazine and the Tax Foundation ranked the state's business climate forty-eighth and seventeenth, respectively.

Population Projections

	2010	2015	2020	2025
Total Population	2,971,412	3,014,409	3,044,812	3,069,420
Median Age	36.5	37.8	39.4	40.6
Population 18 Years of Age and Older	2,211,962	2,261,862	2,307,758	2,351,380
Population 65 Years of Age and Older	379,025	433,428	499,190	573,543

Data: U.S. Census Bureau

Workforce and Industry Profile

Workforce

	2000	2005
Civilian Labor Force	1,267,092	1,338,496
Labor Force Participation Rate	59.4%	62.3%
Unemployment Rate	5.6%	7.9%
Average Earnings per Job (USD)	$25,205	$29,100
Education Attainment (Population 25 Years and Older)	**(%)**	**(%)**
High School Graduate or Higher	72.9	78.5
Bachelors Degree or Higher	16.9	18.7
Graduate or Professional Degree	5.8	6.5

Data: U.S. Census Bureau, American Community Survey; U.S. Department of Labor, Bureau of Labor Statistics

Industry Overview

	1998	2004
Total Employees	937,023	928,313
Total Payroll ($1,000)	21,066,790	24,817,597
Total Establishments	59,771	60,534
Establishments with 1–19 Employees	51,949	52,201
Establishments with 20–49 Employees	4,921	5,377
Establishments with 50–249 Employees	2,430	2,561
Establishments with 250–999 Employees	405	335
Establishments with 1,000+ Employees	66	60

Data: U.S. Census Bureau, County Business Patterns

Major Industries (Ranked by 2004 Employment; Payroll in $1,000s)				
Industry	1998 Employment	2004 Employment	1998 Payroll	2004 Payroll
Manufacturing	230,175	174,494	5,882,128	5,593,663
Retail Trade	138,422	141,965	2,156,337	2,586,994
Health Care and Social Assistance	126,613	141,609	3,309,588	4,550,467
Accommodation and Food Services	93,376	117,820	1,163,591	1,621,951
Construction	49,854	50,665	1,291,418	1,524,086
Admin., Support, Waste Mngt., Remediation Services	43,815	43,179	703,619	855,929
Other Services (except Public Admin.)	39,511	42,176	585,933	716,864
Wholesale Trade	39,464	35,458	1,123,409	1,258,807
Finance and Insurance	34,047	34,641	1,049,663	1,328,519
Transportation and Warehousing	25,871	33,397	693,395	1,043,748

Data: U.S. Census Bureau, County Business Patterns

Taxes and Business Climate

State and Local Taxes		
Combined Revenues ($1,000)	2001–2	2003–4
Revenue from Property Taxes	1,646,563	1,859,756
Revenue from Sales and Gross Receipts Taxes	3,255,263	3,458,788
Revenue from Individual Income Taxes	985,117	1,061,704
Revenue from Corporate Income Taxes	195,814	243,846
Revenue from Other Taxes	440,965	464,625
Total Tax Revenue	6,523,722	7,088,719
Per Capita Taxes		
Property Tax per Capita	579	641
Sales and Gross Receipts Tax per Capita	1,144	1,192
Individual Income Tax per Capita	346	366
Corporate Income Tax per Capita	69	84
Other Taxes per Capita	155	160
Total Taxes per Capita	2,293	2,444

Data: U.S. Census Bureau; Anderson Economic Group, LLC

Business Climate Measures	
Anderson Economic Group: 2006 Business Tax Ranking (1 is Best)	45
Forbes Magazine: 2006 Best States for Business Ranking (1 is Best)	48
Tax Foundation: 2007 Business Tax Climate Ranking (1 is Best)	17
2002–3 Employer Firm Births	5,869
2002–3 Employer Firm Terminations	5,383

Data: Anderson Economic Group; Tax Foundation; Forbes Magazine; U.S. Census, Statistics of U.S. Businesses

Voting Behavior and Elected Officials

Voter Registration and Turnout (%)

	1992	1996	2000	2004
Registered Voters Who Voted	59.9	52.1	57.2	63.9
Citizens Age 18+ Who Voted	52.8	45.4	48.1	54.4

Data: Dave Leip's Atlas of U.S. Presidential Elections

Presidential Election Results (Nationwide Winner Listed First)

2004	Popular Vote (%)	Electoral Votes
George W. Bush (Republican, Incumbent)	59.4	6
John Kerry (Democrat)	39.7	0
Other	0.8	0
2000		
George W. Bush (Republican)	57.6	7
Albert Gore (Democrat)	40.7	0
Ralph Nader (Green)	.8	0
Other	0.9	0
1996		
William Clinton (Democrat, Incumbent)	44.1	0
Robert Dole (Republican)	49.2	7
H. Ross Perot (Reformist)	5.8	0
Other	0.9	0
1992		
William Clinton (Democrat)	40.8	0
George H. W. Bush (Republican, Incumbent)	49.7	7
H. Ross Perot (Independent)	8.7	0
Other	0.8	0

Data: Dave Leip's Atlas of U.S. Presidential Elections

Governor and U.S. Congressional Seats				
Governor	Party	Year Term Began	Term	Max. Consecutive Terms
Haley Barbour	R	2004	First	2
U.S. Senators	Party	Year Elected	Term Expires	
Thad Cochran	R	1978	2009	
Trent Lott	R	1988	2013	
U.S. Representatives		Republican	Democrat	Other
		2	2	0

Data: National Governors Association, U.S. Senate, U.S. House of Representatives

Business and Economic Agencies

Agency	Website Address
Mississippi Economic Council	www.msmec.com
Mississippi Development Authority	www.mississippi.org
Mississippi Small Business Dev. Center	www.olemiss.edu/depts/mssbdc
Mississippi Secretary of State, Business Services	www.sos.state.ms.us/busserv

Data: Various Agency Websites

Missouri

Demographics and Socioeconomics. Missouri, located in the West North Central region of the United States, has a population of 5.6 million people, making it the eighteenth most populous state in 2005. The state's population increased by 36,699 people from 2000 to 2005, and is projected to increase to 6.3 million by 2025. This 0.6 percent projected annual growth rate compares to the projected national average of 1.0 percent. Per capita personal income in Missouri was $31,299 in 2005, ranking the twentieth lowest in the country and $3,196 below the national average. From 2000 to 2005 per capita income in Missouri grew at an average annual rate of 2.8 percent, compared to 2.9 percent nationally.

Workforce and Industry. In 2004 the state's largest industry in terms of employment was health care and social assistance, followed by retail trade. The fastest growing industry was construction, with 22.7 percent growth from 1998 to 2004. In terms of the education level of the workforce, 85.0 percent of Missouri's adult population has a high school diploma or

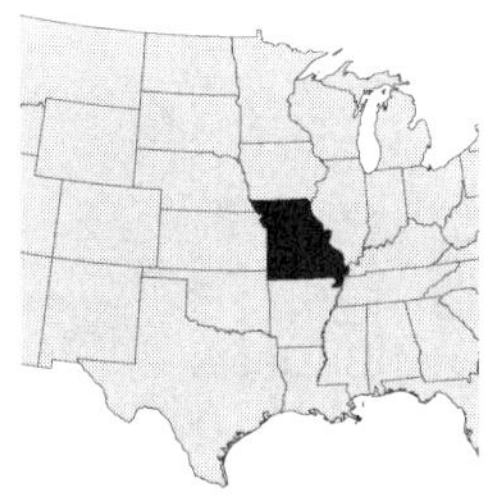

★ State Capitol

Major Urban Area

Major Roadway

Demographic and Socioeconomic Profile

Demographics and Socioeconomic Figures		
Population and Households	**2000**	**2005**
Total Population	5,595,211	5,631,910
Number of Households	2,194,594	2,285,280
Average Household Size	2.5	2.5
Age and Ethnicity		
Median Age	36.1	37.4
Population 18 Years of Age and Older	4,169,109	4,260,766
Population 65 Years of Age and Older	756,038	721,138
Caucasian Population	4,746,952	4,760,327
African-American Population	622,087	627,978
Hispanic Population	116,373	148,994
Asian Population	60,429	78,554
Foreign-Born Population	151,196	193,685
Income		
Per Capita Personal Income (USD)	$27,241	$31,299
Median Household Income (USD)	$37,934	$41,974
Individuals below Poverty Level	11.7%	13.3%

Data: U.S. Census, American Community Survey; U.S. Department of Commerce, Bureau of Economic Analysis

the equivalent, compared to the national average of 84.2 percent; 24.0 percent of Missouri's adult population has a bachelor degree or higher (national average is 27.2 percent); and 8.6 percent hold professional or graduate degrees (national average is 10.0 percent).

Tax Profile and Business Climate. In fiscal year 2003–4 Missouri had total tax revenues of $16.3 billion. The largest share was generated from sales and gross receipts taxes, followed by property taxes. The per capita tax burden in Missouri was $2,822 for 2003–4, some $625 below the national average. In terms of business taxes, the state ranked third in a 2006 report by Anderson Economic Group. Forbes Magazine and the Tax Foundation ranked the state's business climate twenty-second and fifteenth, respectively.

Population Projections

	2010	2015	2020	2025
Total Population	5,922,078	6,069,556	6,199,882	6,315,366
Median Age	37.6	37.9	38.6	39.2
Population 18 Years of Age and Older	4,510,684	4,633,827	4,739,310	4,839,119
Population 65 Years of Age and Older	821,645	922,418	1,047,071	1,189,605

Data: U.S. Census Bureau

Workforce and Industry Profile

Workforce

	2000	2005
Civilian Labor Force	2,806,718	2,940,295
Labor Force Participation Rate	65.2%	66.8%
Unemployment Rate	3.3%	5.4%
Average Earnings per Job (USD)	$31,385	$34,660
Education Attainment (Population 25 Years and Older)	**(%)**	**(%)**
High School Graduate or Higher	81.3	85.0
Bachelors Degree or Higher	21.6	24.0
Graduate or Professional Degree	7.6	8.6

Data: U.S. Census Bureau, American Community Survey; U.S. Department of Labor, Bureau of Labor Statistics

Industry Overview

	1998	2004
Total Employees	2,310,122	2,421,450
Total Payroll ($1,000)	64,669,474	79,157,172
Total Establishments	143,912	153,985
Establishments with 1–19 Employees	123,828	132,554
Establishments with 20–49 Employees	12,250	13,216
Establishments with 50–249 Employees	6,801	7,182
Establishments with 250–999 Employees	885	879
Establishments with 1,000+ Employees	148	154

Data: U.S. Census Bureau, County Business Patterns

Major Industries (Ranked by 2004 Employment; Payroll in $1,000s)				
Industry	1998 Employment	2004 Employment	1998 Payroll	2004 Payroll
Health Care and Social Assistance	320,300	346,641	8,508,854	11,193,368
Retail Trade	304,009	321,135	5,452,695	6,527,449
Manufacturing	382,003	302,760	12,487,544	11,702,622
Accommodation and Food Services	203,301	229,914	2,165,787	2,754,007
Construction	120,864	148,242	4,279,334	5,844,225
Admin., Support, Waste Mngt., Remediation Services	126,561	144,410	2,345,691	3,393,290
Finance and Insurance	123,925	139,920	4,878,339	6,897,780
Wholesale Trade	126,722	131,159	4,638,609	5,049,794
Professional, Scientific, Technical Services	108,911	130,591	4,351,928	6,266,123
Other Services (except Public Admin.)	112,331	122,924	1,957,301	2,509,820

Data: U.S. Census Bureau, County Business Patterns

Taxes and Business Climate

State and Local Taxes		
Combined Revenues ($1,000)	2001–2	2003–4
Revenue from Property Taxes	3,880,344	4,304,387
Revenue from Sales and Gross Receipts Taxes	6,044,079	6,694,944
Revenue from Individual Income Taxes	3,928,546	4,033,495
Revenue from Corporate Income Taxes	300,459	224,366
Revenue from Other Taxes	970,004	998,186
Total Tax Revenue	15,123,432	16,255,378
Per Capita Taxes		
Property Tax per Capita	694	747
Sales and Gross Receipts Tax per Capita	1,080	1,162
Individual Income Tax per Capita	702	700
Corporate Income Tax per Capita	54	39
Other Taxes per Capita	173	173
Total Taxes per Capita	2,703	2,822

Data: U.S. Census Bureau; Anderson Economic Group, LLC

Business Climate Measures	
Anderson Economic Group: 2006 Business Tax Ranking (1 is Best)	3
Forbes Magazine: 2006 Best States for Business Ranking (1 is Best)	22
Tax Foundation: 2007 Business Tax Climate Ranking (1 is Best)	15
2002–3 Employer Firm Births	15,663
2002–3 Employer Firm Terminations	13,516

Data: Anderson Economic Group; Tax Foundation; Forbes Magazine; U.S. Census, Statistics of U.S. Businesses

Voting Behavior and Elected Officials

Voter Registration and Turnout (%)

	1992	1996	2000	2004
Registered Voters Who Voted	77.9	64.6	61.1	65.1
Citizens Age 18+ Who Voted	62.0	54.0	56.6	63.6

Data: Dave Leip's Atlas of U.S. Presidential Elections

Presidential Election Results (Nationwide Winner Listed First)

2004	Popular Vote (%)	Electoral Votes
George W. Bush (Republican, Incumbent)	53.3	11
John Kerry (Democrat)	46.1	0
Other	0.6	0
2000		
George W. Bush (Republican)	50.4	11
Albert Gore (Democrat)	47.1	0
Ralph Nader (Green)	1.6	0
Other	0.9	0
1996		
William Clinton (Democrat, Incumbent)	47.5	11
Robert Dole (Republican)	41.2	0
H. Ross Perot (Reformist)	10.1	0
Other	1.2	0
1992		
William Clinton (Democrat)	44.1	11
George H. W. Bush (Republican, Incumbent)	33.9	0
H. Ross Perot (Independent)	21.7	0
Other	0.3	0

Data: Dave Leip's Atlas of U.S. Presidential Elections

Governor and U.S. Congressional Seats				
Governor	**Party**	**Year Term Began**	**Term**	**Max. Consecutive Terms**
Matt Blunt	D	2005	First	2
U.S. Senators	**Party**	**Year Elected**	**Term Expires**	
Claire McCaskill	D	2006	2013	
Christopher Bond	R	1986	2011	
U.S. Representatives		**Republican**	**Democrat**	**Other**
		5	4	0

Data: National Governors Association, U.S. Senate, U.S. House of Representatives

Business and Economic Agencies

Agency	Website Address
Missouri Chamber of Commerce and Industry	www.mochamber.org
Missouri Department of Economic Development	www.ded.mo.gov
Missouri Small Business Dev. Center	www.missouribusiness.net/sbdc
Missouri Secretary of State, Corporations Division	www.sos.mo.gov/business/corporations

Data: Various Agency Websites

Montana

Demographics and Socioeconomics. Montana, located in the Mountain region of the United States, has a population of 910,651 people, making it the seventh least populous state in 2005. The state's population increased by 8,456 people from 2000 to 2005, and is projected to grow to 1 million by 2025. This 0.7 percent projected annual growth rate is below the projected national average of 1.0 percent. The state's 2005 per capita personal income of $28,906 was the tenth lowest in the United States, some $5,589 below the national average. Per capita income in Montana grew at an average annual rate of 4.7 percent from 2000 to 2005, compared to 2.9 percent nationally.

Workforce and Industry. In 2004 the state's largest industry in terms of employment was retail trade, followed by health care and social assistance. The fastest growing industry was professional, scientific, and technical services, with 35.4 percent growth from 1998 to 2004. In terms of the education level of the workforce, 90.7 percent of Montana's adult population has a high school diploma or the equivalent, compared to the national

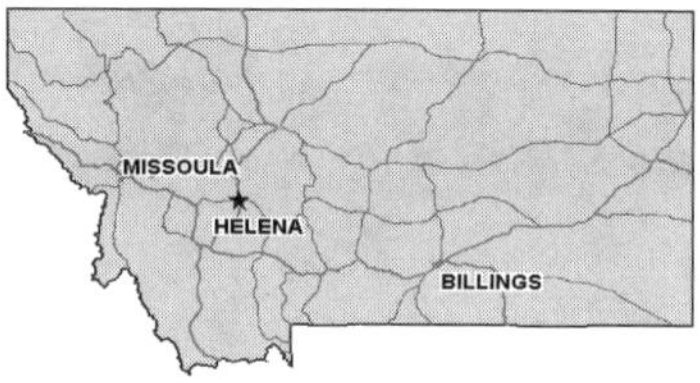

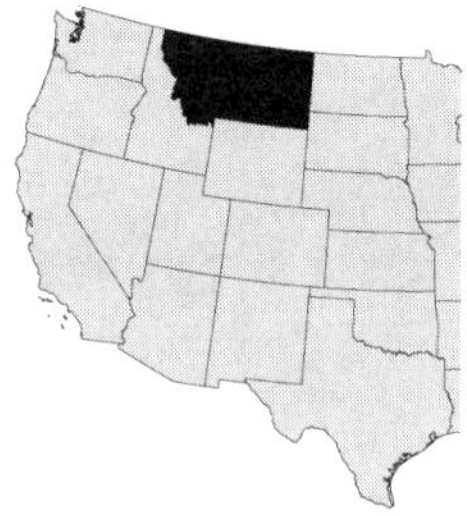

★ State Capitol

Major Urban Area

Major Roadway

Demographic and Socioeconomic Profile

Demographics and Socioeconomic Figures		
Population and Households	**2000**	**2005**
Total Population	902,195	910,651
Number of Households	358,667	368,268
Average Household Size	2.4	2.5
Age and Ethnicity		
Median Age	37.5	40.2
Population 18 Years of Age and Older	672,251	706,921
Population 65 Years of Age and Older	120,931	121,064
Caucasian Population	817,604	824,721
African-American Population	2,359	4,135
Hispanic Population	18,490	20,232
Asian Population	4,363	5,508
Foreign-Born Population	16,396	16,734
Income		
Per Capita Personal Income (USD)	$22,929	$28,906
Median Household Income (USD)	$33,024	$39,301
Individuals below Poverty Level	14.6%	14.4%

Data: U.S. Census, American Community Survey; U.S. Department of Commerce, Bureau of Economic Analysis

average of 84.2 percent. 26.5 percent of Montana's adult population has a bachelor degree or higher (national average is 27.2 percent); and 8.0 percent hold professional or graduate degrees (national average is 10.0 percent).

Tax Profile and Business Climate. In fiscal year 2003–4 Montana had total tax revenues of $2.4 billion. The largest share was generated from property taxes, followed by individual income taxes. The per capita tax burden in Montana was $2,623 for 2003–4, some $824 below the national average. In terms of business taxes, the state ranked fiftieth in a 2006 report by Anderson Economic Group. Forbes Magazine and the Tax Foundation ranked the state's business climate thirty-eighth and eighth, respectively.

Population Projections

	2010	2015	2020	2025
Total Population	968,598	999,489	1,022,735	1,037,387
Median Age	40.4	41.5	42.7	44.3
Population 18 Years of Age and Older	756,286	783,498	804,685	821,871
Population 65 Years of Age and Older	144,961	173,778	211,783	247,769

Data: U.S. Census Bureau

Workforce and Industry Profile

Workforce

	2000	2005
Civilian Labor Force	454,687	492,733
Labor Force Participation Rate	65.4%	67.6%
Unemployment Rate	4.8%	4.0%
Average Earnings per Job (USD)	$24,274	$30,220
Education Attainment (Population 25 Years and Older)	**(%)**	**(%)**
High School Graduate or Higher	87.2	90.7
Bachelors Degree or Higher	24.4	26.5
Graduate or Professional Degree	7.2	8.0

Data: U.S. Census Bureau, American Community Survey; U.S. Department of Labor, Bureau of Labor Statistics

Industry Overview

	1998	2004
Total Employees	277,144	314,865
Total Payroll ($1,000)	5,960,687	8,277,084
Total Establishments	30,957	34,686
Establishments with 1–19 Employees	28,134	31,433
Establishments with 20–49 Employees	2,000	2,307
Establishments with 50–249 Employees	767	876
Establishments with 250–999 Employees	51	64
Establishments with 1,000+ Employees	5	6

Data: U.S. Census Bureau, County Business Patterns

Major Industries (Ranked by 2004 Employment; Payroll in $1,000s)				
Industry	1998 Employment	2004 Employment	1998 Payroll	2004 Payroll
Retail Trade	48,285	55,864	771,476	1,109,658
Health Care and Social Assistance	45,242	53,243	1,067,519	1,578,195
Accommodation and Food Services	37,393	42,712	347,915	456,661
Construction	16,767	21,897	500,826	775,138
Manufacturing	20,686	18,428	599,839	688,391
Professional, Scientific, Technical Services	12,362	16,737	352,733	577,586
Finance and Insurance	12,780	15,980	403,122	600,080
Other Services (except Public Admin.)	13,315	14,422	201,904	267,603
Wholesale Trade	15,025	13,886	398,273	471,388
Admin., Support, Waste Mngt., Remediation Services	11,000	12,123	178,935	238,485

Data: U.S. Census Bureau, County Business Patterns

Taxes and Business Climate

State and Local Taxes		
Combined Revenues ($1,000)	2001–2	2003–4
Revenue from Property Taxes	852,399	958,779
Revenue from Sales and Gross Receipts Taxes	374,039	440,453
Revenue from Individual Income Taxes	517,568	605,582
Revenue from Corporate Income Taxes	68,173	67,723
Revenue from Other Taxes	323,003	358,798
Total Tax Revenue	2,135,182	2,431,335
Per Capita Taxes		
Property Tax per Capita	945	1,034
Sales and Gross Receipts Tax per Capita	415	475
Individual Income Tax per Capita	574	653
Corporate Income Tax per Capita	76	73
Other Taxes per Capita	358	387
Total Taxes per Capita	2,367	2,623

Data: U.S. Census Bureau; Anderson Economic Group, LLC

Business Climate Measures	
Anderson Economic Group: 2006 Business Tax Ranking (1 is Best)	50
Forbes Magazine: 2006 Best States for Business Ranking (1 is Best)	38
Tax Foundation: 2007 Business Tax Climate Ranking (1 is Best)	8
2002–3 Employer Firm Births	3,384
2002–3 Employer Firm Terminations	2,765

Data: Anderson Economic Group; Tax Foundation; Forbes Magazine; U.S. Census, Statistics of U.S. Businesses

Voting Behavior and Elected Officials

Voter Registration and Turnout (%)

	1992	1996	2000	2004
Registered Voters Who Voted	77.5	68.9	58.9	70.6
Citizens Age 18+ Who Voted	70.1	62.1	61.1	64.2

Data: Dave Leip's Atlas of U.S. Presidential Elections

Presidential Election Results (Nationwide Winner Listed First)

2004	Popular Vote (%)	Electoral Votes
George W. Bush (Republican, Incumbent)	59.1	3
John Kerry (Democrat)	38.6	0
Other	2.4	0
2000		
George W. Bush (Republican)	58.4	3
Albert Gore (Democrat)	33.4	0
Ralph Nader (Green)	6.0	0
Other	2.3	0
1996		
William Clinton (Democrat, Incumbent)	41.2	0
Robert Dole (Republican)	44.1	3
H. Ross Perot (Reformist)	13.6	0
Other	1.1	0
1992		
William Clinton (Democrat)	37.6	3
George H. W. Bush (Republican, Incumbent)	35.1	0
H. Ross Perot (Independent)	26.1	0
Other	1.1	0

Data: Dave Leip's Atlas of U.S. Presidential Elections

Governor and U.S. Congressional Seats				
Governor	**Party**	**Year Term Began**	**Term**	**Max. Consecutive Terms**
Brian Schweitzer	D	2005	First	2
U.S. Senators	**Party**	**Year Elected**	**Term Expires**	
Max Baucus	D	1978	2009	
Jon Tester	D	2006	2013	
U.S. Representatives		**Republican**	**Democrat**	**Other**
		1	0	0

Data: National Governors Association, U.S. Senate, U.S. House of Representatives

Business and Economic Agencies

Agency	Website Address
Montana Chamber of Commerce	www.montanachamber.com
Montana Department of Commerce	www.commerce.state.mt.us
Montana Small Business Dev. Center	sbdc.mt.gov
Montana Secretary of State, Business Services Bureau	www.sos.state.mt.us/BSB

Data: Various Agency Websites

Nebraska

Demographics and Socioeconomics. Nebraska, located in the West North Central region of the United States, has a population of 1.7 million people and was the thirteenth least populous state in 2005. The state's population decreased by 4,287 people from 2000 to 2005, but is projected to grow to 1.8 million by 2025. This 0.3 percent projected annual growth rate is below the national average of 1.0 percent. In 2005 Nebraska had a per capita personal income of $32,988, which was $1,507 below the national average. The state's per capita income grew at an average annual rate of 3.6 percent from 2000 to 2005, compared to 2.9 percent nationally.

Workforce and Industry. The state's workforce is generally more educated than that of other states: 89.5 percent of the State's adult population has graduated from high school, compared to an 84.2 percent national average; 27.3 percent hold a bachelor degree or higher (national average is 27.2 percent); and 8.5 percent hold professional or graduate degrees (national average is 10.0). In 2004 the state's largest industry in terms of employment was

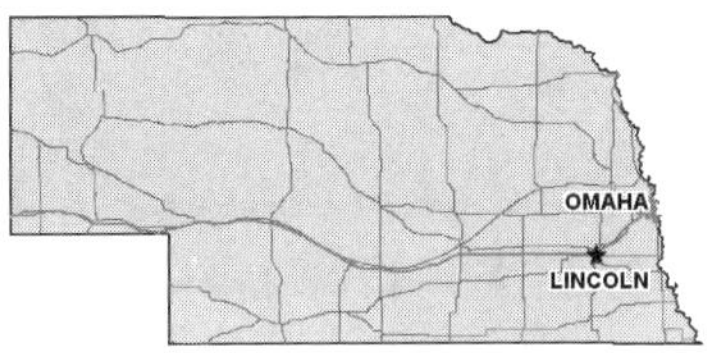

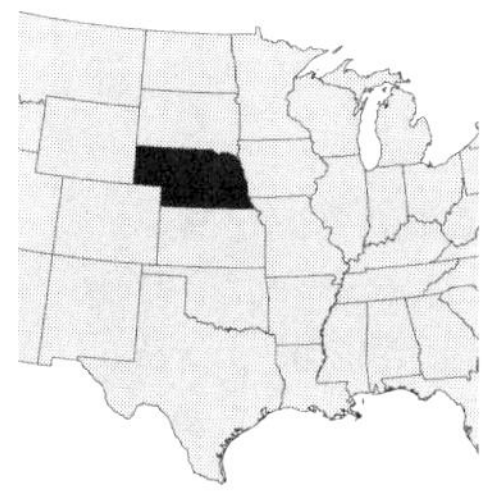

★ State Capitol

Major Urban Area

Major Roadway

Demographic and Socioeconomic Profile

Demographics and Socioeconomic Figures		
Population and Households	**2000**	**2005**
Total Population	1,711,263	1,706,976
Number of Households	666,184	695,592
Average Household Size	2.5	2.5
Age and Ethnicity		
Median Age	35.3	36.2
Population 18 Years of Age and Older	1,261,648	1,278,044
Population 65 Years of Age and Older	232,359	217,917
Caucasian Population	1,533,787	1,529,471
African-American Population	67,435	68,389
Hispanic Population	93,872	122,518
Asian Population	21,126	24,820
Foreign-Born Population	74,638	96,127
Income		
Per Capita Personal Income (USD)	$27,625	$32,988
Median Household Income (USD)	$39,250	$43,841
Individuals below Poverty Level	9.7%	10.9%

Data: U.S. Census, American Community Survey; U.S. Department of Commerce, Bureau of Economic Analysis

retail trade, followed by health care and social assistance. The fastest growing industry was management of companies and enterprises, with 113.0 percent growth from 1998 to 2004.

Tax Profile and Business Climate. In fiscal year 2003–4 Nebraska had total tax revenues of $6.3 billion. The largest share was generated from sales and gross receipts taxes, followed by property taxes. The per capita tax burden in Nebraska was $3,609 for 2003–4, some $162 above the national average. In terms of business taxes, Nebraska ranked twenty-sixth in a 2006 report by Anderson Economic Group. The state's business climate was ranked seventh by Forbes Magazine and forty-fourth by the Tax Foundation.

Population Projections

	2010	2015	2020	2025
Total Population	1,768,997	1,788,508	1,802,678	1,812,787
Median Age	36.7	37.2	37.9	38.3
Population 18 Years of Age and Older	1,322,741	1,334,423	1,344,066	1,355,661
Population 65 Years of Age and Older	243,313	271,379	308,994	347,809

Data: U.S. Census Bureau

Workforce and Industry Profile

Workforce

	2000	2005
Civilian Labor Force	909,524	943,927
Labor Force Participation Rate	69.7%	71.7%
Unemployment Rate	2.7%	3.8%
Average Earnings per Job (USD)	$27,692	$33,310
Education Attainment (Population 25 Years and Older)	**(%)**	**(%)**
High School Graduate or Higher	86.6	89.5
Bachelors Degree or Higher	23.7	27.3
Graduate or Professional Degree	7.3	8.5

Data: U.S. Census Bureau, American Community Survey; U.S. Department of Labor, Bureau of Labor Statistics

Industry Overview

	1998	2004
Total Employees	720,252	774,311
Total Payroll ($1,000)	18,178,238	23,681,558
Total Establishments	48,655	50,928
Establishments with 1–19 Employees	42,487	44,202
Establishments with 20–49 Employees	3,813	4,231
Establishments with 50–249 Employees	2,050	2,173
Establishments with 250–999 Employees	258	268
Establishments with 1,000+ Employees	47	54

Data: U.S. Census Bureau, County Business Patterns

Major Industries (Ranked by 2004 Employment; Payroll in $1,000s)				
Industry	1998 Employment	2004 Employment	1998 Payroll	2004 Payroll
Retail Trade	104,866	107,201	1,675,637	2,088,725
Health Care and Social Assistance	95,015	107,049	2,487,228	3,500,501
Manufacturing	109,645	103,784	3,255,216	3,632,751
Accommodation and Food Services	60,088	66,798	535,911	679,638
Finance and Insurance	47,979	58,595	1,710,584	2,686,536
Admin., Support, Waste Mngt., Remediation Services	52,512	57,991	1,088,358	1,454,125
Construction	38,297	43,247	1,258,732	1,537,272
Professional, Scientific, Technical Services	30,406	40,338	1,143,609	1,772,634
Wholesale Trade	40,357	36,645	1,255,481	1,450,263
Other Services (except Public Admin.)	33,786	35,823	530,062	686,239

Data: U.S. Census Bureau, County Business Patterns

Taxes and Business Climate

State and Local Taxes		
Combined Revenues ($1,000)	**2001–2**	**2003–4**
Revenue from Property Taxes	1,748,841	2,007,118
Revenue from Sales and Gross Receipts Taxes	1,819,154	2,333,889
Revenue from Individual Income Taxes	1,153,444	1,242,603
Revenue from Corporate Income Taxes	107,628	167,429
Revenue from Other Taxes	487,274	556,845
Total Tax Revenue	5,316,341	6,307,884
Per Capita Taxes		
Property Tax per Capita	1,022	1,148
Sales and Gross Receipts Tax per Capita	1,063	1,335
Individual Income Tax per Capita	674	711
Corporate Income Tax per Capita	63	96
Other Taxes per Capita	285	319
Total Taxes per Capita	3,107	3,609

Data: U.S. Census Bureau; Anderson Economic Group, LLC

Business Climate Measures

Anderson Economic Group: 2006 Business Tax Ranking (1 is Best)	26
Forbes Magazine: 2006 Best States for Business Ranking (1 is Best)	7
Tax Foundation: 2007 Business Tax Climate Ranking (1 is Best)	44
2002–3 Employer Firm Births	4,376
2002–3 Employer Firm Terminations	3,939

Data: Anderson Economic Group; Tax Foundation; Forbes Magazine; U.S. Census, Statistics of U.S. Businesses

Voting Behavior and Elected Officials

Voter Registration and Turnout (%)

	1992	1996	2000	2004
Registered Voters Who Voted	77.7	66.7	64.2	67.1
Citizens Age 18+ Who Voted	63.3	55.9	55.2	60.0

Data: Dave Leip's Atlas of U.S. Presidential Elections

Presidential Election Results (Nationwide Winner Listed First)

2004	Popular Vote (%)	Electoral Votes
George W. Bush (Republican, Incumbent)	65.9	5
John Kerry (Democrat)	32.7	0
Other	1.4	0
2000		
George W. Bush (Republican)	62.3	5
Albert Gore (Democrat)	33.3	0
Ralph Nader (Green)	3.5	0
Other	1.0	0
1996		
William Clinton (Democrat, Incumbent)	35.0	0
Robert Dole (Republican)	53.7	5
H. Ross Perot (Reformist)	10.5	0
Other	0.9	0
1992		
William Clinton (Democrat)	29.4	0
George H. W. Bush (Republican, Incumbent)	46.6	5
H. Ross Perot (Independent)	23.6	0
Other	0.4	0

Data: Dave Leip's Atlas of U.S. Presidential Elections

Governor and U.S. Congressional Seats				
Governor	Party	Year Term Began	Term	Max. Consecutive Terms
Dave Heineman	R	2005	First	2
U.S. Senators	Party	Year Elected	Term Expires	
Charles Hagel	R	1996	2009	
Ben Nelson	D	2000	2013	
U.S. Representatives		Republican	Democrat	Other
		3	0	0

Data: National Governors Association, U.S. Senate, U.S. House of Representatives

Business and Economic Agencies

Agency	Website Address
Nebraska Chamber of Commerce and Industry	www.nechamber.com
Nebraska Department of Economic Development	www.neded.org
Nebraska Small Business Dev. Center	nbdc.unomaha.edu
Nebraska Secretary of State, Corporations Division	www.sos.state.ne.us/business/corp_serv

Data: Various Agency Websites

Nevada

Demographics and Socioeconomics. With a population of 2.4 million people, Nevada was the sixteenth least populous state in 2005. From 2000 to 2005 the state's population increased by 383,024 people, and is projected to increase to 3.9 million by 2025. This 2.5 percent projected annual growth rate is one of the highest in the nation and compares to the projected national average of 1.0 percent. In 2005 Nevada had a per capita personal income of $35,780, which was $1,285 above the national average and the fourteenth highest in the country. The state's per capita income grew at an average annual rate of 3.3 percent from 2000 to 2005, compared to 2.9 percent nationally.

Workforce and Industry. In 2004 Nevada's largest industry in terms of employment was accommodation and food services. The fastest growing major industry was administrative and support and waste management and remediation services, with 62.3 percent growth from 1998 to 2004. the state's workforce is generally less educated than that of other states: 82.8 percent of the state's adult population has graduated from high school, compared to an

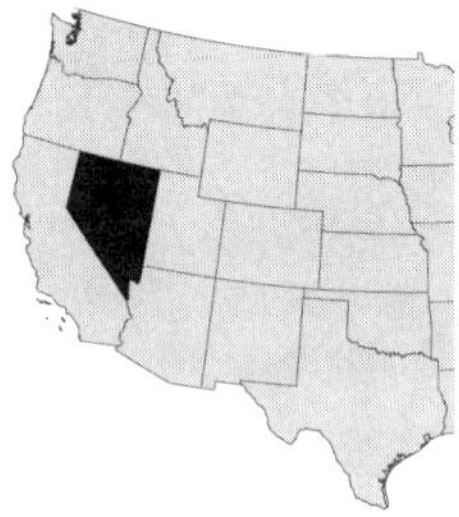

★ State Capitol

Major Urban Area

Major Roadway

Demographic and Socioeconomic Profile

Demographics and Socioeconomic Figures		
Population and Households	**2000**	**2005**
Total Population	1,998,257	2,381,281
Number of Households	751,165	906,719
Average Household Size	2.6	2.6
Age and Ethnicity		
Median Age	35.0	35.2
Population 18 Years of Age and Older	1,488,526	1,762,476
Population 65 Years of Age and Older	218,497	267,676
Caucasian Population	1,503,083	1,811,535
African-American Population	132,490	170,854
Hispanic Population	393,539	563,999
Asian Population	89,121	138,054
Foreign-Born Population	316,593	413,298
Income		
Per Capita Personal Income (USD)	$30,437	$35,780
Median Household Income (USD)	$44,581	$49,169
Individuals below Poverty Level	10.5%	11.1%

Data: U.S. Census, American Community Survey; U.S. Department of Commerce, Bureau of Economic Analysis

84.2 percent national average; 20.6 percent hold a bachelor degree or higher (national average is 27.2 percent); and 11.6 percent hold professional or graduate degrees (national average is 10.0 percent).

Tax Profile and Business Climate. Nevada's total tax revenue was $8.0 billion for fiscal year 2003–4. The largest share of tax revenue in 2003–4 was generated from sales and gross receipts taxes, followed by property taxes. The state does not have an individual income tax or a corporate income tax. On a per capita basis, Nevada had taxes of $3,417, compared to the national average of $3,447 for 2003–4. In terms of business taxes, the state ranked thirty-nineth in a 2006 report by Anderson Economic Group. Forbes Magazine and the Tax Foundation ranked the state's business climate twenty-sixth and fourth, respectively.

Population Projections

	2010	2015	2020	2025
Total Population	2,690,531	3,058,190	3,452,283	3,863,298
Median Age	37.8	38.7	39.0	39.1
Population 18 Years of Age and Older	2,025,446	2,306,302	2,595,522	2,895,136
Population 65 Years of Age and Older	329,621	421,719	531,120	659,700

Data: U.S. Census Bureau

Workforce and Industry Profile

Workforce

	2000	2005
Civilian Labor Force	995,200	1,232,649
Labor Force Participation Rate	65.2%	67.8%
Unemployment Rate	4.5%	4.1%
Average Earnings per Job (USD)	$32,276	$34,750
Education Attainment (Population 25 Years and Older)	**(%)**	**(%)**
High School Graduate or Higher	80.7	82.8
Bachelors Degree or Higher	18.2	20.6
Graduate or Professional Degree	6.1	11.6

Data: U.S. Census Bureau, American Community Survey; U.S. Department of Labor, Bureau of Labor Statistics

Industry Overview

	1998	2004
Total Employees	800,861	1,022,011
Total Payroll ($1,000)	21,847,334	34,848,180
Total Establishments	44,613	55,853
Establishments with 1–19 Employees	38,274	47,705
Establishments with 20–49 Employees	3,946	4,954
Establishments with 50–249 Employees	2,041	2,725
Establishments with 250–999 Employees	263	372
Establishments with 1,000+ Employees	89	97

Data: U.S. Census Bureau, County Business Patterns

Major Industries (Ranked by 2004 Employment; Payroll in $1,000s)				
Industry	1998 Employment	2004 Employment	1998 Payroll	2004 Payroll
Accommodation and Food Services	246,530	280,229	5,121,400	7,093,623
Retail Trade	95,507	127,928	2,038,341	3,179,264
Construction	77,682	104,335	2,705,048	4,441,048
Admin., Support, Waste Mngt., Remediation Services	53,102	86,167	1,172,519	2,486,812
Health Care and Social Assistance	60,524	82,450	1,938,561	3,336,082
Professional, Scientific, Technical Services	33,347	53,874	1,423,080	2,687,098
Manufacturing	39,029	43,080	1,298,552	1,788,537
Finance and Insurance	27,360	37,738	1,012,252	1,817,048
Transportation and Warehousing	25,120	36,742	626,946	1,040,874
Wholesale Trade	29,929	35,215	1,066,396	1,586,291

Data: U.S. Census Bureau, County Business Patterns

Taxes and Business Climate

State and Local Taxes		
Combined Revenues ($1,000)	**2001–2**	**2003–4**
Revenue from Property Taxes	1,702,186	2,147,294
Revenue from Sales and Gross Receipts Taxes	3,840,191	4,568,096
Revenue from Individual Income Taxes	0	0
Revenue from Corporate Income Taxes	0	0
Revenue from Other Taxes	890,187	1,256,208
Total Tax Revenue	6,432,564	7,971,598
Per Capita Taxes		
Property Tax per Capita	852	920
Sales and Gross Receipts Tax per Capita	1,922	1,958
Individual Income Tax per Capita	0	0
Corporate Income Tax per Capita	0	0
Other Taxes per Capita	446	538
Total Taxes per Capita	3,220	3,417

Data: U.S. Census Bureau; Anderson Economic Group, LLC

Business Climate Measures

Anderson Economic Group: 2006 Business Tax Ranking (1 is Best)	39
Forbes Magazine: 2006 Best States for Business Ranking (1 is Best)	26
Tax Foundation: 2007 Business Tax Climate Ranking (1 is Best)	4
2002–3 Employer Firm Births	7,560
2002–3 Employer Firm Terminations	5,677

Data: Anderson Economic Group; Tax Foundation; Forbes Magazine; U.S. Census, Statistics of U.S. Businesses

Voting Behavior and Elected Officials

Voter Registration and Turnout (%)

	1992	1996	2000	2004
Registered Voters Who Voted	77.9	59.7	69.7	77.5
Citizens Age 18+ Who Voted	50.0	38.3	40.9	50.0

Data: Dave Leip's Atlas of U.S. Presidential Elections

Presidential Election Results (Nationwide Winner Listed First)

2004	Popular Vote (%)	Electoral Votes
George W. Bush (Republican, Incumbent)	50.5	5
John Kerry (Democrat)	47.9	0
Other	1.7	0
2000		
George W. Bush (Republican)	49.5	4
Albert Gore (Democrat)	46.0	0
Ralph Nader (Green)	2.5	0
Other	2.0	0
1996		
William Clinton (Democrat, Incumbent)	43.9	4
Robert Dole (Republican)	42.9	0
H. Ross Perot (Reformist)	9.5	0
Other	3.7	0
1992		
William Clinton (Democrat)	37.4	4
George H. W. Bush (Republican, Incumbent)	34.7	0
H. Ross Perot (Independent)	26.2	0
Other	1.7	0

Data: Dave Leip's Atlas of U.S. Presidential Elections

Governor and U.S. Congressional Seats				
Governor	**Party**	**Year Term Began**	**Term**	**Max. Consecutive Terms**
Jim Gibbons	R	2007	First	2
U.S. Senators	**Party**	**Year Elected**	**Term Expires**	
John Ensign	R	2000	2013	
Harry Reid	D	1986	2011	
U.S. Representatives		**Republican**	**Democrat**	**Other**
		2	1	0

Data: National Governors Association, U.S. Senate, U.S. House of Representatives

Business and Economic Agencies

Agency	Website Address
Nevada Commission on Economic Development	www.expand2nevada.com
Nevada Small Business Dev. Center	www.nsbdc.org
Nevada Secretary of State, Commercial Recordings Division	www.sos.state.nv.us/comm_rec

Data: Various Agency Websites

New Hampshire

Demographics and Socioeconomics. New Hampshire, located in the New England region of the United States, has a population of 1.3 million people, making it the tenth least populous state in 2005. The state's population increased by 36,700 people from 2000 to 2005 and is projected to increase to 1.6 million by 2025. This 1.1 percent projected annual growth rate compares to the projected national average of 1.0 percent. The state's 2005 per capita personal income of \$37,835 was the sixth highest in the United States, some \$3,340 above the national average. Per capita income in New Hampshire grew at an average annual rate of 2.5 percent from 2000 to 2005, compared to 2.9 percent nationally.

Workforce and Industry. In 2004 the state's largest industry in terms of employment was retail trade, followed by health care and social assistance. The fastest major growing industry was administrative and support and waste management and remediation services, with 30.9 percent growth from 1998 to 2004. The state's workforce is generally more educated than

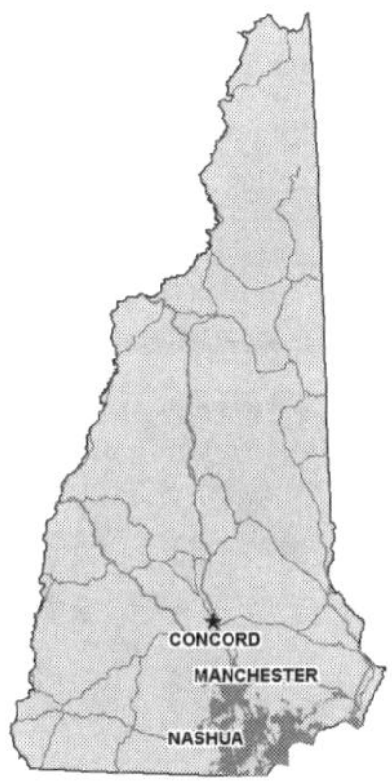

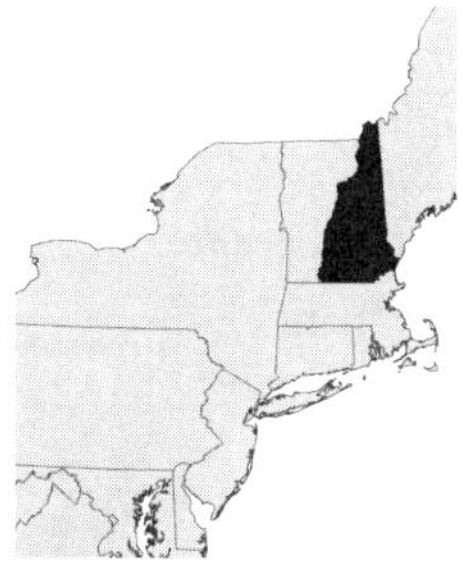

★ State Capitol
Major Urban Area
Major Roadway

Demographic and Socioeconomic Profile

Demographics and Socioeconomic Figures		
Population and Households	**2000**	**2005**
Total Population	1,235,786	1,272,486
Number of Households	474,606	497,054
Average Household Size	2.5	2.6
Age and Ethnicity		
Median Age	37.1	39.5
Population 18 Years of Age and Older	926,885	969,586
Population 65 Years of Age and Older	148,039	151,321
Caucasian Population	1,186,448	1,214,616
African-American Population	8,984	10,456
Hispanic Population	19,910	27,933
Asian Population	15,422	22,850
Foreign-Born Population	54,154	72,480
Income		
Per Capita Personal Income (USD)	\$33,396	\$37,835
Median Household Income (USD)	\$49,467	\$56,768
Individuals below Poverty Level	6.5%	7.5%

Data: U.S. Census, American Community Survey; U.S. Department of Commerce, Bureau of Economic Analysis

that of other states: 89.9 percent of the state's adult population has graduated from high school, compared to an 84.2 percent national average; 31.8 percent hold a bachelor degree or higher (national average is 27.2 percent); and 11.7 percent hold professional or graduate degrees (national average is 10.0 percent).

Tax Profile and Business Climate. In fiscal year 2003–4 New Hampshire had total tax revenues of $4.1 billion. The largest share was generated from property taxes, followed by sales and gross receipts taxes. The per capita tax burden in New Hampshire was $3,133 for 2003–4, some $314 below the national average and. In terms of business taxes, the state ranked forty-sixth in a 2006 report by Anderson Economic Group. Forbes Magazine and the Tax Foundation ranked the state's business climate eighteenth and seventh respectively.

Population Projections

	2010	2015	2020	2025
Total Population	1,385,560	1,456,679	1,524,751	1,586,348
Median Age	39.6	39.8	40.3	41.3
Population 18 Years of Age and Older	1,081,396	1,143,197	1,194,887	1,241,954
Population 65 Years of Age and Older	178,823	217,498	261,856	311,456

Data: U.S. Census Bureau

Workforce and Industry Profile

Workforce

	2000	2005
Civilian Labor Force	676,371	719,073
Labor Force Participation Rate	70.5%	71.6%
Unemployment Rate	2.6%	3.6%
Average Earnings per Job (USD)	$34,738	$37,990
Education Attainment (Population 25 Years and Older)	**(%)**	**(%)**
High School Graduate or Higher	87.4	89.9
Bachelors Degree or Higher	28.7	31.8
Graduate or Professional Degree	10.0	11.7

Data: U.S. Census Bureau, American Community Survey; U.S. Department of Labor, Bureau of Labor Statistics

Industry Overview

	1998	2004
Total Employees	518,526	551,001
Total Payroll ($1,000)	14,863,829	20,005,170
Total Establishments	36,842	38,843
Establishments with 1–19 Employees	32,118	33,718
Establishments with 20–49 Employees	2,969	3,255
Establishments with 50–249 Employees	1,526	1,662
Establishments with 250–999 Employees	211	183
Establishments with 1,000+ Employees	18	25

Data: U.S. Census Bureau, County Business Patterns

Major Industries (Ranked by 2004 Employment; Payroll in $1,000s)				
Industry	1998 Employment	2004 Employment	1998 Payroll	2004 Payroll
Retail Trade	85,811	96,706	1,621,626	2,254,497
Health Care and Social Assistance	68,223	76,319	1,853,351	2,754,076
Manufacturing	101,513	75,999	3,540,699	3,528,528
Accommodation and Food Services	46,138	52,975	530,934	770,372
Admin., Support, Waste Mngt., Remediation Services	30,307	39,686	750,584	1,160,276
Professional, Scientific, Technical Services	22,048	28,418	904,628	1,487,639
Construction	22,749	28,378	831,245	1,282,085
Finance and Insurance	24,936	26,321	958,836	1,471,053
Wholesale Trade	22,912	24,665	946,987	1,399,042
Other Services (except Public Admin.)	19,520	22,009	384,469	522,454

Data: U.S. Census Bureau, County Business Patterns

Taxes and Business Climate

State and Local Taxes		
Combined Revenues ($1,000)	2001–2	2003–4
Revenue from Property Taxes	2,169,494	2,519,714
Revenue from Sales and Gross Receipts Taxes	605,386	674,354
Revenue from Individual Income Taxes	71,433	54,769
Revenue from Corporate Income Taxes	377,313	407,603
Revenue from Other Taxes	375,236	413,231
Total Tax Revenue	3,598,862	4,069,671
Per Capita Taxes		
Property Tax per Capita	1,755	1,940
Sales and Gross Receipts Tax per Capita	490	519
Individual Income Tax per Capita	58	42
Corporate Income Tax per Capita	305	314
Other Taxes per Capita	304	318
Total Taxes per Capita	2,912	3,133

Data: U.S. Census Bureau; Anderson Economic Group, LLC

Business Climate Measures

Anderson Economic Group: 2006 Business Tax Ranking (1 is Best)	46
Forbes Magazine: 2006 Best States for Business Ranking (1 is Best)	18
Tax Foundation: 2007 Business Tax Climate Ranking (1 is Best)	7
2002–3 Employer Firm Births	3,460
2002–3 Employer Firm Terminations	3,315

Data: Anderson Economic Group; Tax Foundation; Forbes Magazine; U.S. Census, Statistics of U.S. Businesses

Voting Behavior and Elected Officials

Voter Registration and Turnout (%)

	1992	1996	2000	2004
Registered Voters Who Voted	81.3	66.1	66.6	79.2
Citizens Age 18+ Who Voted	63.1	57.3	61.4	69.1

Data: Dave Leip's Atlas of U.S. Presidential Elections

Presidential Election Results (Nationwide Winner Listed First)

2004	Popular Vote (%)	Electoral Votes
George W. Bush (Republican, Incumbent)	48.9	0
John Kerry (Democrat)	50.3	4
Other	0.9	0
2000		
George W. Bush (Republican)	48.1	4
Albert Gore (Democrat)	46.8	0
Ralph Nader (Green)	3.9	0
Other	1.2	0
1996		
William Clinton (Democrat, Incumbent)	49.3	4
Robert Dole (Republican)	39.4	0
H. Ross Perot (Reformist)	9.7	0
Other	1.6	0
1992		
William Clinton (Democrat)	38.9	4
George H. W. Bush (Republican, Incumbent)	37.6	0
H. Ross Perot (Independent)	22.6	0
Other	0.9	0

Data: Dave Leip's Atlas of U.S. Presidential Elections

Governor and U.S. Congressional Seats				
Governor	**Party**	**Year Term Began**	**Term**	**Max. Consecutive Terms**
John Lynch	D	2005	First	No limit
U.S. Senators	**Party**	**Year Elected**	**Term Expires**	
John E. Sununu	R	2002	2009	
Judd Gregg	R	1992	2011	
U.S. Representatives		**Republican**	**Democrat**	**Other**
		0	2	0

Data: National Governors Association, U.S. Senate, U.S. House of Representatives

Business and Economic Agencies

Agency	Website Address
Business and Industry Association of New Hampshire	www.nhbia.org
State of New Hampshire Economic Development	www.nheconomy.com
New Hampshire Small Business Dev. Center	www.nhsbdc.org
New Hampshire Secretary of State, Corporate Division	www.sos.nh.gov/corporate

Data: Various Agency Websites

New Jersey

Demographics and Socioeconomics. With a population of 8.5 million people, New Jersey was the tenth most populous state in the United States in 2005. From 2000 to 2005 the state's population increased by 107,077 people and is projected to reach 9.6 million by 2025. This 0.6 percent projected annual growth rate compares to the projected national average of 1.0 percent. Per capita personal income in New Jersey was $43,822 in 2005, the second highest in the country and $9,327 above the national average. From 2000 to 2005 per capita income in New Jersey grew at an average annual rate of 2.7 percent, compared to 2.9 percent nationally.

Workforce and Industry. The state's largest industry in terms of 2004 employment was retail trade. The fastest growing major industry was professional, scientific, and technical services, with 24.8 percent growth from 1998 to 2004. The state's workforce is generally more educated than that of other states: 86.3 percent of the state's adult population has graduated from high school, compared to an 84.2 percent national average; 34.2 percent hold a bachelor degree or higher

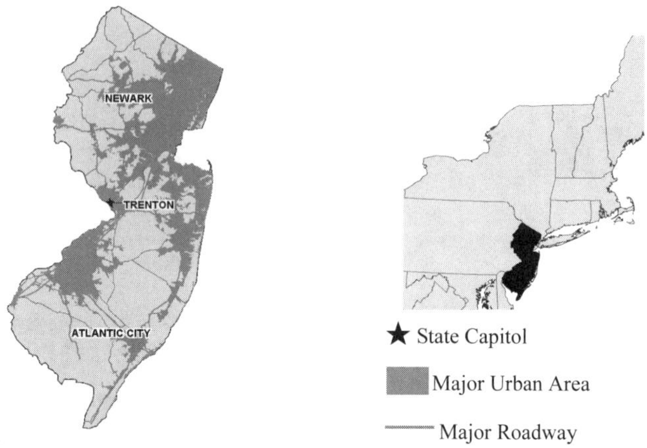

Demographic and Socioeconomic Profile

Demographics and Socioeconomic Figures		
Population and Households	**2000**	**2005**
Total Population	8,414,350	8,521,427
Number of Households	3,064,645	3,141,956
Average Household Size	2.7	2.7
Age and Ethnicity		
Median Age	36.7	38.0
Population 18 Years of Age and Older	6,332,876	6,366,744
Population 65 Years of Age and Older	1,113,035	1,068,010
Caucasian Population	6,099,439	5,954,926
African-American Population	1,127,266	1,130,967
Hispanic Population	1,116,149	1,307,412
Asian Population	481,794	620,588
Foreign-Born Population	1,476,327	1,662,857
Income		
Per Capita Personal Income (USD)	$38,364	$43,822
Median Household Income (USD)	$55,146	$61,672
Individuals below Poverty Level	8.5%	8.7%

Data: U.S. Census, American Community Survey; U.S. Department of Commerce, Bureau of Economic Analysis

(national average is 27.2 percent); and 12.5 percent hold professional or graduate degrees (national average is 10.0 percent).

Tax Profile and Business Climate. New Jersey's total tax revenue was $40 billion for fiscal year 2003–4. The largest share was generated from property taxes, followed by sales and gross receipts taxes. On a per capita basis, New Jersey had taxes of $4,555, compared to the national average of $3,447 for 2003–4. In terms of business taxes, the state ranked thirty-fifth in a 2006 report by Anderson Economic Group. Forbes Magazine and the Tax Foundation ranked the state's business climate sixteenth and forty-eighth, respectively.

Population Projections

	2010	2015	2020	2025
Total Population	9,018,231	9,255,769	9,461,635	9,636,644
Median Age	38.9	39.3	39.6	40.2
Population 18 Years of Age and Older	6,930,007	7,151,894	7,323,271	7,477,125
Population 65 Years of Age and Older	1,231,585	1,385,167	1,552,544	1,762,460

Data: U.S. Census Bureau

Workforce and Industry Profile

Workforce

	2000	2005
Civilian Labor Force	4,193,145	4,389,993
Labor Force Participation Rate	64.2%	66.5%
Unemployment Rate	3.7%	4.4%
Average Earnings per Job (USD)	$43,676	$43,860
Education Attainment (Population 25 Years and Older)	**(%)**	**(%)**
High School Graduate or Higher	82.1	86.3
Bachelors Degree or Higher	29.8	34.2
Graduate or Professional Degree	11.0	12.5

Data: U.S. Census Bureau, American Community Survey; U.S. Department of Labor, Bureau of Labor Statistics

Industry Overview

	1998	2004
Total Employees	3,368,365	3,609,640
Total Payroll ($1,000)	125,787,145	160,237,399
Total Establishments	230,860	240,539
Establishments with 1–19 Employees	202,389	209,777
Establishments with 20–49 Employees	17,103	18,782
Establishments with 50–249 Employees	9,826	10,361
Establishments with 250–999 Employees	1,318	1,369
Establishments with 1,000+ Employees	224	250

Data: U.S. Census Bureau, County Business Patterns

Major Industries (Ranked by 2004 Employment; Payroll in $1,000s)				
Industry	1998 Employment	2004 Employment	1998 Payroll	2004 Payroll
Retail Trade	417,791	470,199	8,693,222	11,168,513
Health Care and Social Assistance	405,935	468,926	13,192,467	18,329,709
Manufacturing	405,275	325,711	16,756,666	17,001,029
Admin., Support, Waste Mngt., Remediation Services	247,799	294,417	5,702,383	8,394,350
Professional, Scientific, Technical Services	234,816	293,046	12,782,239	18,555,619
Wholesale Trade	275,717	272,818	13,355,315	16,273,884
Accommodation and Food Services	249,836	270,112	3,897,674	4,780,515
Finance and Insurance	200,646	218,513	11,166,663	16,728,372
Construction	143,243	176,889	5,828,494	8,756,334
Transportation and Warehousing	151,493	172,046	4,941,082	6,389,105

Data: U.S. Census Bureau, County Business Patterns

Taxes and Business Climate

State and Local Taxes		
Combined Revenues ($1,000)	2001–2	2003–4
Revenue from Property Taxes	16,049,550	18,229,254
Revenue from Sales and Gross Receipts Taxes	8,803,618	9,780,318
Revenue from Individual Income Taxes	6,867,275	7,400,733
Revenue from Corporate Income Taxes	1,101,296	1,896,998
Revenue from Other Taxes	1,807,065	2,250,974
Total Tax Revenue	34,628,804	39,558,277
Per Capita Taxes		
Property Tax per Capita	1,907	2,099
Sales and Gross Receipts Tax per Capita	1,046	1,126
Individual Income Tax per Capita	816	852
Corporate Income Tax per Capita	131	218
Other Taxes per Capita	215	259
Total Taxes per Capita	4,116	4,555

Data: U.S. Census Bureau; Anderson Economic Group, LLC

Business Climate Measures	
Anderson Economic Group: 2006 Business Tax Ranking (1 is Best)	35
Forbes Magazine: 2006 Best States for Business Ranking (1 is Best)	16
Tax Foundation: 2007 Business Tax Climate Ranking (1 is Best)	48
2002–3 Employer Firm Births	23,779
2002–3 Employer Firm Terminations	22,795

Data: Anderson Economic Group; Tax Foundation; Forbes Magazine; U.S. Census, Statistics of U.S. Businesses

Voting Behavior and Elected Officials

Voter Registration and Turnout (%)

	1992	1996	2000	2004
Registered Voters Who Voted	82.3	71.4	67.7	72.1
Citizens Age 18+ Who Voted	56.3	51.0	50.3	55.5

Data: Dave Leip's Atlas of U.S. Presidential Elections

Presidential Election Results (Nationwide Winner Listed First)

2004	Popular Vote (%)	Electoral Votes
George W. Bush (Republican, Incumbent)	46.2	0
John Kerry (Democrat)	52.9	15
Other	0.8	0
2000		
George W. Bush (Republican)	40.3	0
Albert Gore (Democrat)	56.1	15
Ralph Nader (Green)	3.0	0
Other	0.6	0
1996		
William Clinton (Democrat, Incumbent)	53.7	15
Robert Dole (Republican)	35.9	0
H. Ross Perot (Reformist)	8.5	0
Other	1.9	0
1992		
William Clinton (Democrat)	43.0	15
George H. W. Bush (Republican, Incumbent)	40.6	0
H. Ross Perot (Independent)	15.6	0
Other	0.9	0

Data: Dave Leip's Atlas of U.S. Presidential Elections

Governor and U.S. Congressional Seats				
Governor	**Party**	**Year Term Began**	**Term**	**Max. Consecutive Terms**
Jon Corzine	D	2006	First	2
U.S. Senators	**Party**	**Year Elected**	**Term Expires**	
Frank R. Lautenberg	D	1982	2009	
Robert Menendez	D	2006	2013	
U.S. Representatives		**Republican**	**Democrat**	**Other**
		6	7	0

Data: National Governors Association, U.S. Senate, U.S. House of Representatives

Business and Economic Agencies

Agency	Website Address
New Jersey State Chamber of Commerce	www.njchamber.com
New Jersey Economic Development Authority	www.njeda.com
New Jersey Small Business Dev. Center	www.njsbdc.com
New Jersey Department of State, Business and Corporate Information	www.state.nj.us/state/business

Data: Various Agency Websites

New Mexico

Demographics and Socioeconomics. New Mexico, located in the Mountain region of the United States, has a population of 1.9 million people, making it the fifteenth least populous state in 2005. The state's population increased by 68,154 people from 2000 to 2005, and is projected to increase to 2.1 million by 2025. This 0.6 percent projected annual growth rate is below the projected national average of 1.0 percent. The state's 2005 per capita personal income of $27,912 was the sixth lowest in the United States, some $6,583 below the national average. Per capita income in New Mexico grew at an average annual rate of 4.7 percent from 2000 to 2005, compared to 2.9 percent nationally.

Workforce and Industry. In 2004 the state's largest industry in terms of employment was retail trade, followed by health care and social assistance. The fastest growing major industry in New Mexico was health care and social assistance, with 22.3 percent growth from 1998 to 2004. The state's workforce is generally less educated than that of other states: 82.0 percent of the state's adult population

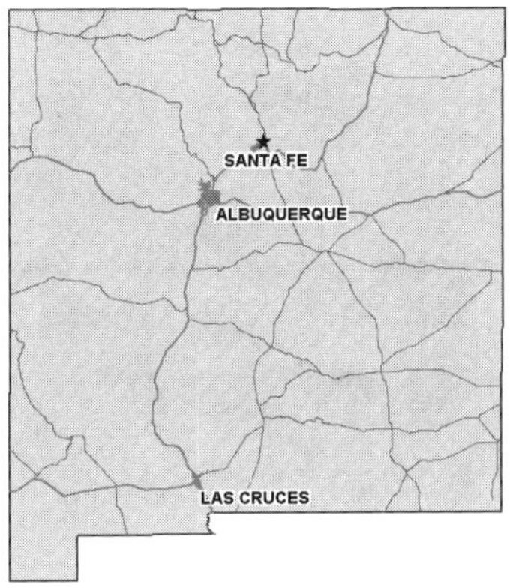

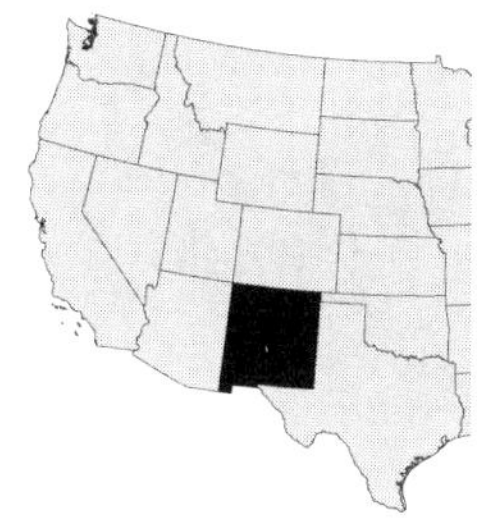

★ State Capitol

Major Urban Area

Major Roadway

Demographic and Socioeconomic Profile

Demographics and Socioeconomic Figures		
Population and Households	**2000**	**2005**
Total Population	1,819,046	1,887,200
Number of Households	677,971	727,820
Average Household Size	2.6	2.6
Age and Ethnicity		
Median Age	34.6	36.2
Population 18 Years of Age and Older	1,311,478	1,400,839
Population 65 Years of Age and Older	212,490	227,685
Caucasian Population	1,214,680	1,311,829
African-American Population	33,513	35,604
Hispanic Population	765,610	822,224
Asian Population	18,286	22,454
Foreign-Born Population	149,606	168,640
Income		
Per Capita Personal Income (USD)	$22,135	$27,912
Median Household Income (USD)	$34,133	$37,492
Individuals below Poverty Level	18.4%	18.5%

Data: U.S. Census, American Community Survey; U.S. Department of Commerce, Bureau of Economic Analysis

has graduated from high school, compared to an 84.2 percent national average; 25.1 percent hold a bachelor degree or higher (national average is 27.2 percent); and 10.9 percent hold professional or graduate degrees (national average is 10.0 percent).

Tax Profile and Business Climate. In fiscal year 2003–4 New Mexico had total tax revenues of $5.4 billion. The largest share was generated from sales and gross receipts taxes, followed by individual income taxes. The per capita tax burden in New Mexico was $2,861 for 2003–4, some $586 below the national average. In terms of business taxes, the state ranked seventh in a 2006 report by Anderson Economic Group. Forbes Magazine and the Tax Foundation ranked the state's business climate twenty-nineth and twenty-third, respectively.

Population Projections

	2010	2015	2020	2025
Total Population	1,980,225	2,041,539	2,084,341	2,106,584
Median Age	38.3	39.7	41.2	42.9
Population 18 Years of Age and Older	1,500,820	1,556,822	1,595,626	1,628,082
Population 65 Years of Age and Older	278,967	343,622	419,690	497,357

Data: U.S. Census Bureau

Workforce and Industry Profile

Workforce

	2000	2005
Civilian Labor Force	823,440	917,697
Labor Force Participation Rate	61.0%	63.4%
Unemployment Rate	5.0%	5.3%
Average Earnings per Job (USD)	$27,497	$33,180
Education Attainment (Population 25 Years and Older)	**(%)**	**(%)**
High School Graduate or Higher	78.9	82.0
Bachelors Degree or Higher	23.5	25.1
Graduate or Professional Degree	9.8	10.9

Data: U.S. Census Bureau, American Community Survey; U.S. Department of Labor, Bureau of Labor Statistics

Industry Overview

	1998	2004
Total Employees	540,186	580,576
Total Payroll ($1,000)	13,133,707	16,811,505
Total Establishments	42,608	44,205
Establishments with 1–19 Employees	37,254	38,295
Establishments with 20–49 Employees	3,544	3,953
Establishments with 50–249 Employees	1,618	1,739
Establishments with 250–999 Employees	173	200
Establishments with 1,000+ Employees	19	18

Data: U.S. Census Bureau, County Business Patterns

Major Industries (Ranked by 2004 Employment; Payroll in $1,000s)				
Industry	1998 Employment	2004 Employment	1998 Payroll	2004 Payroll
Retail Trade	89,883	95,945	1,569,283	2,039,154
Health Care and Social Assistance	76,641	93,699	1,995,230	3,101,682
Accommodation and Food Services	65,149	76,578	672,950	912,020
Construction	42,164	46,786	1,061,850	1,490,189
Professional, Scientific, Technical Services	35,771	34,186	1,514,635	1,570,529
Manufacturing	40,561	33,204	1,216,861	1,297,305
Admin., Support, Waste Mngt., Remediation Services	32,347	32,813	669,284	817,605
Other Services (except Public Admin.)	26,279	26,714	418,964	540,281
Finance and Insurance	21,847	24,984	679,563	979,626
Wholesale Trade	21,672	20,444	652,200	772,144

Data: U.S. Census Bureau, County Business Patterns

Taxes and Business Climate

State and Local Taxes		
Combined Revenues ($1,000)	2001–2	2003–4
Revenue from Property Taxes	755,948	840,068
Revenue from Sales and Gross Receipts Taxes	2,319,455	2,627,794
Revenue from Individual Income Taxes	982,891	1,007,248
Revenue from Corporate Income Taxes	124,327	138,196
Revenue from Other Taxes	694,993	830,852
Total Tax Revenue	4,877,614	5,444,158
Per Capita Taxes		
Property Tax per Capita	416	441
Sales and Gross Receipts Tax per Capita	1,275	1,381
Individual Income Tax per Capita	540	529
Corporate Income Tax per Capita	68	73
Other Taxes per Capita	382	437
Total Taxes per Capita	2,681	2,861

Data: U.S. Census Bureau; Anderson Economic Group, LLC

Business Climate Measures	
Anderson Economic Group: 2006 Business Tax Ranking (1 is Best)	7
Forbes Magazine: 2006 Best States for Business Ranking (1 is Best)	29
Tax Foundation: 2007 Business Tax Climate Ranking (1 is Best)	23
2002–3 Employer Firm Births	4,444
2002–3 Employer Firm Terminations	4,059

Data: Anderson Economic Group; Tax Foundation; Forbes Magazine; U.S. Census, Statistics of U.S. Businesses

Voting Behavior and Elected Officials

Voter Registration and Turnout (%)

	1992	1996	2000	2004
Registered Voters Who Voted	80.6	66.4	61.5	68.4
Citizens Age 18+ Who Voted	51.6	45.4	45.6	55.1

Data: Dave Leip's Atlas of U.S. Presidential Elections

Presidential Election Results (Nationwide Winner Listed First)

2004	Popular Vote (%)	Electoral Votes
George W. Bush (Republican, Incumbent)	49.8	5
John Kerry (Democrat)	49.1	0
Other	1.1	0
2000		
George W. Bush (Republican)	47.9	0
Albert Gore (Democrat)	47.9	5
Ralph Nader (Green)	3.6	0
Other	0.7	0
1996		
William Clinton (Democrat, Incumbent)	49.2	5
Robert Dole (Republican)	41.9	0
H. Ross Perot (Reformist)	5.8	0
Other	3.2	0
1992		
William Clinton (Democrat)	49.5	5
George H. W. Bush (Republican, Incumbent)	37.3	0
H. Ross Perot (Independent)	16.1	0
Other	0.6	0

Data: Dave Leip's Atlas of U.S. Presidential Elections

Governor and U.S. Congressional Seats				
Governor	**Party**	**Year Term Began**	**Term**	**Max. Consecutive Terms**
Bill Richardson	D	2003	Second	2
U.S. Senators	**Party**	**Year Elected**	**Term Expires**	
Pete V. Domenici	R	1972	2009	
Jeff Bingaman	D	1982	2013	
U.S. Representatives		**Republican**	**Democrat**	**Other**
		2	1	0

Data: National Governors Association, U.S. Senate, U.S. House of Representatives

Business and Economic Agencies

Agency	Website Address
Association of Commerce and Industry of New Mexico	www.aci.nm.org
New Mexico Economic Development Department	www.edd.state.nm.us
New Mexico Small Business Dev. Center	www.nmsbdc.org
New Mexico, Public Regulation Commission	www.nmprc.state.nm.us/cb.htm

Data: Various Agency Websites

New York

Demographics and Socio-economics. New York, located in the Middle Atlantic region of the United States, has a population of 18.7 million people, making it the third most populous state in 2005. The state's population decreased by 321,182 people from 2000 to 2005, but is projected to increase to 19.5 million by 2025. This 0.2 percent projected annual growth rate is below national average of 1.0 percent. In 2005 the state's per capita personal income of $40,072 was the fifth highest in the United States and $5,577 above the national average. Per capita income in New York grew at an average annual rate of 2.8 percent from 2000 to 2005, compared to 2.9 percent nationally.

Workforce and Industry. The state's workforce is generally more educated than that of other states: 84.3 percent of the state's adult population has graduated from high school, compared to an 84.2 percent national average; 31.3 percent hold a bachelor degree or higher (national average is 27.2 percent); and 13.4 percent hold professional or graduate degrees (national average is 10.0). In 2004 the state's largest

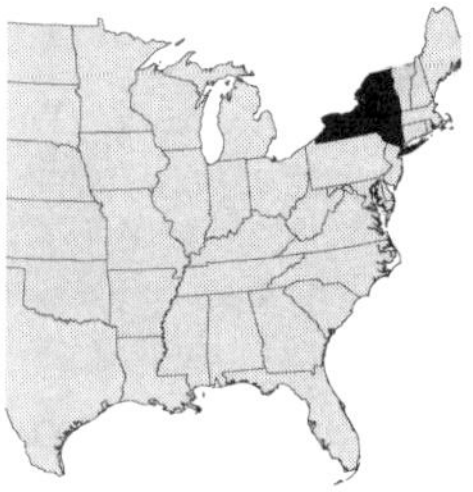

★ State Capitol

Major Urban Area

Major Roadway

Demographic and Socioeconomic Profile

Demographics and Socioeconomic Figures		
Population and Households	**2000**	**2005**
Total Population	18,976,457	18,655,275
Number of Households	7,056,860	7,114,431
Average Household Size	2.6	2.6
Age and Ethnicity		
Median Age	35.9	37.5
Population 18 Years of Age and Older	14,302,266	14,135,504
Population 65 Years of Age and Older	2,450,697	2,370,873
Caucasian Population	12,891,118	12,508,643
African-American Population	2,986,242	2,858,062
Hispanic Population	2,865,016	3,028,658
Asian Population	1,044,423	1,246,567
Foreign-Born Population	3,868,133	3,997,268
Income		
Per Capita Personal Income (USD)	$34,897	$40,072
Median Household Income (USD)	$43,393	$49,480
Individuals below Poverty Level	14.6%	13.8%

Data: U.S. Census, American Community Survey; U.S. Department of Commerce, Bureau of Economic Analysis

industry in terms of employment was health care and social assistance, followed by retail trade. The fastest growing major industry was educational services, with 19.4 percent growth from 1998 to 2004.

Tax Profile and Business Climate. In fiscal year 2003–4 New York had total tax revenues of $101.4 billion. The largest share was generated from property taxes, followed by individual income taxes. The per capita tax burden in New York was $5,260 for 2003–4, some $1,814 above the national average. In terms of business taxes, New York ranked twentieth in a 2006 report by Anderson Economic Group. The state's business climate was ranked thirty-fifth by Forbes Magazine and forty-seventh by the Tax Foundation.

Population Projections

	2010	2015	2020	2025
Total Population	19,443,672	19,546,699	19,576,920	19,540,179
Median Age	37.9	38.1	38.6	39.1
Population 18 Years of Age and Older	15,022,796	15,193,695	15,201,880	15,171,558
Population 65 Years of Age and Older	2,651,655	2,943,496	3,250,020	3,606,687

Data: U.S. Census Bureau

Workforce and Industry Profile

Workforce

	2000	2005
Civilian Labor Force	9,023,096	9,351,711
Labor Force Participation Rate	61.1%	63.9%
Unemployment Rate	4.5%	5.0%
Average Earnings per Job (USD)	$45,357	$44,060
Education Attainment (Population 25 Years and Older)	**(%)**	**(%)**
High School Graduate or Higher	79.1	84.3
Bachelors Degree or Higher	27.4	31.3
Graduate or Professional Degree	11.8	13.4

Data: U.S. Census Bureau, American Community Survey; U.S. Department of Labor, Bureau of Labor Statistics

Industry Overview

	1998	2004
Total Employees	6,993,814	7,433,686
Total Payroll ($1,000)	274,634,982	353,254,114
Total Establishments	481,962	511,440
Establishments with 1–19 Employees	425,442	450,689
Establishments with 20–49 Employees	34,883	37,519
Establishments with 50–249 Employees	18,351	19,795
Establishments with 250–999 Employees	2,737	2,894
Establishments with 1,000+ Employees	549	543

Data: U.S. Census Bureau, County Business Patterns

Major Industries (Ranked by 2004 Employment; Payroll in $1,000s)				
Industry	1998 Employment	2004 Employment	1998 Payroll	2004 Payroll
Health Care and Social Assistance	1,134,481	1,285,963	35,796,990	48,077,400
Retail Trade	800,566	887,747	15,427,452	20,219,526
Manufacturing	752,511	598,622	27,017,165	25,306,968
Finance and Insurance	587,464	586,893	56,877,864	76,857,659
Professional, Scientific, Technical Services	485,199	564,633	26,435,717	36,744,548
Accommodation and Food Services	479,455	542,309	6,912,726	9,364,833
Admin., Support, Waste Mngt., Remediation Services	449,222	476,156	11,375,703	15,608,257
Wholesale Trade	410,877	407,036	18,116,101	21,865,957
Other Services (except Public Admin.)	325,885	356,597	7,337,514	9,577,710
Educational Services	283,373	338,315	7,158,767	10,369,475

Data: U.S. Census Bureau, County Business Patterns

Taxes and Business Climate

State and Local Taxes		
Combined Revenues ($1,000)	2001–2	2003–4
Revenue from Property Taxes	26,825,697	32,333,564
Revenue from Sales and Gross Receipts Taxes	22,490,606	27,397,195
Revenue from Individual Income Taxes	30,207,782	30,744,990
Revenue from Corporate Income Taxes	5,075,411	5,362,907
Revenue from Other Taxes	4,278,616	5,587,606
Total Tax Revenue	88,878,112	101,426,262
Per Capita Taxes		
Property Tax per Capita	1,414	1,677
Sales and Gross Receipts Tax per Capita	1,185	1,421
Individual Income Tax per Capita	1,592	1,595
Corporate Income Tax per Capita	267	278
Other Taxes per Capita	225	290
Total Taxes per Capita	4,684	5,260

Data: U.S. Census Bureau; Anderson Economic Group, LLC

Business Climate Measures	
Anderson Economic Group: 2006 Business Tax Ranking (1 is Best)	20
Forbes Magazine: 2006 Best States for Business Ranking (1 is Best)	35
Tax Foundation: 2007 Business Tax Climate Ranking (1 is Best)	47
2002–3 Employer Firm Births	50,067
2002–3 Employer Firm Terminations	44,670

Data: Anderson Economic Group; Tax Foundation; Forbes Magazine; U.S. Census, Statistics of U.S. Businesses

Voting Behavior and Elected Officials

Voter Registration and Turnout (%)	1992	1996	2000	2004
Registered Voters Who Voted	75.3	62.2	60.6	62.4
Citizens Age 18+ Who Voted	50.9	46.6	47.7	50.4

Data: Dave Leip's Atlas of U.S. Presidential Elections

Presidential Election Results (Nationwide Winner Listed First)		
2004	**Popular Vote (%)**	**Electoral Votes**
George W. Bush (Republican, Incumbent)	40.1	0
John Kerry (Democrat)	58.4	31
Other	1.6	0
2000		
George W. Bush (Republican)	35.2	0
Albert Gore (Democrat)	60.2	33
Ralph Nader (Green)	3.6	0
Other	1.0	0
1996		
William Clinton (Democrat, Incumbent)	59.5	33
Robert Dole (Republican)	30.6	0
H. Ross Perot (Reformist)	8.0	0
Other	2.0	0
1992		
William Clinton (Democrat)	49.7	33
George H. W. Bush (Republican, Incumbent)	33.9	0
H. Ross Perot (Independent)	15.8	0
Other	0.6	0

Data: Dave Leip's Atlas of U.S. Presidential Elections

Governor and U.S. Congressional Seats				
Governor	Party	Year Term Began	Term	Max. Consecutive Terms
Eliot Spitzer	D	2007	First	No limit
U.S. Senators	Party	Year Elected	Term Expires	
Hillary Rodham Clinton	D	2000	2013	
Charles "Chuck" E. Schumer	D	1998	2011	
U.S. Representatives		Republican	Democrat	Other
		6	23	0

Data: National Governors Association, U.S. Senate, U.S. House of Representatives

Business and Economic Agencies

Agency	Website Address
Business Council of New York State, Inc.	www.bcnys.org
Empire State Development	www.nylovesbiz.com/default.asp
New York State Small Business Dev. Center	www.nyssbdc.org
New York Department of State	www.dos.state.ny.us

Data: Various Agency Websites

North Carolina

Demographics and Socioeconomics. North Carolina is located in the South Atlantic region of the United States. The state's 2005 population of 8.4 million made it the eleventh most populous state. The state's population increased by 361,728 people from 2000 to 2005, and is projected to increase to 11.4 million by 2025. This 1.6 percent projected annual growth rate is above the national average of 1.0 percent. In 2005 North Carolina had a per capita personal income of $31,029, which was $3,466 below the national average. The state's per capita income grew at an average annual rate of 2.8 percent, close to the 2.9 percent national average.

Workforce and Industry. The state's workforce is generally less educated than that of other states: 82.3 percent of the state's adult population has graduated from high school, compared to an 84.2 percent national average; 25.1 percent hold a bachelor degree or higher (national average is 27.2 percent); and 8.0 percent hold professional or graduate degrees (national average is 10.0). In 2004 the state's largest industry in terms of employment was

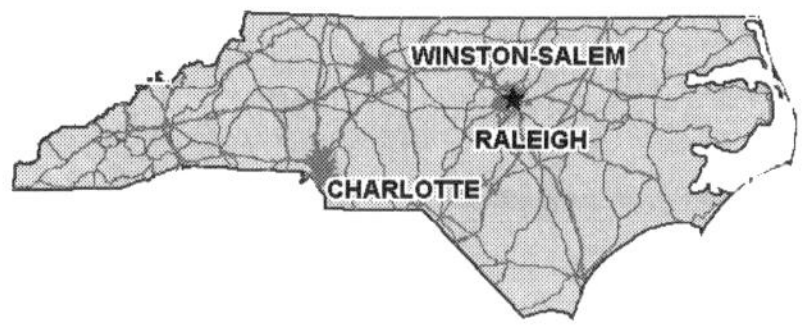

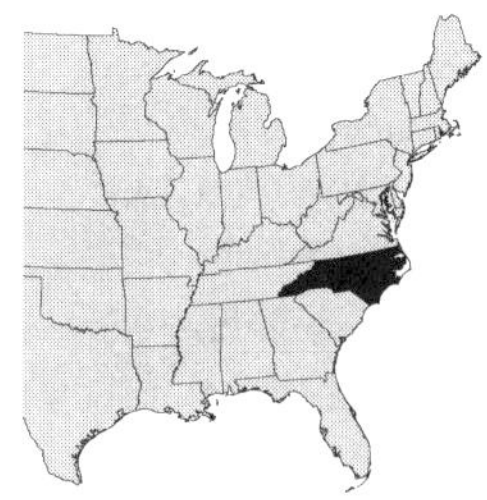

★ State Capitol

Major Urban Area

Major Roadway

Demographic and Socioeconomic Profile

Demographics and Socioeconomic Figures

Population and Households	2000	2005
Total Population	8,049,313	8,411,041
Number of Households	3,132,013	3,409,840
Average Household Size	2.5	2.5
Age and Ethnicity		
Median Age	35.3	36.2
Population 18 Years of Age and Older	6,087,996	6,279,024
Population 65 Years of Age and Older	969,822	985,875
Caucasian Population	5,802,165	6,005,471
African-American Population	1,734,154	1,765,698
Hispanic Population	372,964	533,087
Asian Population	111,292	146,795
Foreign-Born Population	430,000	560,753
Income		
Per Capita Personal Income (USD)	$27,068	$31,029
Median Household Income (USD)	$39,184	$40,729
Individuals below Poverty Level	12.3%	15.1%

Data: U.S. Census, American Community Survey; U.S. Department of Commerce, Bureau of Economic Analysis

manufacturing, followed by retail trade. The fastest growing industry was finance and insurance, with 36.7 percent growth from 1998 to 2004.

Tax Profile and Business Climate. In fiscal year 2003–4 North Carolina had total tax revenues of $25.0 billion. The largest share was generated from sales and gross receipts taxes, followed by individual income taxes. The per capita tax burden in North Carolina was $2,929 for 2003–4, some $518 below the national average. In terms of business taxes, North Carolina ranked fifth in a 2006 report by Anderson Economic Group. The state's business climate was ranked third by Forbes Magazine and fortieth by the Tax Foundation.

Population Projections

	2010	2015	2020	2025
Total Population	9,345,823	10,010,770	10,709,289	11,449,153
Median Age	36.9	37.3	37.2	36.8
Population 18 Years of Age and Older	7,076,985	7,572,393	8,083,886	8,609,911
Population 65 Years of Age and Older	1,161,164	1,374,754	1,618,578	1,897,902

Data: U.S. Census Bureau

Workforce and Industry Profile

Workforce

	2000	2005
Civilian Labor Force	4,039,732	4,300,012
Labor Force Participation Rate	65.7%	66.6%
Unemployment Rate	3.8%	5.2%
Average Earnings per Job (USD)	$31,068	$34,460
Education Attainment (Population 25 Years and Older)	**(%)**	**(%)**
High School Graduate or Higher	78.1	82.3
Bachelors Degree or Higher	22.5	25.1
Graduate or Professional Degree	7.2	8.0

Data: U.S. Census Bureau, American Community Survey; U.S. Department of Labor, Bureau of Labor Statistics

Industry Overview

	1998	2004
Total Employees	3,223,178	3,365,633
Total Payroll ($1,000)	86,780,877	109,572,059
Total Establishments	198,690	213,057
Establishments with 1–19 Employees	170,676	181,555
Establishments with 20–49 Employees	17,002	19,828
Establishments with 50–249 Employees	9,411	10,211
Establishments with 250–999 Employees	1,426	1,279
Establishments with 1,000+ Employees	175	184

Data: U.S. Census Bureau, County Business Patterns

Major Industries (Ranked by 2004 Employment; Payroll in $1,000s)				
Industry	1998 Employment	2004 Employment	1998 Payroll	2004 Payroll
Manufacturing	771,282	571,164	22,452,407	20,690,512
Retail Trade	430,667	458,404	7,424,839	9,290,241
Health Care and Social Assistance	375,399	458,395	10,495,546	15,548,206
Accommodation and Food Services	260,453	307,230	2,668,813	3,697,738
Admin., Support, Waste Mngt., Remediation Services	188,349	222,661	3,608,799	5,281,691
Construction	205,750	216,086	5,926,419	7,107,204
Finance and Insurance	133,120	181,941	5,316,012	9,962,881
Professional, Scientific, Technical Services	126,888	170,712	5,000,972	8,803,507
Wholesale Trade	161,459	165,335	6,121,068	7,261,578
Other Services (except Public Admin.)	134,043	148,477	2,313,119	2,916,872

Data: U.S. Census Bureau, County Business Patterns

Taxes and Business Climate

State and Local Taxes		
Combined Revenues ($1,000)	2001–2	2003–4
Revenue from Property Taxes	5,421,740	6,093,170
Revenue from Sales and Gross Receipts Taxes	7,851,733	8,951,045
Revenue from Individual Income Taxes	7,265,242	7,510,978
Revenue from Corporate Income Taxes	668,124	837,085
Revenue from Other Taxes	1,369,580	1,620,186
Total Tax Revenue	22,576,419	25,012,464
Per Capita Taxes		
Property Tax per Capita	674	713
Sales and Gross Receipts Tax per Capita	975	1,048
Individual Income Tax per Capita	903	880
Corporate Income Tax per Capita	83	98
Other Taxes per Capita	170	190
Total Taxes per Capita	2,805	2,929

Data: U.S. Census Bureau; Anderson Economic Group, LLC

Business Climate Measures	
Anderson Economic Group: 2006 Business Tax Ranking (1 is Best)	5
Forbes Magazine: 2006 Best States for Business Ranking (1 is Best)	3
Tax Foundation: 2007 Business Tax Climate Ranking (1 is Best)	40
2002–3 Employer Firm Births	20,808
2002–3 Employer Firm Terminations	19,305

Data: Anderson Economic Group; Tax Foundation; Forbes Magazine; U.S. Census, Statistics of U.S. Businesses

Voting Behavior and Elected Officials

Voter Registration and Turnout (%)	1992	1996	2000	2004
Registered Voters Who Voted	68.4	58.3	56.8	64.0
Citizens Age 18+ Who Voted	50.1	45.6	47.8	55.4

Data: Dave Leip's Atlas of U.S. Presidential Elections

Presidential Election Results (Nationwide Winner Listed First)		
2004	**Popular Vote (%)**	**Electoral Votes**
George W. Bush (Republican, Incumbent)	56.0	15
John Kerry (Democrat)	43.6	0
Other	0.4	0
2000		
George W. Bush (Republican)	56.0	14
Albert Gore (Democrat)	43.2	0
Ralph Nader (Green)	.0	0
Other	0.8	0
1996		
William Clinton (Democrat, Incumbent)	44.0	0
Robert Dole (Republican)	48.7	14
H. Ross Perot (Reformist)	6.7	0
Other	0.6	0
1992		
William Clinton (Democrat)	42.7	0
George H. W. Bush (Republican, Incumbent)	43.4	14
H. Ross Perot (Independent)	13.7	0
Other	0.2	0

Data: Dave Leip's Atlas of U.S. Presidential Elections

Governor and U.S. Congressional Seats				
Governor	**Party**	**Year Term Began**	**Term**	**Max. Consecutive Terms**
Michael F. Easley	D	2001	First	2
U.S. Senators	**Party**	**Year Elected**	**Term Expires**	
Elizabeth Dole	R	2002	2009	
Richard Burr	R	2004	2011	
U.S. Representatives		**Republican**	**Democrat**	**Other**
		6	7	0

Data: National Governors Association, U.S. Senate, U.S. House of Representatives

Business and Economic Agencies

Agency	Website Address
North Carolina Citizens for Business and Industry	www.nccbi.org
North Carolina Department of Commerce	www.commerce.state.nc.us
North Carolina Small Business and Tech Dev. Center	www.sbtdc.org
Employment Security Commission	www.ncesc.com

Data: Various Agency Websites

North Dakota

Demographics and Socio-economics. North Dakota, located in the West North Central region of the United States, has a population of 609,645 people, making it the third least populous state in 2005. The state's population decreased by 32,555 people from 2000 to 2005, but is projected to increase to 620,777 by 2025. This 0.1 percent projected annual growth rate compares to the projected national average of 1.0 percent. Per capita personal income in North Dakota was $31,230 in 2005, ranking the nineteenth lowest in the country and $3,265 below the national average. From 2000 to 2005 per capita income in the state grew at an average annual rate of 4.5 percent, compared to 2.9 percent nationally.

Workforce and Industry. In 2004 the state's largest industry in terms of employment was health care and social assistance, followed by retail trade. The fastest growing industry was professional, scientific, and technical services, with 51.6 percent growth from 1998 to 2004. In terms of the education level of the workforce, 88.2 percent of North Dakota's adult population has a high school

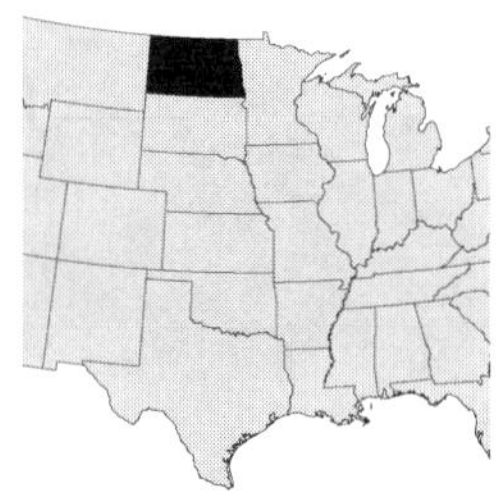

★ State Capitol

Major Urban Area

Major Roadway

Demographic and Socioeconomic Profile

Demographics and Socioeconomic Figures		
Population and Households	**2000**	**2005**
Total Population	642,200	609,645
Number of Households	257,152	270,437
Average Household Size	2.4	2.3
Age and Ethnicity		
Median Age	36.2	39.1
Population 18 Years of Age and Older	481,301	474,382
Population 65 Years of Age and Older	94,597	86,655
Caucasian Population	593,785	557,952
African-American Population	3,673	4,981
Hispanic Population	7,568	8,553
Asian Population	3,342	5,459
Foreign-Born Population	12,114	11,968
Income		
Per Capita Personal Income (USD)	$25,106	$31,230
Median Household Income (USD)	$34,604	$41,030
Individuals below Poverty Level	11.9%	11.2%

Data: U.S. Census, American Community Survey; U.S. Department of Commerce, Bureau of Economic Analysis

diploma or the equivalent, compared to the national average of 84.2 percent; 25.5 percent of North Dakota's adult population has a bachelor degree or higher (national average is 27.2 percent); and 6.7 percent hold professional or graduate degrees (national average is 10.0 percent).

Tax Profile and Business Climate. In fiscal year 2003–4 North Dakota had total tax revenues of $1.9 billion. The largest share was generated from sales and gross receipts taxes, followed by property taxes. The per capita tax burden in North Dakota was $2,989 for 2003–4, some $458 below the national average. In terms of business taxes, the state ranked forty-fourth in a 2006 report by Anderson Economic Group. Forbes Magazine and the Tax Foundation ranked the state's business climate thirteenth and thirty-third, respectively.

Population Projections

	2010	2015	2020	2025
Total Population	636,623	635,133	630,112	620,777
Median Age	38.4	39.3	40.6	41.9
Population 18 Years of Age and Older	494,659	496,436	492,483	486,949
Population 65 Years of Age and Older	97,108	107,900	125,023	142,195

Data: U.S. Census Bureau

Workforce and Industry Profile

Workforce

	2000	2005
Civilian Labor Force	331,889	345,602
Labor Force Participation Rate	67.5%	71.1%
Unemployment Rate	2.9%	3.4%
Average Earnings per Job (USD)	$24,683	$30,850
Education Attainment (Population 25 Years and Older)	**(%)**	**(%)**
High School Graduate or Higher	83.9	88.2
Bachelors Degree or Higher	22.0	25.5
Graduate or Professional Degree	5.5	6.7

Data: U.S. Census Bureau, American Community Survey; U.S. Department of Labor, Bureau of Labor Statistics

Industry Overview

	1998	2004
Total Employees	249,476	265,663
Total Payroll ($1,000)	5,533,810	7,314,026
Total Establishments	20,288	20,822
Establishments with 1–19 Employees	17,815	18,229
Establishments with 20–49 Employees	1,618	1,632
Establishments with 50–249 Employees	774	860
Establishments with 250–999 Employees	72	92
Establishments with 1,000+ Employees	9	9

Data: U.S. Census Bureau, County Business Patterns

Major Industries (Ranked by 2004 Employment; Payroll in $1,000s)				
Industry	1998 Employment	2004 Employment	1998 Payroll	2004 Payroll
Health Care and Social Assistance	45,894	51,535	1,089,193	1,528,625
Retail Trade	41,402	42,669	655,415	809,704
Accommodation and Food Services	25,850	27,588	208,591	281,335
Manufacturing	23,209	23,558	670,183	779,822
Wholesale Trade	17,000	16,854	476,356	623,528
Construction	13,980	15,110	451,087	603,307
Finance and Insurance	12,526	14,417	371,331	519,543
Other Services (except Public Admin.)	13,819	13,212	184,901	223,018
Professional, Scientific, Technical Services	7,596	11,514	233,272	400,045
Admin., Support, Waste Mngt., Remediation Services	10,953	10,589	177,802	194,893

Data: U.S. Census Bureau, County Business Patterns

Taxes and Business Climate

State and Local Taxes		
Combined Revenues ($1,000)	2001–2	2003–4
Revenue from Property Taxes	532,340	584,622
Revenue from Sales and Gross Receipts Taxes	688,643	742,116
Revenue from Individual Income Taxes	199,590	213,982
Revenue from Corporate Income Taxes	49,990	49,807
Revenue from Other Taxes	258,192	310,520
Total Tax Revenue	1,728,755	1,901,047
Per Capita Taxes		
Property Tax per Capita	829	919
Sales and Gross Receipts Tax per Capita	1,073	1,167
Individual Income Tax per Capita	311	336
Corporate Income Tax per Capita	78	78
Other Taxes per Capita	402	488
Total Taxes per Capita	2,693	2,989

Data: U.S. Census Bureau; Anderson Economic Group, LLC

Business Climate Measures	
Anderson Economic Group: 2006 Business Tax Ranking (1 is Best)	44
Forbes Magazine: 2006 Best States for Business Ranking (1 is Best)	13
Tax Foundation: 2007 Business Tax Climate Ranking (1 is Best)	33
2002–3 Employer Firm Births	1,496
2002–3 Employer Firm Terminations	1,447

Data: Anderson Economic Group; Tax Foundation; Forbes Magazine; U.S. Census, Statistics of U.S. Businesses

Voting Behavior and Elected Officials

Voter Registration and Turnout (%)

	1992	1996	2000	2004
Registered Voters Who Voted	n/a	n/a	n/a	n/a
Citizens Age 18+ Who Voted	67.3	56.0	59.9	64.2

Data: Dave Leip's Atlas of U.S. Presidential Elections

Presidential Election Results (Nationwide Winner Listed First)

2004	Popular Vote (%)	Electoral Votes
George W. Bush (Republican, Incumbent)	62.9	3
John Kerry (Democrat)	35.5	0
Other	1.6	0
2000		
George W. Bush (Republican)	60.7	3
Albert Gore (Democrat)	33.1	0
Ralph Nader (Green)	3.3	0
Other	3.0	0
1996		
William Clinton (Democrat, Incumbent)	40.1	0
Robert Dole (Republican)	46.9	3
H. Ross Perot (Reformist)	12.2	0
Other	0.7	0
1992		
William Clinton (Democrat)	32.2	0
George H. W. Bush (Republican, Incumbent)	44.2	3
H. Ross Perot (Independent)	23.1	0
Other	0.5	0

Data: Dave Leip's Atlas of U.S. Presidential Elections

Governor and U.S. Congressional Seats				
Governor	**Party**	**Year Term Began**	**Term**	**Max. Consecutive Terms**
John Hoeven	R	2000	First	No limit
U.S. Senators	**Party**	**Year Elected**	**Term Expires**	
Kent Conrad	D	1986	2013	
Byron L. Dorgan	D	1992	2011	
U.S. Representatives		**Republican**	**Democrat**	**Other**
		0	1	0

Data: National Governors Association, U.S. Senate, U.S. House of Representatives

Business and Economic Agencies

Agency	Website Address
Greater North Dakota Chamber of Commerce	www.gnda.com
North Dakota Department of Commerce	www.growingnd.com
North Dakota Small Business Dev. Center	www.und.nodak.edu/dept/ndsbdc
North Dakota Secretary of State	www.nd.gov/sos/businessserv

Data: Various Agency Websites

Ohio

Demographics and Socioeconomics. Ohio, located in the East North Central region of the United States, has a population of 11.2 million people, making it the seventh most populous state in 2005. The state's population decreased by 197,534 people from 2000 to 2005, but is projected to increase to 11.6 million by 2025. This 0.2 percent projected annual growth rate compares to the projected national average of 1.0 percent. The state's 2005 per capita personal income of $31,867 was the twenty-second lowest in the United States, some $2,628 below the national average. Per capita income in Ohio grew at an average annual rate of 2.5 percent from 2000 to 2005, compared to 2.9 percent nationally.

Workforce and Industry. In 2004 the state's largest industry in terms of employment was manufacturing, followed by health care and social assistance. The fastest growing major industry was professional, scientific, and technical services, with 14.3 percent growth from 1998 to 2004. In terms of the education level of the workforce, 86.3 percent of Ohio's adult population has a high school

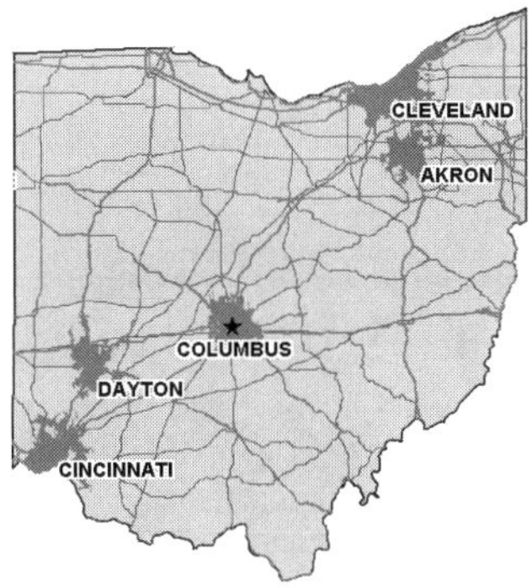

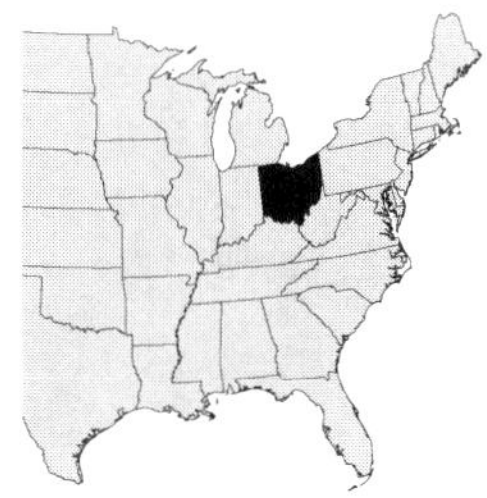

★ State Capitol

Major Urban Area

Major Roadway

Demographic and Socioeconomic Profile

Demographics and Socioeconomic Figures		
Population and Households	**2000**	**2005**
Total Population	11,353,140	11,155,606
Number of Households	4,445,773	4,507,821
Average Household Size	2.5	2.5
Age and Ethnicity		
Median Age	36.2	37.6
Population 18 Years of Age and Older	8,467,999	8,401,998
Population 65 Years of Age and Older	1,508,095	1,430,984
Caucasian Population	9,640,523	9,408,020
African-American Population	1,288,359	1,283,908
Hispanic Population	213,889	253,889
Asian Population	132,131	162,117
Foreign-Born Population	339,279	387,216
Income		
Per Capita Personal Income (USD)	$28,207	$31,867
Median Household Income (USD)	$40,956	$43,493
Individuals below Poverty Level	10.6%	13.0%

Data: U.S. Census, American Community Survey; U.S. Department of Commerce, Bureau of Economic Analysis

diploma or the equivalent, compared to the national average of 84.2 percent: 23.3 percent of Ohio's adult population has a bachelor degree or higher (national average is 27.2 percent); and 7.5 percent hold professional or graduate degrees (national average is 10.0 percent).

Tax Profile and Business Climate. In fiscal year 2003–4 Ohio had total tax revenues of $39.1 billion. The largest share was generated from sales and gross receipts taxes, followed by individual income taxes. The per capita tax burden in Ohio was $3,419 for 2003–4, very close to the national average per capita tax burden of $3,447. In terms of business taxes, the state ranked eleventh in a 2006 report by Anderson Economic Group. Forbes Magazine and the Tax Foundation ranked the state's business climate thirty-fourth and forty-nineth, respectively.

Population Projections

	2010	2015	2020	2025
Total Population	11,576,181	11,635,446	11,644,058	11,605,738
Median Age	38.1	38.3	39.0	39.7
Population 18 Years of Age and Older	8,831,750	8,912,543	8,940,542	8,932,576
Population 65 Years of Age and Older	1,586,981	1,766,239	1,978,464	2,206,698

Data: U.S. Census Bureau

Workforce and Industry Profile

Workforce

	2000	2005
Civilian Labor Force	5,684,790	5,745,886
Labor Force Participation Rate	64.8%	66.0%
Unemployment Rate	4.0%	5.9%
Average Earnings per Job (USD)	$32,507	$36,270
Education Attainment (Population 25 Years and Older)	**(%)**	**(%)**
High School Graduate or Higher	83.0	86.3
Bachelors Degree or Higher	21.1	23.3
Graduate or Professional Degree	7.4	7.5

Data: U.S. Census Bureau, American Community Survey; U.S. Department of Labor, Bureau of Labor Statistics

Industry Overview

	1998	2004
Total Employees	4,806,046	4,762,205
Total Payroll ($1,000)	140,265,358	162,559,634
Total Establishments	270,343	271,733
Establishments with 1–19 Employees	227,768	228,346
Establishments with 20–49 Employees	25,666	26,358
Establishments with 50–249 Employees	14,702	14,957
Establishments with 250–999 Employees	1,927	1,793
Establishments with 1,000+ Employees	280	279

Data: U.S. Census Bureau, County Business Patterns

Major Industries (Ranked by 2004 Employment; Payroll in $1,000s)				
Industry	1998 Employment	2004 Employment	1998 Payroll	2004 Payroll
Manufacturing	994,788	814,662	37,590,541	35,718,653
Health Care and Social Assistance	628,383	706,108	17,364,658	23,715,778
Retail Trade	632,285	619,078	10,789,385	12,432,636
Accommodation and Food Services	404,645	426,820	3,839,217	4,672,684
Admin., Support, Waste Mngt., Remediation Services	298,272	318,081	5,734,863	7,710,847
Finance and Insurance	246,164	258,015	9,522,859	12,447,215
Professional, Scientific, Technical Services	207,796	237,590	8,391,803	11,771,883
Wholesale Trade	254,997	235,090	9,446,007	10,706,447
Other Services (except Public Admin.)	228,028	231,321	3,907,272	4,688,399
Construction	222,637	227,414	7,898,182	9,114,809

Data: U.S. Census Bureau, County Business Patterns

Taxes and Business Climate

State and Local Taxes		
Combined Revenues ($1,000)	2001–2	2003–4
Revenue from Property Taxes	10,643,420	11,232,828
Revenue from Sales and Gross Receipts Taxes	10,765,580	12,318,284
Revenue from Individual Income Taxes	11,793,667	12,183,380
Revenue from Corporate Income Taxes	761,050	1,060,594
Revenue from Other Taxes	2,201,473	2,356,137
Total Tax Revenue	36,165,190	39,151,223
Per Capita Taxes		
Property Tax per Capita	937	981
Sales and Gross Receipts Tax per Capita	948	1,076
Individual Income Tax per Capita	1,039	1,064
Corporate Income Tax per Capita	67	93
Other Taxes per Capita	194	206
Total Taxes per Capita	3,186	3,419

Data: U.S. Census Bureau; Anderson Economic Group, LLC

Business Climate Measures

Anderson Economic Group: 2006 Business Tax Ranking (1 is Best)	11
Forbes Magazine: 2006 Best States for Business Ranking (1 is Best)	34
Tax Foundation: 2007 Business Tax Climate Ranking (1 is Best)	49
2002–3 Employer Firm Births	22,439
2002–3 Employer Firm Terminations	22,644

Data: Anderson Economic Group; Tax Foundation; Forbes Magazine; U.S. Census, Statistics of U.S. Businesses

Voting Behavior and Elected Officials

Voter Registration and Turnout (%)

	1992	1996	2000	2004
Registered Voters Who Voted	75.6	66.3	62.4	70.6
Citizens Age 18+ Who Voted	60.6	54.3	55.6	65.3

Data: Dave Leip's Atlas of U.S. Presidential Elections

Presidential Election Results (Nationwide Winner Listed First)

2004	Popular Vote (%)	Electoral Votes
George W. Bush (Republican, Incumbent)	50.8	20
John Kerry (Democrat)	48.7	0
Other	0.5	0
2000		
George W. Bush (Republican)	50.0	21
Albert Gore (Democrat)	46.5	0
Ralph Nader (Green)	2.5	0
Other	1.1	0
1996		
William Clinton (Democrat, Incumbent)	47.4	21
Robert Dole (Republican)	41.0	0
H. Ross Perot (Reformist)	10.7	0
Other	1.0	0
1992		
William Clinton (Democrat)	40.2	21
George H. W. Bush (Republican, Incumbent)	38.4	0
H. Ross Perot (Independent)	21.0	0
Other	0.5	0

Data: Dave Leip's Atlas of U.S. Presidential Elections

Governor and U.S. Congressional Seats				
Governor	**Party**	**Year Term Began**	**Term**	**Max. Consecutive Terms**
Ted Strickland	D	2007	First	2
U.S. Senators	**Party**	**Year Elected**	**Term Expires**	
Sherrod Brown	D	2006	2013	
George V. Voinovich	R	1998	2011	
U.S. Representatives		**Republican**	**Democrat**	**Other**
		11	7	0

Data: National Governors Association, U.S. Senate, U.S. House of Representatives

Business and Economic Agencies

Agency	Website Address
Ohio Chamber of Commerce	www.ohiochamber.com
Ohio Department of Development	www.odod.state.oh.us
Ohio Small Business Dev. Center	www.odod.state.oh.us/edd/osb/sbdc
Ohio Secretary of State	www.sos.state.oh.us

Data: Various Agency Websites

Oklahoma

Demographics and Socioeconomics. With a population of 3.4 million people, Oklahoma was the twenty-third least populous state in the United States in 2005. From 2000 to 2005 the state's population decreased by 17,158 people, but is projected to increase to 3.8 million by 2025. This 0.5 percent projected annual growth rate compares to the projected national average of 1.0 percent. Per capita personal income in Oklahoma was $29,908 in 2005, ranking twelfth lowest in the country and $4,587 below the national average. From 2000 to 2005 per capita income in Oklahoma grew at an average annual rate of 4.1 percent, compared to 2.9 percent nationally.

Workforce and Industry. The state's largest industry in terms of 2004 employment was health care and social assistance. The fastest growing major industry in Oklahoma was professional, scientific, and technical services, with 22.8 percent growth from 1998 to 2004. In terms of the education level of the workforce, 84.3 percent of Oklahoma's adult population has a high school diploma or the equivalent, compared to the national

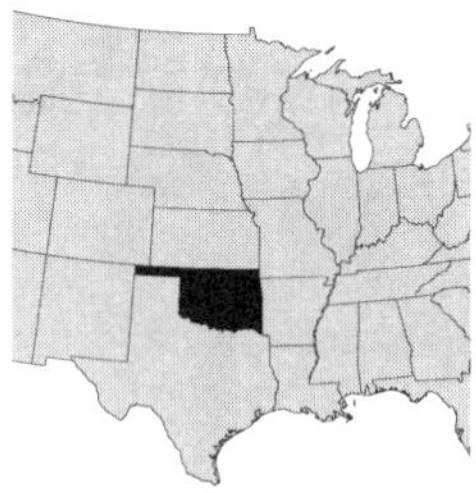

★ State Capitol

Major Urban Area

Major Roadway

Demographic and Socioeconomic Profile

Demographics and Socioeconomic Figures		
Population and Households	**2000**	**2005**
Total Population	3,450,654	3,433,496
Number of Households	1,342,293	1,380,595
Average Household Size	2.5	2.5
Age and Ethnicity		
Median Age	35.5	36.5
Population 18 Years of Age and Older	2,560,390	2,585,083
Population 65 Years of Age and Older	455,700	441,763
Caucasian Population	2,624,679	2,589,660
African-American Population	258,532	243,094
Hispanic Population	177,768	227,767
Asian Population	45,546	54,270
Foreign-Born Population	131,747	155,880
Income		
Per Capita Personal Income (USD)	$24,407	$29,908
Median Household Income (USD)	$33,400	$37,063
Individuals below Poverty Level	14.7%	16.5%

Data: U.S. Census, American Community Survey; U.S. Department of Commerce, Bureau of Economic Analysis

average of 84.2 percent. 22.4 percent of Oklahoma's adult population has a bachelor degree or higher (national average is 27.2 percent); and 7.2 percent hold professional or graduate degrees (national average is 10.0 percent).

Tax Profile and Business Climate. Oklahoma's total tax revenue was $9.4 billion for fiscal year 2003–4. The largest share of tax revenue was generated from sales and gross receipts taxes, followed by individual income taxes. On a per capita basis, Oklahoma had total taxes of $2,677, compared to the national average of $3,447 for 2003–4. In terms of business taxes, the state ranked seventeenth in a 2006 report by Anderson Economic Group. Forbes Magazine and the Tax Foundation ranked the state's business climate nineteenth and twenty-first, respectively.

Population Projections

	2010	2015	2020	2025
Total Population	3,591,516	3,661,694	3,735,690	3,820,994
Median Age	36.8	37.3	37.9	38.0
Population 18 Years of Age and Older	2,696,443	2,746,485	2,801,647	2,870,485
Population 65 Years of Age and Older	494,966	553,761	625,384	702,307

Data: U.S. Census Bureau

Workforce and Industry Profile

Workforce

	2000	2005
Civilian Labor Force	1,632,128	1,709,179
Labor Force Participation Rate	62.1%	64.2%
Unemployment Rate	3.1%	4.4%
Average Earnings per Job (USD)	$26,988	$31,460
Education Attainment (Population 25 Years and Older)	**(%)**	**(%)**
High School Graduate or Higher	80.6	84.3
Bachelors Degree or Higher	20.3	22.4
Graduate or Professional Degree	6.8	7.2

Data: U.S. Census Bureau, American Community Survey; U.S. Department of Labor, Bureau of Labor Statistics

Industry Overview

	1998	2004
Total Employees	1,167,709	1,195,043
Total Payroll ($1,000)	28,667,008	35,597,604
Total Establishments	84,881	87,440
Establishments with 1–19 Employees	73,827	76,061
Establishments with 20–49 Employees	7,124	7,363
Establishments with 50–249 Employees	3,453	3,527
Establishments with 250–999 Employees	420	423
Establishments with 1,000+ Employees	57	66

Data: U.S. Census Bureau, County Business Patterns

Major Industries (Ranked by 2004 Employment; Payroll in $1,000s)				
Industry	1998 Employment	2004 Employment	1998 Payroll	2004 Payroll
Health Care and Social Assistance	171,498	184,166	4,149,804	5,594,854
Retail Trade	165,852	170,914	2,605,428	3,272,724
Manufacturing	168,140	141,126	5,241,720	5,370,741
Accommodation and Food Services	104,489	117,314	956,839	1,214,637
Admin., Support, Waste Mngt., Remediation Services	79,011	93,656	1,404,856	2,284,789
Other Services (except Public Admin.)	61,363	61,406	962,404	1,101,187
Professional, Scientific, Technical Services	49,645	60,972	1,721,291	2,527,764
Construction	54,900	60,313	1,478,200	1,853,437
Finance and Insurance	57,364	58,890	1,825,437	2,319,277
Wholesale Trade	61,096	53,677	1,919,885	2,110,878

Data: U.S. Census Bureau, County Business Patterns

Taxes and Business Climate

State and Local Taxes		
Combined Revenues ($1,000)	2001–2	2003–4
Revenue from Property Taxes	1,482,139	1,637,457
Revenue from Sales and Gross Receipts Taxes	3,446,259	3,638,525
Revenue from Individual Income Taxes	2,286,110	2,319,123
Revenue from Corporate Income Taxes	173,701	133,309
Revenue from Other Taxes	1,393,680	1,706,529
Total Tax Revenue	8,781,889	9,434,943
Per Capita Taxes		
Property Tax per Capita	429	465
Sales and Gross Receipts Tax per Capita	999	1,032
Individual Income Tax per Capita	662	658
Corporate Income Tax per Capita	50	38
Other Taxes per Capita	404	484
Total Taxes per Capita	2,545	2,677

Data: U.S. Census Bureau; Anderson Economic Group, LLC

Business Climate Measures	
Anderson Economic Group: 2006 Business Tax Ranking (1 is Best)	17
Forbes Magazine: 2006 Best States for Business Ranking (1 is Best)	19
Tax Foundation: 2007 Business Tax Climate Ranking (1 is Best)	21
2002–3 Employer Firm Births	8,263
2002–3 Employer Firm Terminations	7,704

Data: Anderson Economic Group; Tax Foundation; Forbes Magazine; U.S. Census, Statistics of U.S. Businesses

Voting Behavior and Elected Officials

Voter Registration and Turnout (%)	1992	1996	2000	2004
Registered Voters Who Voted	60.4	61.0	55.3	68.3
Citizens Age 18+ Who Voted	59.7	49.7	48.2	55.6

Data: Dave Leip's Atlas of U.S. Presidential Elections

Presidential Election Results (Nationwide Winner Listed First)		
2004	**Popular Vote (%)**	**Electoral Votes**
George W. Bush (Republican, Incumbent)	65.6	7
John Kerry (Democrat)	34.4	0
Other	0.0	0
2000		
George W. Bush (Republican)	60.3	8
Albert Gore (Democrat)	38.4	0
Ralph Nader (Green)	0.0	0
Other	1.3	0
1996		
William Clinton (Democrat, Incumbent)	40.5	0
Robert Dole (Republican)	48.3	8
H. Ross Perot (Reformist)	10.8	0
Other	0.5	0
1992		
William Clinton (Democrat)	34.0	0
George H. W. Bush (Republican, Incumbent)	42.7	8
H. Ross Perot (Independent)	23.0	0
Other	0.3	0

Data: Dave Leip's Atlas of U.S. Presidential Elections

Governor and U.S. Congressional Seats				
Governor	**Party**	**Year Term Began**	**Term**	**Max. Consecutive Terms**
Brad Henry	D	2003	Second	2
U.S. Senators	**Party**	**Year Elected**	**Term Expires**	
James M. Inhofe	R	1994	2009	
Tom Coburn	R	2004	2011	
U.S. Representatives		**Republican**	**Democrat**	**Other**
		4	1	0

Data: National Governors Association, U.S. Senate, U.S. House of Representatives

Business and Economic Agencies

Agency	Website Address
The State Chamber	www.okstatechamber.com
Oklahoma Advantage, Oklahoma Department of Commerce	www.okcommerce.gov
Oklahoma Small Business Dev. Center	www.osbdc.org
Oklahoma Secretary of State	www.sos.state.ok.us/business/business_filing.htm

Data: Various Agency Websites

Oregon

Demographics and Socioeconomics. With a population of 3.6 million people, Oregon was the twenty-fourth least populous state in the United States in 2005. From 2000 to 2005 the state's population increased by 138,710 people, and is projected to increase to 4.5 million by 2025. This 1.2 percent projected annual growth rate compares to the projected national average of 1.0 percent. The state's 2005 per capita personal income of $32,174 was the twenty-third lowest in the United States, some $2,321 below the national average. Per capita income in Oregon grew at an average annual rate of 2.7 percent from 2000 to 2005, compared to 2.9 percent nationally.

Workforce and Industry. Oregon's largest industry in terms of 2004 employment was retail trade. The fastest growing major industry was health care and social assistance, with 16.3 percent growth from 1998 to 2004. The state's workforce is generally more educated than that of other states: 87.5 percent of the state's adult population has graduated from high school, compared to an 84.2 percent national

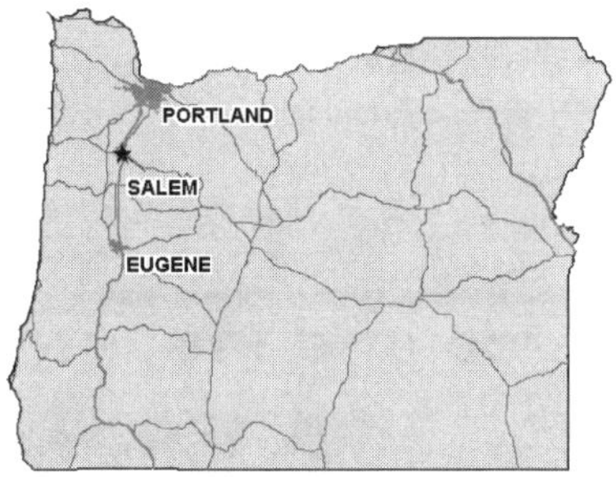

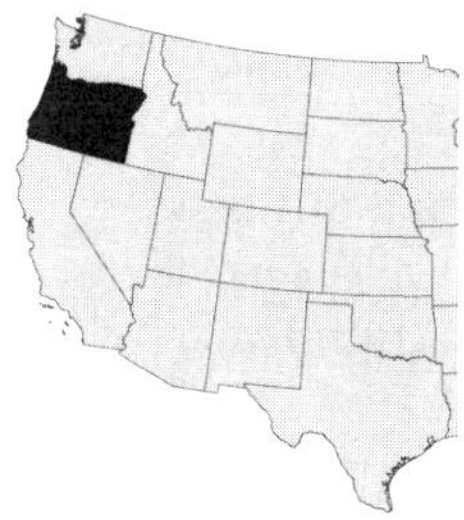

★ State Capitol

Major Urban Area

Major Roadway

Demographic and Socioeconomic Profile

Demographics and Socioeconomic Figures		
Population and Households	**2000**	**2005**
Total Population	3,421,399	3,560,109
Number of Households	1,333,723	1,425,340
Average Household Size	2.5	2.5
Age and Ethnicity		
Median Age	36.3	37.0
Population 18 Years of Age and Older	2,577,129	2,713,648
Population 65 Years of Age and Older	437,887	447,408
Caucasian Population	2,957,510	3,089,729
African-American Population	53,032	58,309
Hispanic Population	273,938	353,433
Asian Population	99,136	125,049
Foreign-Born Population	289,702	344,575
Income		
Per Capita Personal Income (USD)	$28,097	$32,174
Median Household Income (USD)	$40,916	$42,944
Individuals below Poverty Level	11.6%	14.1%

Data: U.S. Census, American Community Survey; U.S. Department of Commerce, Bureau of Economic Analysis

average; 27.7 percent hold a bachelor degree or higher (national average is 27.2 percent); and 10.0 percent hold professional or graduate degrees (national average is 10.0 percent).

Tax Profile and Business Climate. Oregon's total tax revenue was $10.5 billion for fiscal year 2003–4. The largest share of this tax revenue was generated from individual income taxes, followed by property taxes. Total Taxes per Capita in Oregon were $2,917 in 2003–4, compared to the national average of $3,447. In terms of business taxes, the state ranked 34th in a 2006 report by Anderson Economic Group. Forbes Magazine and the Tax Foundation ranked the state's business climate thirty-first and tenth, respectively.

Population Projections

	2010	2015	2020	2025
Total Population	3,790,996	4,012,924	4,260,393	4,536,418
Median Age	37.6	37.9	38.5	38.9
Population 18 Years of Age and Older	2,927,830	3,097,346	3,279,891	3,483,880
Population 65 Years of Age and Older	494,328	590,784	704,866	805,717

Data: U.S. Census Bureau

Workforce and Industry Profile

Workforce

	2000	2005
Civilian Labor Force	1,740,298	1,713,126
Labor Force Participation Rate	65.2%	66.0%
Unemployment Rate	5.2%	6.1%
Average Earnings per Job (USD)	$32,774	$37,280
Education Attainment (Population 25 Years and Older)	**(%)**	**(%)**
High School Graduate or Higher	85.1	87.5
Bachelors Degree or Higher	25.1	27.7
Graduate or Professional Degree	8.7	10.0

Data: U.S. Census Bureau, American Community Survey; U.S. Department of Labor, Bureau of Labor Statistics

Industry Overview

	1998	2004
Total Employees	1,310,750	1,355,542
Total Payroll ($1,000)	37,722,920	46,346,936
Total Establishments	99,183	105,449
Establishments with 1–19 Employees	86,688	92,522
Establishments with 20–49 Employees	8,151	8,383
Establishments with 50–249 Employees	3,831	4,036
Establishments with 250–999 Employees	456	439
Establishments with 1,000+ Employees	57	69

Data: U.S. Census Bureau, County Business Patterns

Major Industries (Ranked by 2004 Employment; Payroll in $1,000s)				
Industry	1998 Employment	2004 Employment	1998 Payroll	2004 Payroll
Retail Trade	182,706	194,645	3,622,503	4,410,788
Manufacturing	211,636	176,847	7,624,969	7,531,806
Health Care and Social Assistance	150,105	174,617	4,199,706	6,268,492
Accommodation and Food Services	125,462	135,163	1,363,861	1,828,469
Admin., Support, Waste Mngt., Remediation Services	81,555	84,998	1,621,416	2,061,896
Construction	78,753	77,808	2,718,801	3,130,538
Wholesale Trade	77,517	73,231	2,950,647	3,359,048
Professional, Scientific, Technical Services	62,828	72,597	2,380,263	3,446,258
Finance and Insurance	59,843	64,513	2,501,220	3,294,545
Other Services (except Public Admin.)	57,303	61,020	1,028,385	1,343,305

Data: U.S. Census Bureau, County Business Patterns

Taxes and Business Climate

State and Local Taxes		
Combined Revenues ($1,000)	**2001–2**	**2003–4**
Revenue from Property Taxes	3,138,875	3,459,371
Revenue from Sales and Gross Receipts Taxes	888,828	1,014,307
Revenue from Individual Income Taxes	3,674,962	4,370,854
Revenue from Corporate Income Taxes	196,257	320,065
Revenue from Other Taxes	1,095,882	1,309,613
Total Tax Revenue	8,994,804	10,474,210
Per Capita Taxes		
Property Tax per Capita	918	963
Sales and Gross Receipts Tax per Capita	260	282
Individual Income Tax per Capita	1,074	1,217
Corporate Income Tax per Capita	57	89
Other Taxes per Capita	320	365
Total Taxes per Capita	2,629	2,917

Data: U.S. Census Bureau; Anderson Economic Group, LLC

Business Climate Measures	
Anderson Economic Group: 2006 Business Tax Ranking (1 is Best)	34
Forbes Magazine: 2006 Best States for Business Ranking (1 is Best)	31
Tax Foundation: 2007 Business Tax Climate Ranking (1 is Best)	10
2002–3 Employer Firm Births	10,689
2002–3 Employer Firm Terminations	9,298

Data: Anderson Economic Group; Tax Foundation; Forbes Magazine; U.S. Census, Statistics of U.S. Businesses

Voting Behavior and Elected Officials

Voter Registration and Turnout (%)	1992	1996	2000	2004
Registered Voters Who Voted	82.4	70.2	78.5	85.8
Citizens Age 18+ Who Voted	65.7	57.1	59.5	67.8

Data: Dave Leip's Atlas of U.S. Presidential Elections

Presidential Election Results (Nationwide Winner Listed First)		
2004	**Popular Vote (%)**	**Electoral Votes**
George W. Bush (Republican, Incumbent)	47.2	0
John Kerry (Democrat)	51.4	7
Other	1.5	0
2000		
George W. Bush (Republican)	46.5	0
Albert Gore (Democrat)	47.0	7
Ralph Nader (Green)	5.0	0
Other	1.5	0
1996		
William Clinton (Democrat, Incumbent)	47.2	7
Robert Dole (Republican)	39.1	0
H. Ross Perot (Reformist)	8.8	0
Other	5.0	0
1992		
William Clinton (Democrat)	42.5	7
George H. W. Bush (Republican, Incumbent)	32.5	0
H. Ross Perot (Independent)	24.2	0
Other	0.8	0

Data: Dave Leip's Atlas of U.S. Presidential Elections

Governor and U.S. Congressional Seats				
Governor	**Party**	**Year Term Began**	**Term**	**Max. Consecutive Terms**
Ted Kulongoski	D	2003	Second	2
U.S. Senators	**Party**	**Year Elected**	**Term Expires**	
Gordon H. Smith	R	1996	2009	
Ron Wyden	D	1996	2011	
U.S. Representatives		**Republican**	**Democrat**	**Other**
		1	4	0

Data: National Governors Association, U.S. Senate, U.S. House of Representatives

Business and Economic Agencies

Agency	Website Address
Associated Oregon Industries, Inc.	www.aoi.org
Oregon Economic and Community Development Department	econ.oregon.gov
Oregon Small Business Development Center	www.bizcenter.org
Oregon Secretary of State, Corporation Division	www.filinginoregon.com

Data: Various Agency Websites

Pennsylvania

Demographics and Socioeconomics. Pennsylvania, located in the Mid-Atlantic region of the United States, has a population of 12.0 million people, making it the sixth most populous state in 2005. The state's population decreased by 301,907 people from 2000 to 2005, but is projected to increase to 12.8 million by 2025. This 0.3 percent projected annual growth rate compares to the projected national average of 1.0 percent. The state's 2005 per capita personal income of $34,848 was the eighteenth highest in the United States, some $353 above the national average. Per capita income in Pennsylvania grew at an average annual rate of 3.3 percent from 2000 to 2005, compared to 2.9 percent nationally.

Workforce and Industry. In 2004 the state's largest industry in terms of employment was health care and social assistance, followed by retail trade. The fastest growing industry was transportation and warehousing, with 29.3 percent growth from 1998 to 2004. Overall, the transportation and warehousing industry ranked twelfth in terms of 2004 employment. In terms of the education level of the

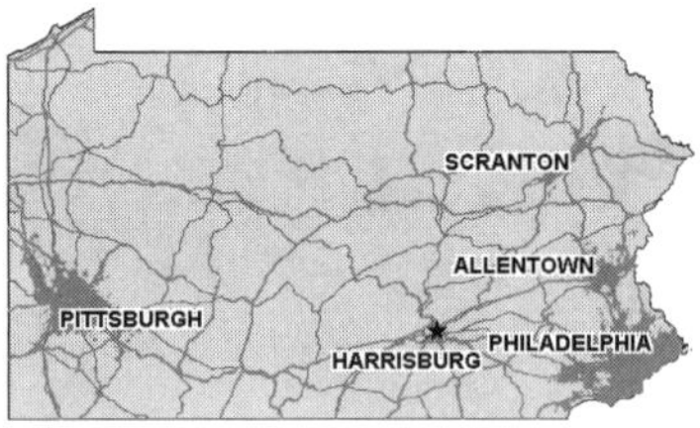

★ State Capitol

Major Urban Area

Major Roadway

Demographic and Socioeconomic Profile

Demographics and Socioeconomic Figures		
Population and Households	**2000**	**2005**
Total Population	12,281,054	11,979,147
Number of Households	4,777,003	4,860,140
Average Household Size	2.5	2.5
Age and Ethnicity		
Median Age	38.0	39.7
Population 18 Years of Age and Older	9,362,066	9,179,373
Population 65 Years of Age and Older	1,920,257	1,754,466
Caucasian Population	10,486,177	10,132,144
African-American Population	1,211,669	1,208,536
Hispanic Population	392,121	484,679
Asian Population	216,631	266,473
Foreign-Born Population	508,291	603,674
Income		
Per Capita Personal Income (USD)	$29,695	$34,848
Median Household Income (USD)	$40,106	$44,537
Individuals below Poverty Level	11.0%	11.9%

Data: U.S. Census, American Community Survey; U.S. Department of Commerce, Bureau of Economic Analysis

workforce, 86.7 percent of Pennsylvania's adult population has a high school diploma or the equivalent, compared to the national average of 84.2 percent: 25.7 percent of the state's adult population has a bachelor degree or higher (national average is 27.2 percent); and 9.8 percent hold professional or graduate degrees (national average is 10.0 percent).

Tax Profile and Business Climate. In fiscal year 2003–4 Pennsylvania had total tax revenues of $42.7 billion. The largest share was generated from sales and gross receipts taxes, followed by property taxes. The per capita tax burden in Pennsylvania was $3,447, which equaled the national average. In terms of business taxes, the state ranked twenty-third in a 2006 report by Anderson Economic Group. Forbes Magazine and the Tax Foundation ranked the state's business climate forty-first and twenty-second, respectively.

Population Projections

	2010	2015	2020	2025
Total Population	12,584,487	12,710,938	12,787,354	12,801,945
Median Age	40.0	40.3	40.6	41.4
Population 18 Years of Age and Older	9,836,892	9,970,245	10,016,274	10,023,766
Population 65 Years of Age and Older	1,956,235	2,148,982	2,403,118	2,688,781

Data: U.S. Census Bureau

Workforce and Industry Profile

Workforce

	2000	2005
Civilian Labor Force	5,992,886	6,091,791
Labor Force Participation Rate	61.9%	64.1%
Unemployment Rate	4.2%	5.0%
Average Earnings per Job (USD)	$34,015	$36,320
Education Attainment (Population 25 Years and Older)	**(%)**	**(%)**
High School Graduate or Higher	81.9	86.7
Bachelors Degree or Higher	22.4	25.7
Graduate or Professional Degree	8.4	9.8

Data: U.S. Census Bureau, American Community Survey; U.S. Department of Labor, Bureau of Labor Statistics

Industry Overview

	1998	2004
Total Employees	4,906,190	5,107,044
Total Payroll ($1,000)	145,569,019	181,784,478
Total Establishments	292,659	301,557
Establishments with 1–19 Employees	250,822	256,868
Establishments with 20–49 Employees	25,263	27,113
Establishments with 50–249 Employees	14,282	15,214
Establishments with 250–999 Employees	1,971	2,050
Establishments with 1,000+ Employees	321	312

Data: U.S. Census Bureau, County Business Patterns

Major Industries (Ranked by 2004 Employment; Payroll in $1,000s)				
Industry	1998 Employment	2004 Employment	1998 Payroll	2004 Payroll
Health Care and Social Assistance	740,333	822,824	20,979,688	28,073,329
Retail Trade	645,472	678,236	11,092,400	13,898,143
Manufacturing	818,215	667,829	28,636,023	27,930,501
Accommodation and Food Services	364,480	403,150	3,736,716	4,777,797
Professional, Scientific, Technical Services	266,917	308,253	12,571,204	17,757,464
Finance and Insurance	272,427	299,033	11,510,271	16,197,060
Admin., Support, Waste Mngt., Remediation Services	278,403	290,143	5,632,982	7,363,540
Construction	225,797	256,193	8,279,710	10,729,128
Other Services (except Public Admin.)	239,673	248,940	4,148,515	5,132,493
Wholesale Trade	234,940	245,044	9,203,086	11,987,747

Data: U.S. Census Bureau, County Business Patterns

Taxes and Business Climate

State and Local Taxes		
Combined Revenues ($1,000)	2001–2	2003–4
Revenue from Property Taxes	10,910,756	12,518,226
Revenue from Sales and Gross Receipts Taxes	11,290,873	12,917,786
Revenue from Individual Income Taxes	9,509,821	10,311,095
Revenue from Corporate Income Taxes	1,198,438	1,677,998
Revenue from Other Taxes	4,716,732	5,292,752
Total Tax Revenue	37,626,620	42,717,857
Per Capita Taxes		
Property Tax per Capita	888	1,010
Sales and Gross Receipts Tax per Capita	919	1,042
Individual Income Tax per Capita	774	832
Corporate Income Tax per Capita	98	135
Other Taxes per Capita	384	427
Total Taxes per Capita	3,064	3,447

Data: U.S. Census Bureau; Anderson Economic Group, LLC

Business Climate Measures	
Anderson Economic Group: 2006 Business Tax Ranking (1 is Best)	23
Forbes Magazine: 2006 Best States for Business Ranking (1 is Best)	41
Tax Foundation: 2007 Business Tax Climate Ranking (1 is Best)	22
2002–3 Employer Firm Births	24,912
2002–3 Employer Firm Terminations	23,977

Data: Anderson Economic Group; Tax Foundation; Forbes Magazine; U.S. Census, Statistics of U.S. Businesses

Voting Behavior and Elected Officials

Voter Registration and Turnout (%)	1992	1996	2000	2004
Registered Voters Who Voted	82.8	66.2	63.1	69.0
Citizens Age 18+ Who Voted	54.3	49.0	52.5	60.5

Data: Dave Leip's Atlas of U.S. Presidential Elections

Presidential Election Results (Nationwide Winner Listed First)		
2004	**Popular Vote (%)**	**Electoral Votes**
George W. Bush (Republican, Incumbent)	48.4	0
John Kerry (Democrat)	50.9	21
Other	0.7	0
2000		
George W. Bush (Republican)	46.4	0
Albert Gore (Democrat)	50.6	23
Ralph Nader (Green)	2.1	0
Other	0.9	0
1996		
William Clinton (Democrat, Incumbent)	49.2	23
Robert Dole (Republican)	40.0	0
H. Ross Perot (Reformist)	9.6	0
Other	1.3	0
1992		
William Clinton (Democrat)	45.2	23
George H. W. Bush (Republican, Incumbent)	36.1	0
H. Ross Perot (Independent)	18.2	0
Other	0.5	0

Data: Dave Leip's Atlas of U.S. Presidential Elections

Governor and U.S. Congressional Seats				
Governor	**Party**	**Year Term Began**	**Term**	**Max. Consecutive Terms**
Edward G. Rendell	D	2003	Second	2
U.S. Senators	**Party**	**Year Elected**	**Term Expires**	
Bob Casey, Jr.	D	2006	2013	
Arlen Specter	R	1980	2011	
U.S. Representatives		**Republican**	**Democrat**	**Other**
		8	11	0

Data: National Governors Association, U.S. Senate, U.S. House of Representatives

Business and Economic Agencies

Agency	Website Address
Pennsylvania Chamber of Business and Industry	www.pachamber.org
Pennsylvania Department of Community and Economic Development	www.newpa.com
Pennsylvania Small Business Dev. Center	www.pasbdc.org
Pennsylvania Department of State	www.dos.state.pa.us/corps

Data: Various Agency Websites

Rhode Island

Demographics and Socioeconomics. With a population of 1.0 million people, Rhode Island was the eighth least populous state in the United States in 2005. From 2000 to 2005 the state's population decreased by 15,657 people, but is projected to increase to 1.2 million by 2025. This 0.6 percent projected annual growth rate compares to the projected national average of 1.0 percent. Per capita personal income in Rhode Island was $35,219 in 2005, ranking the seventeenth highest in the country and $724 above the national average. From 2000 to 2005 per capita income in the state grew at an average annual rate of 3.8 percent, compared to 2.9 percent nationally.

Workforce and Industry. In 2004 Rhode Island's largest industry in terms of employment was health care and social assistance. The fastest growing industry was transportation and warehousing, with 78.4 percent growth from 1998 to 2004. Overall, the transportation and warehousing industry ranked twelfth in terms of 2004 employment. In terms of the education level of the

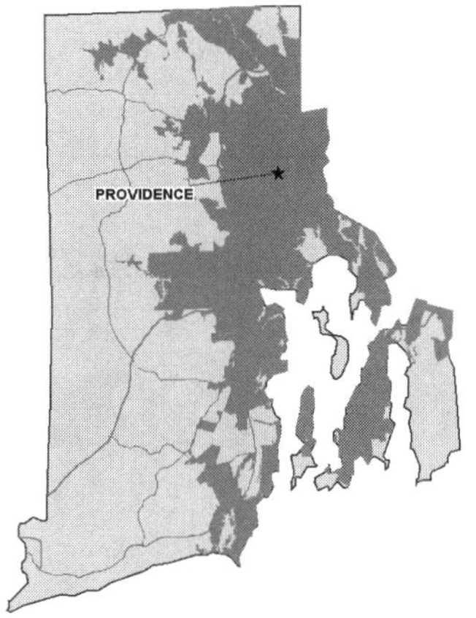

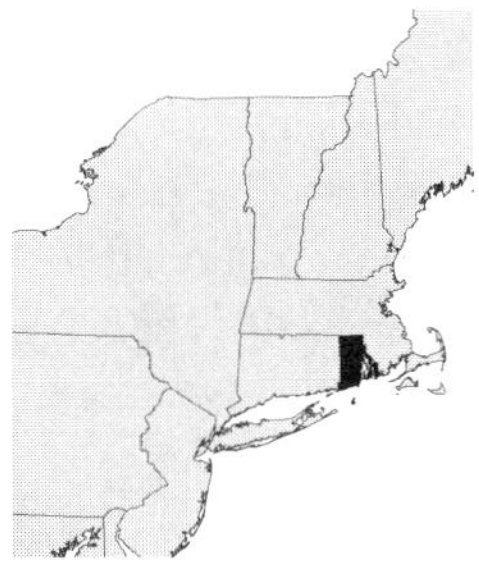

★ State Capitol
Major Urban Area
Major Roadway

Demographic and Socioeconomic Profile

Demographics and Socioeconomic Figures		
Population and Households	**2000**	**2005**
Total Population	1,048,319	1,032,662
Number of Households	408,424	406,089
Average Household Size	2.5	2.5
Age and Ethnicity		
Median Age	36.7	38.4
Population 18 Years of Age and Older	800,810	788,331
Population 65 Years of Age and Older	152,719	139,961
Caucasian Population	890,766	856,314
African-American Population	45,236	51,843
Hispanic Population	90,452	112,722
Asian Population	23,825	26,803
Foreign-Born Population	119,277	130,517
Income		
Per Capita Personal Income (USD)	$29,214	$35,219
Median Household Income (USD)	$42,090	$51,458
Individuals below Poverty Level	11.9%	12.3%

Data: U.S. Census, American Community Survey; U.S. Department of Commerce, Bureau of Economic Analysis

workforce, 83.5 percent of Rhode Island's adult population has a high school diploma or the equivalent, compared to the national average of 84.2 percent; 29.3 percent of Rhode Island's adult population has a bachelor degree or higher (national average is 27.2 percent); and 11.5 percent hold professional or graduate degrees (national average is 10.0 percent).

Tax Profile and Business Climate. Rhode Island's total tax revenue was $4.2 billion for fiscal year 2003–4. The largest share of tax revenue was generated from property taxes, followed by sales and gross receipts taxes. On a per capita basis Rhode Island had taxes of $3,891, compared to the national average of $3,447 for 2003–4. In terms of business taxes, the state ranked thirty-sixth in a 2006 report by Anderson Economic Group. Forbes Magazine and the Tax Foundation ranked the state's business climate forty-third and fiftieth, respectively.

Population Projections

	2010	2015	2020	2025
Total Population	1,116,652	1,139,543	1,154,230	1,157,855
Median Age	38.2	38.2	39.2	39.7
Population 18 Years of Age and Older	867,379	891,204	900,219	901,037
Population 65 Years of Age and Older	157,358	175,242	197,972	224,508

Data: U.S. Census Bureau

Workforce and Industry Profile

Workforce

	2000	2005
Civilian Labor Force	530,590	551,545
Labor Force Participation Rate	64.6%	67.8%
Unemployment Rate	4.1%	5.0%
Average Earnings per Job (USD)	$32,615	$38,980
Education Attainment (Population 25 Years and Older)	**(%)**	**(%)**
High School Graduate or Higher	78.0	83.5
Bachelors Degree or Higher	25.6	29.3
Graduate or Professional Degree	9.7	11.5

Data: U.S. Census Bureau, American Community Survey; U.S. Department of Labor, Bureau of Labor Statistics

Industry Overview

	1998	2004
Total Employees	402,485	434,706
Total Payroll ($1,000)	11,115,638	15,025,183
Total Establishments	28,245	30,011
Establishments with 1–19 Employees	24,651	25,940
Establishments with 20–49 Employees	2,242	2,556
Establishments with 50–249 Employees	1,165	1,344
Establishments with 250–999 Employees	162	146
Establishments with 1,000+ Employees	25	25

Data: U.S. Census Bureau, County Business Patterns

Major Industries (Ranked by 2004 Employment; Payroll in $1,000s)				
Industry	1998 Employment	2004 Employment	1998 Payroll	2004 Payroll
Health Care and Social Assistance	68,633	79,393	1,914,868	2,671,808
Manufacturing	74,181	58,151	2,341,311	2,260,927
Retail Trade	46,781	54,716	834,011	1,272,043
Accommodation and Food Services	33,837	41,425	384,469	596,542
Finance and Insurance	24,277	29,633	917,996	1,768,095
Professional, Scientific, Technical Services	15,973	23,564	632,606	1,082,150
Educational Services	18,410	22,631	429,108	667,470
Admin., Support, Waste Mngt., Remediation Services	28,065	21,556	563,833	552,091
Construction	16,290	20,323	614,594	923,012
Other Services (except Public Admin.)	16,913	19,638	314,071	446,533

Data: U.S. Census Bureau, County Business Patterns

Taxes and Business Climate

State and Local Taxes		
Combined Revenues ($1,000)	**2001–2**	**2003–4**
Revenue from Property Taxes	1,462,064	1,759,134
Revenue from Sales and Gross Receipts Taxes	1,164,485	1,310,984
Revenue from Individual Income Taxes	823,521	899,939
Revenue from Corporate Income Taxes	28,273	69,479
Revenue from Other Taxes	143,901	162,730
Total Tax Revenue	3,622,244	4,202,266
Per Capita Taxes		
Property Tax per Capita	1,395	1,629
Sales and Gross Receipts Tax per Capita	1,111	1,214
Individual Income Tax per Capita	786	833
Corporate Income Tax per Capita	27	64
Other Taxes per Capita	137	151
Total Taxes per Capita	3,456	3,891

Data: U.S. Census Bureau; Anderson Economic Group, LLC

Business Climate Measures	
Anderson Economic Group: 2006 Business Tax Ranking (1 is Best)	36
Forbes Magazine: 2006 Best States for Business Ranking (1 is Best)	43
Tax Foundation: 2007 Business Tax Climate Ranking (1 is Best)	50
2002–3 Employer Firm Births	2,680
2002–3 Employer Firm Terminations	2,424

Data: Anderson Economic Group; Tax Foundation; Forbes Magazine; U.S. Census, Statistics of U.S. Businesses

Voting Behavior and Elected Officials

Voter Registration and Turnout (%)

	1992	1996	2000	2004
Registered Voters Who Voted	81.8	64.8	60.9	61.7
Citizens Age 18+ Who Voted	58.4	52.0	51.1	52.5

Data: Dave Leip's Atlas of U.S. Presidential Elections

Presidential Election Results (Nationwide Winner Listed First)

2004	Popular Vote (%)	Electoral Votes
George W. Bush (Republican, Incumbent)	38.7	0
John Kerry (Democrat)	59.4	4
Other	1.9	0
2000		
George W. Bush (Republican)	31.9	0
Albert Gore (Democrat)	61.0	4
Ralph Nader (Green)	6.1	0
Other	1.0	0
1996		
William Clinton (Democrat, Incumbent)	59.7	4
Robert Dole (Republican)	26.8	0
H. Ross Perot (Reformist)	11.2	0
Other	2.3	0
1992		
William Clinton (Democrat)	47.0	4
George H. W. Bush (Republican, Incumbent)	29.0	0
H. Ross Perot (Independent)	23.2	0
Other	0.8	0

Data: Dave Leip's Atlas of U.S. Presidential Elections

Governor and U.S. Congressional Seats				
Governor	**Party**	**Year Term Began**	**Term**	**Max. Consecutive Terms**
Don Carcieri	R	2003	Second	2
U.S. Senators	**Party**	**Year Elected**	**Term Expires**	
Jack Reed	D	1996	2009	
Sheldon Whitehouse	D	2006	2013	
U.S. Representatives		**Republican**	**Democrat**	**Other**
		0	2	0

Data: National Governors Association, U.S. Senate, U.S. House of Representatives

Business and Economic Agencies

Agency	Website Address
Rhode Island Economic Development Corporation	www.riedc.com
Rhode Island Small Business Dev. Center	www.risbdc.org
Rhode Island Secretary of State	www.sec.state.ri.us/corps

Data: Various Agency Websites

South Carolina

Demographics and Socioeconomics. South Carolina is located in the South Atlantic region of the United States. The state, with a population of 4.1 million, was the twenty-fifth most populous in 2005. The state's population increased by 101,949 people from 2000 to 2005, and is projected to increase to 5.0 million by 2025. This 1.0 percent projected annual growth rate is in line with the national average. In 2005 South Carolina had a per capita personal income of \$28,212, which was \$6,283 below the national average and the seventh lowest in the country. The state's per capita income grew at an average annual rate of 2.9 percent, which is equal to the national average.

Workforce and Industry. The state's workforce is generally less educated than that of other states: 81.7 percent of the State's adult population has graduated from high school, compared to an 84.2 percent national average; 23.0 percent hold a bachelor degree or higher (national average is 27.2 percent); and 7.9 percent hold professional or graduate degrees (national average is 10.0). In 2004 the state's largest industry in

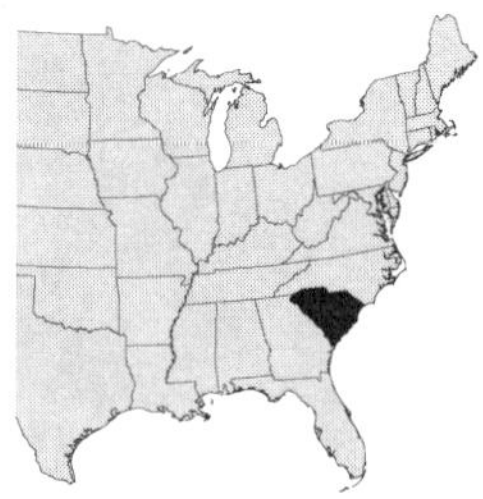

★ State Capitol

Major Urban Area

Major Roadway

Demographic and Socioeconomic Profile

Demographics and Socioeconomic Figures		
Population and Households	**2000**	**2005**
Total Population	4,012,012	4,113,961
Number of Households	1,533,854	1,635,907
Average Household Size	2.5	2.5
Age and Ethnicity		
Median Age	35.4	37.1
Population 18 Years of Age and Older	3,002,919	3,091,757
Population 65 Years of Age and Older	485,845	505,588
Caucasian Population	2,695,678	2,774,429
African-American Population	1,182,727	1,174,488
Hispanic Population	92,828	135,041
Asian Population	36,505	44,560
Foreign-Born Population	115,978	170,750
Income		
Per Capita Personal Income (USD)	\$24,424	\$28,212
Median Household Income (USD)	\$37,082	\$39,316
Individuals below Poverty Level	14.1%	15.6%

Data: U.S. Census, American Community Survey; U.S. Department of Commerce, Bureau of Economic Analysis

terms of employment was manufacturing, followed by retail trade. The fastest growing industry was transportation and warehousing, with 44.9 percent growth from 1998 to 2004. The transportation and warehousing industry ranked 11th in terms of 2004 employment.

Tax Profile and Business Climate. In fiscal year 2003–4 South Carolina had total tax revenues of $11.2 billion. The largest share was generated from sales and gross receipts taxes, followed by property taxes. In terms of business taxes, South Carolina ranked thirty-seventh in a 2006 report by Anderson Economic Group. The state's business climate was ranked twenty-seventh by Forbes Magazine and twenty-sixth by the tax foundation.

Population Projections

	2010	2015	2020	2025
Total Population	4,446,704	4,642,137	4,822,577	4,989,550
Median Age	38.4	39.4	40.3	41.0
Population 18 Years of Age and Older	3,410,355	3,580,984	3,737,193	3,878,805
Population 65 Years of Age and Older	605,660	729,179	866,250	1,009,242

Data: U.S. Census Bureau

Workforce and Industry Profile

Workforce

	2000	2005
Civilian Labor Force	1,938,195	2,060,548
Labor Force Participation Rate	63.4%	64.6%
Unemployment Rate	3.5%	6.8%
Average Earnings per Job (USD)	$28,179	$32,250
Education Attainment (Population 25 Years and Older)	**(%)**	**(%)**
High School Graduate or Higher	76.3	81.7
Bachelors Degree or Higher	20.4	23.0
Graduate or Professional Degree	6.9	7.9

Data: U.S. Census Bureau, American Community Survey; U.S. Department of Labor, Bureau of Labor Statistics

Industry Overview

	1998	2004
Total Employees	1,526,106	1,560,573
Total Payroll ($1,000)	38,559,169	46,656,784
Total Establishments	94,985	101,165
Establishments with 1–19 Employees	82,048	86,748
Establishments with 20–49 Employees	7,980	9,134
Establishments with 50–249 Employees	4,195	4,605
Establishments with 250–999 Employees	670	594
Establishments with 1,000+ Employees	92	84

Data: U.S. Census Bureau, County Business Patterns

Major Industries (Ranked by 2004 Employment; Payroll in $1,000s)				
Industry	1998 Employment	2004 Employment	1998 Payroll	2004 Payroll
Manufacturing	343,295	274,793	10,898,250	10,796,357
Retail Trade	213,800	222,629	3,393,667	4,325,877
Health Care and Social Assistance	161,581	190,779	4,600,631	6,529,671
Accommodation and Food Services	145,493	166,575	1,490,773	2,022,427
Admin., Support, Waste Mngt., Remediation Services	122,913	121,168	2,183,375	2,698,641
Construction	111,427	104,648	2,973,943	3,116,482
Other Services (except Public Admin.)	67,783	78,100	1,076,923	1,492,192
Professional, Scientific, Technical Services	58,476	70,666	2,264,270	3,267,182
Finance and Insurance	58,771	66,961	1,972,715	2,699,628
Wholesale Trade	60,762	63,752	2,056,717	2,560,621

Data: U.S. Census Bureau, County Business Patterns

Taxes and Business Climate

State and Local Taxes		
Combined Revenues ($1,000)	2001–2	2003–4
Revenue from Property Taxes	3,096,431	3,704,419
Revenue from Sales and Gross Receipts Taxes	3,424,549	4,011,717
Revenue from Individual Income Taxes	2,349,195	2,438,712
Revenue from Corporate Income Taxes	159,837	196,510
Revenue from Other Taxes	721,689	825,248
Total Tax Revenue	9,751,701	11,176,606
Per Capita Taxes		
Property Tax per Capita	772	882
Sales and Gross Receipts Tax per Capita	854	956
Individual Income Tax per Capita	586	581
Corporate Income Tax per Capita	40	47
Other Taxes per Capita	180	197
Total Taxes per Capita	2,431	2,662

Data: U.S. Census Bureau; Anderson Economic Group, LLC

Business Climate Measures	
Anderson Economic Group: 2006 Business Tax Ranking (1 is Best)	37
Forbes Magazine: 2006 Best States for Business Ranking (1 is Best)	27
Tax Foundation: 2007 Business Tax Climate Ranking (1 is Best)	26
2002–3 Employer Firm Births	10,033
2002–3 Employer Firm Terminations	8,963

Data: Anderson Economic Group; Tax Foundation; Forbes Magazine; U.S. Census, Statistics of U.S. Businesses

Voting Behavior and Elected Officials

Voter Registration and Turnout (%)	1992	1996	2000	2004
Registered Voters Who Voted	78.2	63.3	61.1	69.9
Citizens Age 18+ Who Voted	45.0	41.5	46.1	51.8

Data: Dave Leip's Atlas of U.S. Presidential Elections

Presidential Election Results (Nationwide Winner Listed First)		
2004	**Popular Vote (%)**	**Electoral Votes**
George W. Bush (Republican, Incumbent)	58.0	8
John Kerry (Democrat)	40.9	0
Other	1.1	0
2000		
George W. Bush (Republican)	56.8	8
Albert Gore (Democrat)	40.9	0
Ralph Nader (Green)	1.5	0
Other	0.8	0
1996		
William Clinton (Democrat, Incumbent)	44.0	0
Robert Dole (Republican)	49.9	8
H. Ross Perot (Reformist)	5.6	0
Other	0.7	0
1992		
William Clinton (Democrat)	39.9	0
George H. W. Bush (Republican, Incumbent)	48.0	8
H. Ross Perot (Independent)	11.6	0
Other	0.6	0

Data: Dave Leip's Atlas of U.S. Presidential Elections

Governor and U.S. Congressional Seats				
Governor	**Party**	**Year Term Began**	**Term**	**Max. Consecutive Terms**
Mark Sanford	R	2003	Second	2
U.S. Senators	**Party**	**Year Elected**	**Term Expires**	
Lindsey Graham	R	2002	2009	
Jim DeMint	R	2004	2011	
U.S. Representatives		**Republican**	**Democrat**	**Other**
		4	2	0

Data: National Governors Association, U.S. Senate, U.S. House of Representatives

Business and Economic Agencies

Agency	Website Address
South Carolina Chamber of Commerce	www.sccc.org
South Carolina Economic Development Directory	www.sciway.net/econ
South Carolina Small Business Dev. Center	scsbdc.moore.sc.edu
South Carolina Secretary of State	www.scsos.com

Data: Various Agency Websites

South Dakota

Demographics and Socioeconomics. South Dakota, located in the West North Central region of the United States, has a population of 746,033 people, making it the fifth least populous state in 2005. The state's population decreased by 8,811 people from 2000 to 2005, but is projected to grow to 801,845 by 2025. This 0.4 percent projected annual growth rate is below the projected national average of 1.0 percent. Per capita personal income in South Dakota was $32,642 in 2005, some $1,853 below the national average. From 2000 to 2005 per capita income in South Dakota grew at an average annual rate of 4.9 percent, compared to 2.9 percent nationally.

Workforce and Industry. In 2004 the state's largest industry in terms of employment was health care and social assistance, followed by retail trade. The fastest growing major industry was professional, scientific, and technical services, with 39.3 percent growth from 1998 to 2004. In terms of the education level of the workforce, 88.2 percent of South Dakota's adult population has

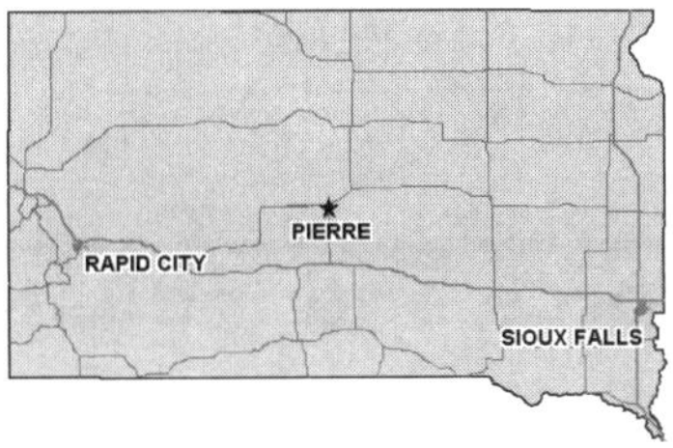

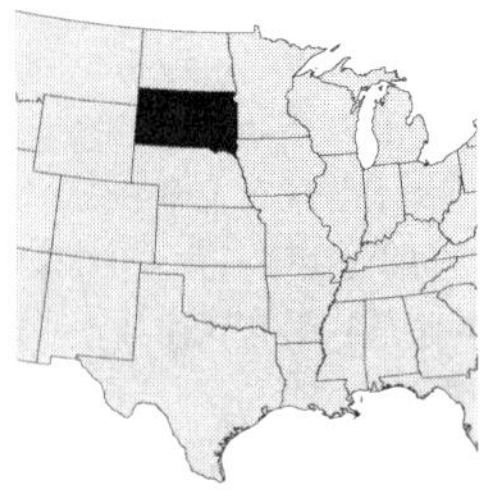

★ State Capitol

Major Urban Area

Major Roadway

Demographic and Socioeconomic Profile

Demographics and Socioeconomic Figures		
Population and Households	**2000**	**2005**
Total Population	754,844	746,033
Number of Households	290,245	310,331
Average Household Size	2.5	2.4
Age and Ethnicity		
Median Age	35.6	37.0
Population 18 Years of Age and Older	552,118	559,788
Population 65 Years of Age and Older	108,116	101,090
Caucasian Population	669,477	656,165
African-American Population	4,518	6,166
Hispanic Population	10,386	14,140
Asian Population	4,729	4,756
Foreign-Born Population	13,495	17,269
Income		
Per Capita Personal Income (USD)	$25,720	$32,642
Median Household Income (USD)	$35,282	$40,310
Individuals below Poverty Level	13.2%	13.6%

Data: U.S. Census, American Community Survey; U.S. Department of Commerce, Bureau of Economic Analysis

a high school diploma or the equivalent, compared to the national average of 84.2 percent; 25.5 percent of South Dakota's adult population has a bachelor degree or higher (national average is 27.2 percent); and 6.7 percent hold professional or graduate degrees (national average is 10.0 percent).

Tax Profile and Business Climate. In fiscal year 2003–4 South Dakota had total tax revenues of $2.0 billion. The largest share was generated from sales and gross receipts taxes, followed by property taxes. There is no individual income tax at the state level. The per capita tax burden in South Dakota was $2,615 for 2003–4, some $832 below the national average. In terms of business taxes, the state ranked eighth in a 2006 report by Anderson Economic Group. Forbes Magazine and the Tax Foundation ranked the state's business climate seventeenth and second, respectively.

Population Projections

	2010	2015	2020	2025
Total Population	786,399	796,954	801,939	801,845
Median Age	37.5	38.3	39.6	40.8
Population 18 Years of Age and Older	592,247	600,551	604,727	605,728
Population 65 Years of Age and Older	114,459	127,974	148,398	169,663

Data: U.S. Census Bureau

Workforce and Industry Profile

Workforce

	2000	2005
Civilian Labor Force	391,594	409,054
Labor Force Participation Rate	68.4%	70.7%
Unemployment Rate	2.7%	3.9%
Average Earnings per Job (USD)	$24,802	$29,170
Education Attainment (Population 25 Years and Older)	**(%)**	**(%)**
High School Graduate or Higher	84.6	88.6
Bachelors Degree or Higher	21.5	24.7
Graduate or Professional Degree	6.0	7.0

Data: U.S. Census Bureau, American Community Survey; U.S. Department of Labor, Bureau of Labor Statistics

Industry Overview

	1998	2004
Total Employees	289,422	308,010
Total Payroll ($1,000)	6,403,476	8,433,346
Total Establishments	23,521	24,787
Establishments with 1–19 Employees	20,842	21,863
Establishments with 20–49 Employees	1,762	1,892
Establishments with 50–249 Employees	815	929
Establishments with 250–999 Employees	93	94
Establishments with 1,000+ Employees	9	9

Data: U.S. Census Bureau, County Business Patterns

Major Industries (Ranked by 2004 Employment; Payroll in $1,000s)				
Industry	1998 Employment	2004 Employment	1998 Payroll	2004 Payroll
Health Care and Social Assistance	48,237	54,844	1,200,868	1,892,979
Retail Trade	47,784	49,866	771,746	971,121
Manufacturing	48,082	39,639	1,371,454	1,273,772
Accommodation and Food Services	29,168	34,028	254,740	361,888
Finance and Insurance	20,034	23,871	564,637	857,797
Construction	13,992	17,087	402,173	585,601
Wholesale Trade	16,089	15,224	431,329	525,746
Other Services (except Public Admin.)	12,924	14,195	186,226	254,471
Professional, Scientific, Technical Services	7,499	10,447	193,922	317,864
Admin., Support, Waste Mngt., Remediation Services	8,289	9,002	134,475	184,138

Data: U.S. Census Bureau, County Business Patterns

Taxes and Business Climate

State and Local Taxes		
Combined Revenues ($1,000)	2001–2	2003–4
Revenue from Property Taxes	668,048	705,183
Revenue from Sales and Gross Receipts Taxes	929,968	1,070,896
Revenue from Individual Income Taxes	0	11
Revenue from Corporate Income Taxes	40,547	47,108
Revenue from Other Taxes	202,885	192,730
Total Tax Revenue	1,841,448	2,015,928
Per Capita Taxes		
Property Tax per Capita	885	915
Sales and Gross Receipts Tax per Capita	1,232	1,389
Individual Income Tax per Capita	0	0
Corporate Income Tax per Capita	54	61
Other Taxes per Capita	269	250
Total Taxes per Capita	2,439	2,615

Data: U.S. Census Bureau; Anderson Economic Group, LLC

Business Climate Measures	
Anderson Economic Group: 2006 Business Tax Ranking (1 is Best)	8
Forbes Magazine: 2006 Best States for Business Ranking (1 is Best)	17
Tax Foundation: 2007 Business Tax Climate Ranking (1 is Best)	2
2002–3 Employer Firm Births	2,115
2002–3 Employer Firm Terminations	2,076

Data: Anderson Economic Group; Tax Foundation; Forbes Magazine; U.S. Census, Statistics of U.S. Businesses

Voting Behavior and Elected Officials

Voter Registration and Turnout (%)	1992	1996	2000	2004
Registered Voters Who Voted	75.0	70.4	67.1	77.3
Citizens Age 18+ Who Voted	67.0	60.5	57.3	68.2

Data: Dave Leip's Atlas of U.S. Presidential Elections

Presidential Election Results (Nationwide Winner Listed First)		
2004	**Popular Vote (%)**	**Electoral Votes**
George W. Bush (Republican, Incumbent)	59.9	3
John Kerry (Democrat)	38.4	0
Other	1.7	0
2000		
George W. Bush (Republican)	60.3	3
Albert Gore (Democrat)	37.6	0
Ralph Nader (Green)	0.0	0
Other	2.1	0
1996		
William Clinton (Democrat, Incumbent)	43.0	0
Robert Dole (Republican)	46.5	3
H. Ross Perot (Reformist)	9.7	0
Other	0.8	0
1992		
William Clinton (Democrat)	37.1	0
George H. W. Bush (Republican, Incumbent)	40.7	3
H. Ross Perot (Independent)	21.8	0
Other	0.4	0

Data: Dave Leip's Atlas of U.S. Presidential Elections

Governor and U.S. Congressional Seats				
Governor	**Party**	**Year Term Began**	**Term**	**Max. Consecutive Terms**
Michael Rounds	R	2003	Second	2
U.S. Senators	**Party**	**Year Elected**	**Term Expires**	
Tim Johnson	D	1996	2009	
John Thune	R	2004	2011	
U.S. Representatives		**Republican**	**Democrat**	**Other**
		0	1	0

Data: National Governors Association, U.S. Senate, U.S. House of Representatives

Business and Economic Agencies

Agency	Website Address
South Dakota Chamber of Commerce and Industry	www.sdchamber.biz
South Dakota's Governor's Office of Economic Development	www.sdreadytowork.com
South Dakota Small Business Dev. Center	www.sdsbdc.org
South Dakota Secretary of State	www.sdsos.gov/busineservices/busineservices_overview.shtm

Data: Various Agency Websites

Tennessee

Demographics and Socioeconomics. Tennessee, located in the East South Central region of the United States, has a population of 5.8 million people, making it the seventeenth most populous state in 2005. The state's population increased by 121,307 people from 2000 to 2005, and is projected to increase to 7.1 million by 2025. This 1.0 percent projected annual growth rate is equal to the national average. The state's 2005 per capita personal income of $30,952 was the fifteenth lowest in the United States, some $3,543 below the national average. Per capita income in Tennessee grew at an average annual rate of 3.5 percent from 2000 to 2005, compared to 2.9 percent nationally.

Workforce and Industry. In 2004 the state's largest industry in terms of employment was manufacturing, followed by health care and social assistance. The fastest growing major industry was transportation and warehousing, with 37.2 percent growth from 1998 to 2004. The state's workforce is generally less educated than that of other states: 81.2 percent of the state's adult population has graduated from high

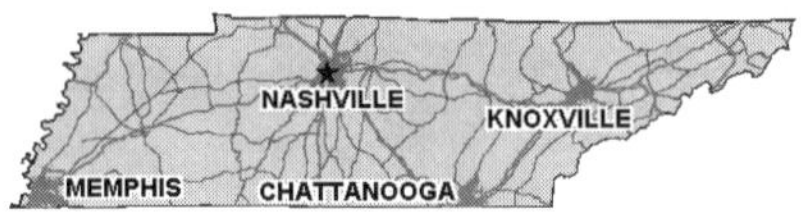

★ State Capitol

Major Urban Area

Major Roadway

Demographic and Socioeconomic Profile

Demographics and Socioeconomic Figures		
Population and Households	**2000**	**2005**
Total Population	5,689,283	5,810,590
Number of Households	2,232,905	2,366,130
Average Household Size	2.5	2.5
Age and Ethnicity		
Median Age	35.9	37.3
Population 18 Years of Age and Older	4,292,047	4,427,784
Population 65 Years of Age and Older	702,839	708,653
Caucasian Population	4,562,454	4,625,715
African-American Population	929,864	954,287
Hispanic Population	119,425	172,704
Asian Population	54,132	73,824
Foreign-Born Population	159,004	223,118
Income		
Per Capita Personal Income (USD)	$26,097	$30,952
Median Household Income (USD)	$36,360	$38,874
Individuals below Poverty Level	13.5%	15.5%

Data: U.S. Census, American Community Survey; U.S. Department of Commerce, Bureau of Economic Analysis

school, compared to an 84.2 percent national average; 21.8 percent hold a bachelor degree or higher (national average is 27.2 percent); and 7.6 percent hold professional or graduate degrees (national average is 10.0 percent).

Tax Profile and Business Climate. In fiscal year 2003–4 Tennessee had total tax revenues of $14.9 billion. The largest share was generated from sales and gross receipts taxes, followed by property taxes. The per capita tax burden in Tennessee was $2,536 for 2003–4, some $910 below the national average. In terms of business taxes, the state ranked 4th in a 2006 report by Anderson Economic Group. Forbes Magazine and the Tax Foundation ranked the state's business climate twentieth and eighteenth, respectively.

Population Projections

	2010	2015	2020	2025
Total Population	6,230,852	6,502,017	6,780,670	7,073,125
Median Age	37.9	38.2	38.6	38.5
Population 18 Years of Age and Older	4,751,937	4,963,306	5,173,458	5,383,849
Population 65 Years of Age and Older	829,023	968,919	1,121,063	1,279,981

Data: U.S. Census Bureau

Workforce and Industry Profile

Workforce

	2000	2005
Civilian Labor Force	2,805,234	2,930,779
Labor Force Participation Rate	63.5%	64.3%
Unemployment Rate	4.0%	5.6%
Average Earnings per Job (USD)	$30,554	$33,260
Education Attainment (Population 25 Years and Older)	**(%)**	**(%)**
High School Graduate or Higher	75.9	81.2
Bachelors Degree or Higher	19.6	21.8
Graduate or Professional Degree	6.8	7.6

Data: U.S. Census Bureau, American Community Survey; U.S. Department of Labor, Bureau of Labor Statistics

Industry Overview

	1998	2004
Total Employees	2,299,348	2,347,335
Total Payroll ($1,000)	62,441,176	76,922,192
Total Establishments	131,110	131,691
Establishments with 1–19 Employees	111,021	110,585
Establishments with 20–49 Employees	12,072	12,920
Establishments with 50–249 Employees	6,894	7,067
Establishments with 250–999 Employees	992	986
Establishments with 1,000+ Employees	131	133

Data: U.S. Census Bureau, County Business Patterns

Major Industries (Ranked by 2004 Employment; Payroll in $1,000s)				
Industry	1998 Employment	2004 Employment	1998 Payroll	2004 Payroll
Manufacturing	482,811	392,084	15,020,254	15,267,826
Health Care and Social Assistance	281,083	324,140	8,307,173	11,323,187
Retail Trade	311,720	320,482	5,322,361	6,590,237
Accommodation and Food Services	189,001	215,426	2,078,502	2,580,012
Admin., Support, Waste Mngt., Remediation Services	157,976	169,390	3,011,742	4,164,543
Transportation and Warehousing	86,518	118,692	2,745,830	4,157,983
Wholesale Trade	125,204	117,856	4,390,902	5,259,537
Construction	120,575	114,329	3,762,360	4,087,323
Other Services (except Public Admin.)	109,070	113,037	1,858,267	2,258,157
Finance and Insurance	101,293	111,769	4,003,336	5,815,301

Data: U.S. Census Bureau, County Business Patterns

Taxes and Business Climate

State and Local Taxes		
Combined Revenues ($1,000)	2001–2	2003–4
Revenue from Property Taxes	3,453,047	3,585,440
Revenue from Sales and Gross Receipts Taxes	7,460,508	8,846,308
Revenue from Individual Income Taxes	146,293	139,991
Revenue from Corporate Income Taxes	502,977	694,798
Revenue from Other Taxes	1,410,943	1,680,101
Total Tax Revenue	12,973,768	14,946,638
Per Capita Taxes		
Property Tax per Capita	607	608
Sales and Gross Receipts Tax per Capita	1,311	1,501
Individual Income Tax per Capita	26	24
Corporate Income Tax per Capita	88	118
Other Taxes per Capita	248	285
Total Taxes per Capita	2,281	2,536

Data: U.S. Census Bureau; Anderson Economic Group, LLC

Business Climate Measures	
Anderson Economic Group: 2006 Business Tax Ranking (1 is Best)	4
Forbes Magazine: 2006 Best States for Business Ranking (1 is Best)	20
Tax Foundation: 2007 Business Tax Climate Ranking (1 is Best)	18
2002–3 Employer Firm Births	12,612
2002–3 Employer Firm Terminations	12,276

Data: Anderson Economic Group; Tax Foundation; Forbes Magazine; U.S. Census, Statistics of U.S. Businesses

Voting Behavior and Elected Officials

Voter Registration and Turnout (%)

	1992	1996	2000	2004
Registered Voters Who Voted	72.7	66.5	65.3	73.1
Citizens Age 18+ Who Voted	52.4	46.9	48.4	54.8

Data: Dave Leip's Atlas of U.S. Presidential Elections

Presidential Election Results (Nationwide Winner Listed First)

2004	Popular Vote (%)	Electoral Votes
George W. Bush (Republican, Incumbent)	56.8	11
John Kerry (Democrat)	42.5	0
Other	0.7	0
2000		
George W. Bush (Republican)	51.2	11
Albert Gore (Democrat)	47.3	0
Ralph Nader (Green)	1.0	0
Other	0.6	0
1996		
William Clinton (Democrat, Incumbent)	48.0	11
Robert Dole (Republican)	45.6	0
H. Ross Perot (Reformist)	5.6	0
Other	0.8	0
1992		
William Clinton (Democrat)	47.1	11
George H. W. Bush (Republican, Incumbent)	42.4	0
H. Ross Perot (Independent)	10.1	0
Other	0.4	0

Data: Dave Leip's Atlas of U.S. Presidential Elections

Governor and U.S. Congressional Seats				
Governor	**Party**	**Year Term Began**	**Term**	**Max. Consecutive Terms**
Phil Bredesen	D	2003	Second	2
U.S. Senators	**Party**	**Year Elected**	**Term Expires**	
Lamar Alexandar	R	2002	2009	
Bob Corker	R	2006	2013	
U.S. Representatives		**Republican**	**Democrat**	**Other**
		4	5	0

Data: National Governors Association, U.S. Senate, U.S. House of Representatives

Business and Economic Agencies

Agency	Website Address
Tennessee Chamber of Commerce and Industry	www.tnchamber.org
Tennessee Department of Economic and Community Development	www.state.tn.us/ecd
Tennessee Small Business Development Centers	www.tsbdc.org
Tennessee Department of State, Division of Business Services	www.state.tn.us/sos/bus_svc

Data: Various Agency Websites

Texas

Demographics and Socio-economics. With a population of 22.3 million people, Texas was the second most populous state in the United States in 2005. From 2000 to 2005 the state's population increased by 1.4 million people, and is projected to increase to 30.1 million by 2025. This 1.7 percent projected annual growth rate compares to the projected national average of 1.0 percent. Per capita personal income in Texas was $32,604 in 2005, which was $1,891 below the national average. From 2000 to 2005 the per capita income in Texas grew at an average annual rate of 2.9 percent, which equals the national rate.

Workforce and Industry. The state's largest industry in terms of 2004 employment was health care and social assistance. The fastest growing major industry was finance and insurance, with 24.9 percent growth from 1998 to 2004. The state's workforce is generally less educated than that of other states: 78.8 percent of the state's adult population has graduated from high school, compared to an 84.2 percent national average;

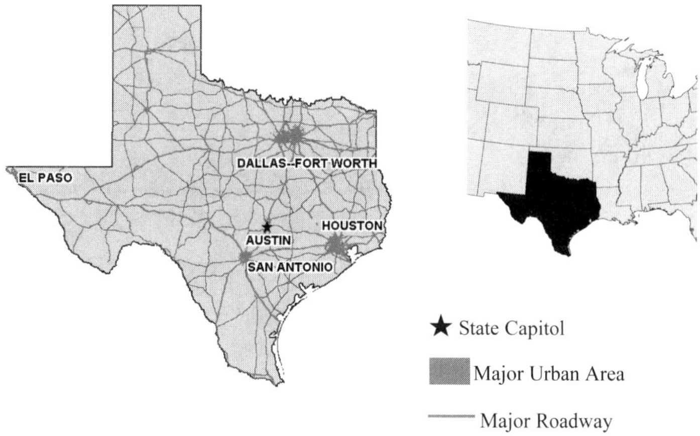

Demographic and Socioeconomic Profile

Demographics and Socioeconomic Figures

Population and Households	2000	2005
Total Population	20,851,820	22,270,165
Number of Households	7,393,354	7,978,095
Average Household Size	2.7	2.8
Age and Ethnicity		
Median Age	32.3	33.2
Population 18 Years of Age and Older	14,977,890	15,969,874
Population 65 Years of Age and Older	2,067,467	2,147,849
Caucasian Population	14,797,985	16,021,256
African-American Population	2,385,554	2,442,350
Hispanic Population	6,670,122	7,903,079
Asian Population	555,928	726,027
Foreign-Born Population	2,899,642	3,542,513
Income		
Per Capita Personal Income (USD)	$28,313	$32,604
Median Household Income (USD)	$39,927	$42,139
Individuals below Poverty Level	15.4%	17.6%

Data: U.S. Census, American Community Survey; U.S. Department of Commerce, Bureau of Economic Analysis

25.1 percent hold a bachelor degree or higher (national average is 27.2 percent); and 8.2 percent hold professional or graduate degrees (national average is 10.0 percent).

Tax Profile and Business Climate. Texas' total tax revenue was $64.7 billion for fiscal year 2003–4. The largest share of tax revenue in 2003–4 was generated from sales and gross receipts taxes, followed by property taxes. There is not an individual or corporate income tax in Texas. On a per capita basis, Texas had taxes of $2,881, compared to the national average of $3,447 for 2003–4. In terms of business taxes, the state ranked thirty-third in a 2006 report by Anderson Economic Group. Forbes Magazine and the Tax Foundation ranked the state's business climate second and sixth, respectively.

Population Projections

	2010	2015	2020	2025
Total Population	24,648,888	26,585,801	28,634,896	30,865,134
Median Age	33.4	33.8	34.3	34.6
Population 18 Years of Age and Older	17,863,480	19,209,583	20,666,629	22,405,639
Population 65 Years of Age and Older	2,587,383	3,112,883	3,755,814	4,500,152

Data: U.S. Census Bureau

Workforce and Industry Profile

Workforce

	2000	2005
Civilian Labor Force	9,830,559	11,024,191
Labor Force Participation Rate	63.6%	66.7%
Unemployment Rate	4.4%	5.3%
Average Earnings per Job (USD)	$34,941	$35,470
Education Attainment (Population 25 Years and Older)	**(%)**	**(%)**
High School Graduate or Higher	75.7	78.8
Bachelors Degree or Higher	23.2	25.1
Graduate or Professional Degree	7.6	8.2

Data: U.S. Census Bureau, American Community Survey; U.S. Department of Labor, Bureau of Labor Statistics

Industry Overview

	1998	2004
Total Employees	7,570,820	8,118,483
Total Payroll ($1,000)	229,185,833	293,572,510
Total Establishments	462,875	491,092
Establishments with 1–19 Employees	395,406	418,144
Establishments with 20–49 Employees	41,631	44,948
Establishments with 50–249 Employees	22,411	24,363
Establishments with 250–999 Employees	2,981	3,138
Establishments with 1,000+ Employees	446	499

Data: U.S. Census Bureau, County Business Patterns

Major Industries (Ranked by 2004 Employment; Payroll in $1,000s)				
Industry	1998 Employment	2004 Employment	1998 Payroll	2004 Payroll
Health Care and Social Assistance	911,042	1,070,421	24,604,759	36,009,816
Retail Trade	977,678	1,060,647	18,492,576	22,698,473
Manufacturing	986,892	829,133	36,331,404	36,255,368
Accommodation and Food Services	661,430	773,538	7,361,124	9,689,579
Admin., Support, Waste Mngt., Remediation Services	678,374	688,558	14,845,110	18,469,109
Professional, Scientific, Technical Services	413,798	515,243	19,768,171	29,851,491
Construction	457,076	490,170	14,281,869	17,579,200
Finance and Insurance	360,254	450,042	15,639,191	23,100,145
Wholesale Trade	436,035	437,778	17,141,752	21,679,833
Other Services (except Public Admin.)	373,791	403,238	6,532,243	8,341,718

Data: U.S. Census Bureau, County Business Patterns

Taxes and Business Climate

State and Local Taxes		
Combined Revenues ($1,000)	2001–2	2003–4
Revenue from Property Taxes	24,520,989	28,176,329
Revenue from Sales and Gross Receipts Taxes	28,639,281	29,656,098
Revenue from Individual Income Taxes	29	0
Revenue from Corporate Income Taxes	0	0
Revenue from Other Taxes	5,820,209	6,906,345
Total Tax Revenue	58,980,508	64,738,772
Per Capita Taxes		
Property Tax per Capita	1,176	1,254
Sales and Gross Receipts Tax per Capita	1,373	1,320
Individual Income Tax per Capita	0	0
Corporate Income Tax per Capita	0	0
Other Taxes per Capita	279	307
Total Taxes per Capita	2,829	2,881

Data: U.S. Census Bureau; Anderson Economic Group, LLC

Business Climate Measures	
Anderson Economic Group: 2006 Business Tax Ranking (1 is Best)	33
Forbes Magazine: 2006 Best States for Business Ranking (1 is Best)	2
Tax Foundation: 2007 Business Tax Climate Ranking (1 is Best)	6
2002–3 Employer Firm Births	52,677
2002–3 Employer Firm Terminations	48,494

Data: Anderson Economic Group; Tax Foundation; Forbes Magazine; U.S. Census, Statistics of U.S. Businesses

Voting Behavior and Elected Officials

Voter Registration and Turnout (%)

	1992	1996	2000	2004
Registered Voters Who Voted	72.9	58.8	62.4	67.4
Citizens Age 18+ Who Voted	49.1	41.3	42.8	46.7

Data: Dave Leip's Atlas of U.S. Presidential Elections

Presidential Election Results (Nationwide Winner Listed First)

2004	Popular Vote (%)	Electoral Votes
George W. Bush (Republican, Incumbent)	61.1	34
John Kerry (Democrat)	38.2	0
Other	0.7	0
2000		
George W. Bush (Republican)	59.3	32
Albert Gore (Democrat)	38.0	0
Ralph Nader (Green)	2.2	0
Other	0.6	0
1996		
William Clinton (Democrat, Incumbent)	43.8	0
Robert Dole (Republican)	48.8	32
H. Ross Perot (Reformist)	6.8	0
Other	0.7	0
1992		
William Clinton (Democrat)	37.1	0
George H. W. Bush (Republican, Incumbent)	40.6	32
H. Ross Perot (Independent)	22.0	0
Other	0.4	0

Data: Dave Leip's Atlas of U.S. Presidential Elections

Governor and U.S. Congressional Seats				
Governor	**Party**	**Year Term Began**	**Term**	**Max. Consecutive Terms**
Rick Perry	R	2000	Second	No limit
U.S. Senators	**Party**	**Year Elected**	**Term Expires**	
John Cornyn	R	2002	2009	
Kay Bailey Hutchison	R	1993	2013	
U.S. Representatives		**Republican**	**Democrat**	**Other**
		19	13	0

Data: National Governors Association, U.S. Senate, U.S. House of Representatives

Business and Economic Agencies

Agency	Website Address
Texas Association of Business	www.txbiz.org
Office of the Governor, Economic Development Office and Tourism	www.governor.state.tx.us/ecodevo
Texas Small Business Development Center	www.business.txstate.edu/sbdc
Texas Secretary of State, Corporations Section	www.sos.state.tx.us/corp

Data: Various Agency Websites

Utah

Demographics and Socioeconomics. Utah, located in the Mountain region of the United States, has a population of 2.4 million people, making it the seventeenth least populous state in 2005. The state's population increased by 194,181 people from 2000 to 2005, and is projected to increase to 3.2 million by 2025. This 1.4 percent projected annual growth rate is above the national average of 1.0 percent. In 2005 Utah had a per capita personal income of $27,497, which was $6,998 below the national average and the fifth lowest in the country. The state's per capita income grew at an average annual rate of 2.9 percent, which was equal to the national average.

Workforce and Industry. The state's workforce is generally more educated than that of other states: 90.1 percent of Utah's adult population has graduated form high school, compared to an 84.2 percent national average; 27.9 percent hold a bachelor degree or higher (national average is 27.2 percent); and 8.7 percent hold professional or graduate degrees (national average is 10.0). In 2004 Utah's largest industry in terms of employment was

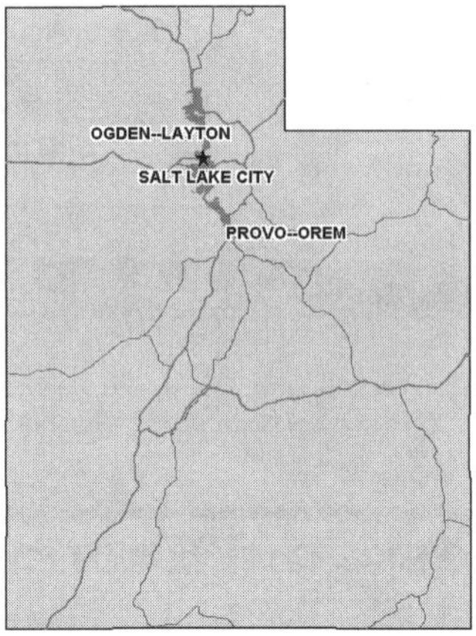

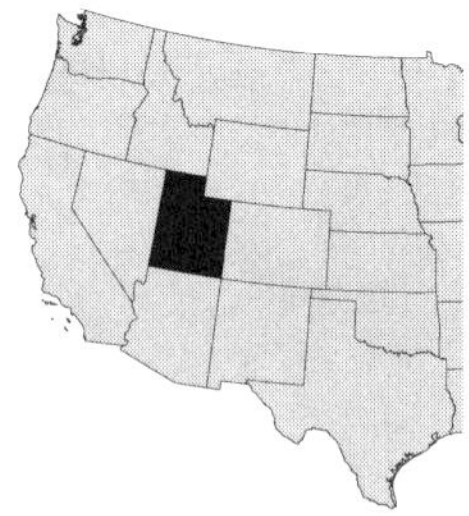

Demographic and Socioeconomic Profile

Demographics and Socioeconomic Figures		
Population and Households	**2000**	**2005**
Total Population	2,233,169	2,427,350
Number of Households	701,281	791,929
Average Household Size	3.1	3.1
Age and Ethnicity		
Median Age	27.1	28.5
Population 18 Years of Age and Older	1,516,338	1,688,413
Population 65 Years of Age and Older	190,531	205,548
Caucasian Population	1,991,560	2,178,777
African-American Population	16,150	18,325
Hispanic Population	200,005	264,084
Asian Population	36,878	46,962
Foreign-Born Population	158,664	192,916
Income		
Per Capita Personal Income (USD)	$23,878	$27,497
Median Household Income (USD)	$45,726	$47,934
Individuals below Poverty Level	9.4%	10.2%

Data: U.S. Census, American Community Survey; U.S. Department of Commerce, Bureau of Economic Analysis

retail trade, followed by manufacturing. The fastest growing industry was professional, scientific, and technical services, with 49.0 percent growth from 1998 to 2004.

Tax Profile and Business Climate. In fiscal year 2003–4 Utah had total tax revenues of $6.6 billion. The largest share was generated from sales and gross receipts taxes, followed by individual income taxes. The per capita tax burden in Utah was $2,735 for 2003–4, some $712 below the national average. In terms of business taxes, Utah ranked nineth in a 2006 report by Anderson Economic Group. The state's business climate was ranked fourth by Forbes Magazine and sixteenth by the Tax Foundation.

Population Projections

	2010	2015	2020	2025
Total Population	2,595,013	2,783,040	2,990,094	3,225,680
Median Age	29.5	30.1	30.3	30.4
Population 18 Years of Age and Older	1,776,028	1,910,568	2,069,975	2,244,888
Population 65 Years of Age and Older	234,798	280,969	341,095	405,543

Data: U.S. Census Bureau

Workforce and Industry Profile

Workforce

	2000	2005
Civilian Labor Force	1,098,923	1,244,025
Labor Force Participation Rate	69.0%	70.9%
Unemployment Rate	3.4%	4.3%
Average Earnings per Job (USD)	$29,229	$34,280
Education Attainment (Population 25 Years and Older)	**(%)**	**(%)**
High School Graduate or Higher	87.7	90.1
Bachelors Degree or Higher	26.1	27.9
Graduate or Professional Degree	8.3	8.7

Data: U.S. Census Bureau, American Community Survey; U.S. Department of Labor, Bureau of Labor Statistics

Industry Overview

	1998	2004
Total Employees	866,146	935,126
Total Payroll ($1,000)	22,199,933	28,602,403
Total Establishments	52,025	62,834
Establishments with 1–19 Employees	44,560	54,604
Establishments with 20–49 Employees	4,716	5,138
Establishments with 50–249 Employees	2,355	2,711
Establishments with 250–999 Employees	341	330
Establishments with 1,000+ Employees	53	51

Data: U.S. Census Bureau, County Business Patterns

Major Industries (Ranked by 2004 Employment; Payroll in $1,000s)				
Industry	1998 Employment	2004 Employment	1998 Payroll	2004 Payroll
Retail Trade	117,336	127,731	2,014,702	2,674,435
Manufacturing	124,504	111,020	3,923,759	4,320,540
Health Care and Social Assistance	83,229	103,305	2,278,267	3,213,628
Accommodation and Food Services	76,781	84,816	736,994	946,175
Admin., Support, Waste Mngt., Remediation Services	78,929	81,057	1,437,965	2,018,168
Professional, Scientific, Technical Services	43,350	64,593	1,618,657	2,520,712
Construction	58,005	63,944	1,732,765	2,149,501
Finance and Insurance	40,957	46,898	1,385,462	2,079,687
Other Services (except Public Admin.)	45,158	44,891	936,360	1,123,896
Wholesale Trade	44,727	44,848	1,515,979	1,855,171

Data: U.S. Census Bureau, County Business Patterns

Taxes and Business Climate

State and Local Taxes		
Combined Revenues ($1,000)	2001–2	2003–4
Revenue from Property Taxes	1,419,769	1,668,988
Revenue from Sales and Gross Receipts Taxes	2,618,575	2,770,235
Revenue from Individual Income Taxes	1,605,310	1,692,035
Revenue from Corporate Income Taxes	110,989	145,005
Revenue from Other Taxes	271,499	344,962
Total Tax Revenue	6,026,142	6,621,225
Per Capita Taxes		
Property Tax per Capita	636	689
Sales and Gross Receipts Tax per Capita	1,173	1,144
Individual Income Tax per Capita	719	699
Corporate Income Tax per Capita	50	60
Other Taxes per Capita	122	142
Total Taxes per Capita	$2,699	$2,735

Data: U.S. Census Bureau; Anderson Economic Group, LLC

Business Climate Measures	
Anderson Economic Group: 2006 Business Tax Ranking (1 is Best)	9
Forbes Magazine: 2006 Best States for Business Ranking (1 is Best)	4
Tax Foundation: 2007 Business Tax Climate Ranking (1 is Best)	16
2002–3 Employer Firm Births	7,786
2002–3 Employer Firm Terminations	6,341

Data: Anderson Economic Group; Tax Foundation; Forbes Magazine; U.S. Census, Statistics of U.S. Businesses

Voting Behavior and Elected Officials

Voter Registration and Turnout (%)

	1992	1996	2000	2004
Registered Voters Who Voted	77.1	63.4	68.6	72.6
Citizens Age 18+ Who Voted	65.1	49.9	50.8	57.7

Data: Dave Leip's Atlas of U.S. Presidential Elections

Presidential Election Results (Nationwide Winner Listed First)

2004	Popular Vote (%)	Electoral Votes
George W. Bush (Republican, Incumbent)	71.5	5
John Kerry (Democrat)	26.0	0
Other	2.5	0
2000		
George W. Bush (Republican)	66.8	5
Albert Gore (Democrat)	26.3	0
Ralph Nader (Green)	4.7	0
Other	2.2	0
1996		
William Clinton (Democrat, Incumbent)	33.3	0
Robert Dole (Republican)	54.4	5
H. Ross Perot (Reformist)	10.0	0
Other	2.4	0
1992		
William Clinton (Democrat)	24.7	0
George H. W. Bush (Republican, Incumbent)	43.4	5
H. Ross Perot (Independent)	27.3	0
Other	4.7	0

Data: Dave Leip's Atlas of U.S. Presidential Elections

Governor and U.S. Congressional Seats				
Governor	**Party**	**Year Term Began**	**Term**	**Max. Consecutive Terms**
Jon Huntsman	R	2005	First	3
U.S. Senators	**Party**	**Year Elected**	**Term Expires**	
Robert Bennett	R	1992	2011	
Orrin Hatch	R	1976	2013	
U.S. Representatives		**Republican**	**Democrat**	**Other**
		2	1	0

Data: National Governors Association, U.S. Senate, U.S. House of Representatives

Business and Economic Agencies

Agency	Website Address
Utah Governor's Office of Economic Development	goed.utah.gov
Utah Small Business Dev. Center	www.utahsbdc.org
Utah Department of Commerce	www.commerce.utah.gov

Data: Various Agency Websites

Vermont

Demographics and Socioeconomics. With a population of 602,290 people, Vermont was the second least populous state in the United States in 2005. From 2000 to 2005 the state's population decreased by 6,537 people, but is projected to reach 703,288 by 2025. This 0.8 percent projected annual growth rate compares to the projected national average of 1.0 percent. Per capita personal income in Vermont was $32,731 in 2005, some $1,764 below the national average. From 2000 to 2005 per capita income in Vermont grew at an average annual rate of 3.4 percent, compared to 2.9 percent nationally.

Workforce and Industry. Vermont's largest industry in terms of 2004 employment was retail trade. The fastest growing major industry was professional, scientific, and technical services, with 35.3 percent growth from 1998 to 2004. The state's workforce is generally more educated than that of other states: 89.5 percent of the state's adult population has graduated from high school, compared to an 84.2 percent national average; 32.5 percent hold a

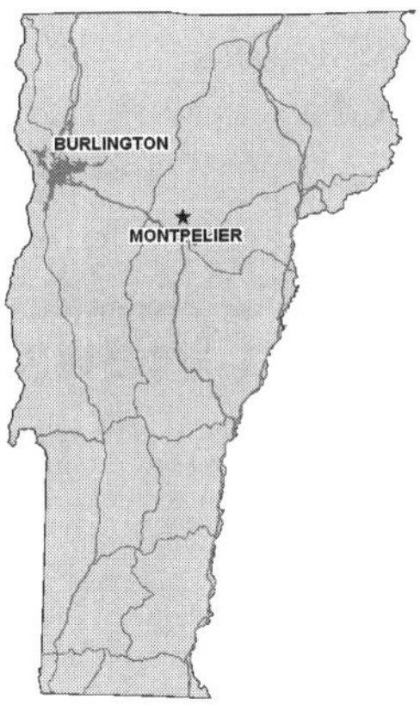

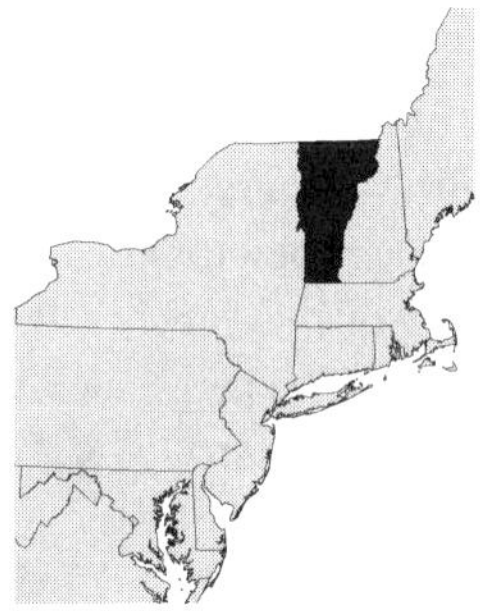

★ State Capitol

Major Urban Area

Major Roadway

Demographic and Socioeconomic Profile

Demographics and Socioeconomic Figures		
Population and Households	**2000**	**2005**
Total Population	608,827	602,290
Number of Households	240,634	248,825
Average Household Size	2.4	2.4
Age and Ethnicity		
Median Age	37.7	40.7
Population 18 Years of Age and Older	461,248	469,721
Population 65 Years of Age and Older	77,295	76,815
Caucasian Population	588,836	581,874
African-American Population	2,981	2,932
Hispanic Population	5,316	5,214
Asian Population	4,851	6,659
Foreign-Born Population	23,245	21,843
Income		
Per Capita Personal Income (USD)	$27,680	$32,731
Median Household Income (USD)	$40,856	$45,686
Individuals below Poverty Level	9.4%	11.5%

Data: U.S. Census, American Community Survey; U.S. Department of Commerce, Bureau of Economic Analysis

bachelor degree or higher (national average is 27.2 percent); and 12.3 percent hold professional or graduate degrees (national average is 10.0 percent).

Tax Profile and Business Climate. Vermont's total tax revenue was $2.3 billion for fiscal year 2003–4. The largest share of this was generated from property taxes, followed by sales and gross receipts taxes. On a per capita basis, Vermont had taxes of $3,681, compared to the national average of $3,447 for 2003–4. In terms of business taxes, the state ranked forty-eighth in a 2006 report by Anderson Economic Group. Forbes Magazine and the Tax Foundation ranked the state's business climate thirtieth and forty-sixth, respectively.

Population Projections

	2010	2015	2020	2025
Total Population	652,512	673,169	690,686	703,288
Median Age	40.6	41.1	41.5	42.8
Population 18 Years of Age and Older	520,140	541,204	554,847	563,723
Population 65 Years of Age and Older	93,442	113,487	136,449	158,159

Data: U.S. Census Bureau

Workforce and Industry Profile

Workforce

	2000	2005
Civilian Labor Force	331,131	343,427
Labor Force Participation Rate	69.3%	70.6%
Unemployment Rate	2.6%	3.5%
Average Earnings per Job (USD)	$28,914	$35,070
Education Attainment (Population 25 Years and Older)	**(%)**	**(%)**
High School Graduate or Higher	86.4	89.5
Bachelors Degree or Higher	29.4	32.5
Graduate or Professional Degree	11.1	12.3

Data: U.S. Census Bureau, American Community Survey; U.S. Department of Labor, Bureau of Labor Statistics

Industry Overview

	1998	2004
Total Employees	239,034	256,132
Total Payroll ($1,000)	5,907,989	7,952,582
Total Establishments	21,261	22,133
Establishments with 1–19 Employees	19,113	19,816
Establishments with 20–49 Employees	1,406	1,558
Establishments with 50–249 Employees	657	663
Establishments with 250–999 Employees	75	84
Establishments with 1,000+ Employees	10	12

Data: U.S. Census Bureau, County Business Patterns

Major Industries (Ranked by 2004 Employment; Payroll in $1,000s)				
Industry	1998 Employment	2004 Employment	1998 Payroll	2004 Payroll
Retail Trade	37,212	40,384	645,573	915,893
Health Care and Social Assistance	32,784	38,877	819,150	1,220,407
Manufacturing	44,836	38,523	1,495,644	1,638,185
Accommodation and Food Services	27,550	28,518	298,343	386,551
Construction	12,699	14,622	385,573	584,396
Educational Services	12,254	13,465	217,795	309,535
Professional, Scientific, Technical Services	9,228	12,481	353,212	513,520
Wholesale Trade	10,792	10,414	348,198	460,956
Finance and Insurance	9,370	10,352	355,166	498,066
Other Services (except Public Admin.)	8,675	9,618	153,936	206,603

Data: U.S. Census Bureau, County Business Patterns

Taxes and Business Climate

State and Local Taxes		
Combined Revenues ($1,000)	2001–2	2003–4
Revenue from Property Taxes	823,610	950,456
Revenue from Sales and Gross Receipts Taxes	572,821	693,232
Revenue from Individual Income Taxes	407,835	429,817
Revenue from Corporate Income Taxes	37,306	62,228
Revenue from Other Taxes	123,560	150,450
Total Tax Revenue	1,965,132	2,286,183
Per Capita Taxes		
Property Tax per Capita	1,352	1,531
Sales and Gross Receipts Tax per Capita	941	1,116
Individual Income Tax per Capita	670	692
Corporate Income Tax per Capita	61	100
Other Taxes per Capita	203	242
Total Taxes per Capita	3,227	3,681

Data: U.S. Census Bureau; Anderson Economic Group, LLC

Business Climate Measures	
Anderson Economic Group: 2006 Business Tax Ranking (1 is Best)	48
Forbes Magazine: 2006 Best States for Business Ranking (1 is Best)	30
Tax Foundation: 2007 Business Tax Climate Ranking (1 is Best)	46
2002–3 Employer Firm Births	1,888
2002–3 Employer Firm Terminations	1,686

Data: Anderson Economic Group; Tax Foundation; Forbes Magazine; U.S. Census, Statistics of U.S. Businesses

Voting Behavior and Elected Officials

Voter Registration and Turnout (%)

	1992	1996	2000	2004
Registered Voters Who Voted	75.6	67.1	68.9	70.3
Citizens Age 18+ Who Voted	67.5	58.1	63.8	64.8

Data: Dave Leip's Atlas of U.S. Presidential Elections

Presidential Election Results (Nationwide Winner Listed First)

2004	Popular Vote (%)	Electoral Votes
George W. Bush (Republican, Incumbent)	38.8	0
John Kerry (Democrat)	58.9	3
Other	2.3	0
2000		
George W. Bush (Republican)	40.7	0
Albert Gore (Democrat)	50.6	3
Ralph Nader (Green)	6.9	0
Other	1.8	0
1996		
William Clinton (Democrat, Incumbent)	53.4	3
Robert Dole (Republican)	31.1	0
H. Ross Perot (Reformist)	12.0	0
Other	3.6	0
1992		
William Clinton (Democrat)	46.1	3
George H. W. Bush (Republican, Incumbent)	30.4	0
H. Ross Perot (Independent)	22.8	0
Other	0.7	0

Data: Dave Leip's Atlas of U.S. Presidential Elections

Governor and U.S. Congressional Seats				
Governor	**Party**	**Year Term Began**	**Term**	**Max. Consecutive Terms**
Jim Douglas	R	2003	Second	No limit
U.S. Senators	**Party**	**Year Elected**	**Term Expires**	
Bernie Sanders	I	2006	2013	
Patrick Leahy	D	1974	2011	
U.S. Representatives		**Republican**	**Democrat**	**Other**
		0	1	0

Data: National Governors Association, U.S. Senate, U.S. House of Representatives

Business and Economic Agencies

Agency	Website Address
Vermont Chamber of Commerce	www.vtchamber.com
Vermont Department of Economic Development	www.thinkvermont.com
Vermont Small Business Dev. Center	www.vtsbdc.org
Vermont Secretary of State, Corporations	www.sec.state.vt.us/corps

Data: Various Agency Websites

Virginia

Demographics and Socioeconomics. Virginia, located in the South Atlantic region of the United States, has a population of 7.3 million people and was the twelfth most populous state in 2005. The state's population increased by 254,093 people from 2000 to 2005, and is projected to increase to 9.4 million by 2025. This 1.2 percent projected annual growth rate is above the national average of 1.0 percent. In 2005 Vermont had a per capita personal income of $37,552, which was $3,057 above the national average and the seventh highest in the country. The state's per capita income grew at an average annual rate of 3.9 percent from 2000 to 2005, compared to 2.9 percent nationally.

Workforce and Industry. The state's workforce is generally more educated than that of other states: 85.4 percent of the state's adult population has graduated form high school, compared to an 84.2 percent national average; 33.2 percent hold a bachelor degree or higher (national average is 27.2 percent); and 13.4 percent hold professional or graduate degrees (national average is 10.0). In 2004 the state's largest

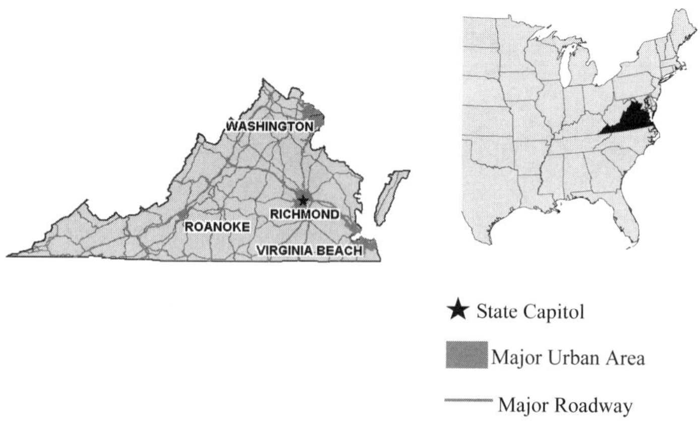

Demographic and Socioeconomic Profile

Demographics and Socioeconomic Figures		
Population and Households	**2000**	**2005**
Total Population	7,078,515	7,332,608
Number of Households	2,699,173	2,889,688
Average Household Size	2.5	2.5
Age and Ethnicity		
Median Age	35.7	37.2
Population 18 Years of Age and Older	5,342,691	5,520,020
Population 65 Years of Age and Older	790,567	823,048
Caucasian Population	5,116,929	5,259,281
African-American Population	1,384,008	1,397,192
Hispanic Population	327,273	438,789
Asian Population	256,355	342,239
Foreign-Born Population	570,279	723,667
Income		
Per Capita Personal Income (USD)	$31,087	$37,552
Median Household Income (USD)	$46,677	$54,240
Individuals below Poverty Level	9.6%	10.0%

Data: U.S. Census, American Community Survey; U.S. Department of Commerce, Bureau of Economic Analysis

industry in terms of employment was retail trade, followed by professional, scientific, and technical services. Professional, scientific, and technical services was also the fastest growing industry, with 35.0 percent growth from 1998 to 2004.

Tax Profile and Business Climate. In fiscal year 2003–4 Virginia had total tax revenues of $25.0 billion. The largest share was generated from property taxes, followed by individual income taxes. The per capita tax burden in Virginia was $3,342 for 2003–4, some $105 below the national average. In terms of business taxes, Virginia ranked eighteenth in a 2006 report by Anderson Economic Group. The state's business climate was ranked as the nation's best by Forbes Magazine and thirteenth by the Tax Foundation.

Population Projections

	2010	2015	2020	2025
Total Population	8,010,245	8,466,864	8,917,395	9,364,304
Median Age	37.2	37.2	37.3	37.5
Population 18 Years of Age and Older	6,130,061	6,484,801	6,817,484	7,155,835
Population 65 Years of Age and Older	994,359	1,193,453	1,404,580	1,634,012

Data: U.S. Census Bureau

Workforce and Industry Profile

Workforce

	2000	2005
Civilian Labor Force	3,563,772	3,828,517
Labor Force Participation Rate	66.8%	68.2%
Unemployment Rate	2.3%	3.5%
Average Earnings per Job (USD)	$35,172	$39,760
Education Attainment (Population 25 Years and Older)	**(%)**	**(%)**
High School Graduate or Higher	81.5	85.4
Bachelors Degree or Higher	29.5	33.2
Graduate or Professional Degree	11.6	13.4

Data: U.S. Census Bureau, American Community Survey; U.S. Department of Labor, Bureau of Labor Statistics

Industry Overview

	1998	2004
Total Employees	2,700,589	3,054,816
Total Payroll ($1,000)	81,261,075	114,893,068
Total Establishments	172,182	188,989
Establishments with 1–19 Employees	147,954	160,922
Establishments with 20–49 Employees	15,065	17,549
Establishments with 50–249 Employees	7,933	9,138
Establishments with 250–999 Employees	1,080	1,196
Establishments with 1,000+ Employees	150	184

Data: U.S. Census Bureau, County Business Patterns

Major Industries (Ranked by 2004 Employment; Payroll in $1,000s)				
Industry	1998 Employment	2004 Employment	1998 Payroll	2004 Payroll
Retail Trade	381,550	432,816	6,814,272	9,154,493
Professional, Scientific, Technical Services	252,923	341,324	12,668,638	22,020,238
Health Care and Social Assistance	293,642	340,794	8,276,316	12,313,666
Manufacturing	368,397	294,951	12,148,259	12,026,041
Accommodation and Food Services	234,205	280,719	2,583,716	3,718,735
Admin., Support, Waste Mngt., Remediation Services	193,746	231,750	3,863,555	6,529,610
Construction	178,057	218,483	5,235,341	8,250,445
Finance and Insurance	131,159	172,970	5,444,898	10,000,388
Other Services (except Public Admin.)	141,679	163,051	3,105,675	4,363,688
Information	101,530	113,141	6,283,070	7,065,023

Data: U.S. Census Bureau, County Business Patterns

Taxes and Business Climate

State and Local Taxes		
Combined Revenues ($1,000)	2001–2	2003–4
Revenue from Property Taxes	6,710,588	7,715,220
Revenue from Sales and Gross Receipts Taxes	6,542,184	7,249,089
Revenue from Individual Income Taxes	6,710,995	7,422,071
Revenue from Corporate Income Taxes	308,554	422,119
Revenue from Other Taxes	1,858,925	2,193,806
Total Tax Revenue	22,131,246	25,002,305
Per Capita Taxes		
Property Tax per Capita	948	1,031
Sales and Gross Receipts Tax per Capita	924	969
Individual Income Tax per Capita	948	992
Corporate Income Tax per Capita	44	56
Other Taxes per Capita	263	293
Total Taxes per Capita	3,126	3,342

Data: U.S. Census Bureau; Anderson Economic Group, LLC

Business Climate Measures	
Anderson Economic Group: 2006 Business Tax Ranking (1 is Best)	18
Forbes Magazine: 2006 Best States for Business Ranking (1 is Best)	1
Tax Foundation: 2007 Business Tax Climate Ranking (1 is Best)	13
2002–3 Employer Firm Births	18,709
2002–3 Employer Firm Terminations	16,066

Data: Anderson Economic Group; Tax Foundation; Forbes Magazine; U.S. Census, Statistics of U.S. Businesses

Voting Behavior and Elected Officials

Voter Registration and Turnout (%)	1992	1996	2000	2004
Registered Voters Who Voted	83.7	72.7	72.6	76.5
Citizens Age 18+ Who Voted	52.8	47.5	51.3	57.2

Data: Dave Leip's Atlas of U.S. Presidential Elections

Presidential Election Results (Nationwide Winner Listed First)		
2004	**Popular Vote (%)**	**Electoral Votes**
George W. Bush (Republican, Incumbent)	53.7	13
John Kerry (Democrat)	45.5	0
Other	0.8	0
2000		
George W. Bush (Republican)	52.5	13
Albert Gore (Democrat)	44.4	0
Ralph Nader (Green)	2.2	0
Other	0.9	0
1996		
William Clinton (Democrat, Incumbent)	45.2	0
Robert Dole (Republican)	47.1	13
H. Ross Perot (Reformist)	6.6	0
Other	1.1	0
1992		
William Clinton (Democrat)	40.6	0
George H. W. Bush (Republican, Incumbent)	45.0	13
H. Ross Perot (Independent)	13.6	0
Other	0.8	0

Data: Dave Leip's Atlas of U.S. Presidential Elections

Governor and U.S. Congressional Seats				
Governor	**Party**	**Year Term Began**	**Term**	**Max. Consecutive Terms**
Timothy M. Kaine	D	2006	First	1
U.S. Senators	**Party**	**Year Elected**	**Term Expires**	
John W. Warner	R	1978	2009	
Jim Webb	D	2006	2013	
U.S. Representatives		**Republican**	**Democrat**	**Other**
		8	3	0

Data: National Governors Association, U.S. Senate, U.S. House of Representatives

Business and Economic Agencies

Agency	Website Address
Virginia Chamber of Commerce	www.vachamber.com
Virginia Economic Development Partnership	www.yesvirginia.org
Virginia Small Business Dev. Center	www.virginiasbdc.com
Virginia State Corporation Commission	www.scc.virginia.gov/division/clk

Data: Various Agency Websites

Washington

Demographics and Socioeconomics. Washington, located in the Pacific region of the United States, has a population of 6.1 million people, making it the fourteenth most populous state in 2005. The state's population increased by 252,217 people from 2000 to 2005, and is projected to increase to 8.0 million by 2025. This 1.3 percent projected annual growth rate compares to the projected national average of 1.0 percent. The state's 2005 per capita personal income of $35,234 was the sixteenth highest in the United States, some $739 above the national average. Per capita income in Washington grew at an average annual rate of 2.1 percent from 2000 to 2005, compared to 2.9 percent nationally.

Workforce and Industry. In 2004 the state's largest industry in terms of employment was retail trade, followed by health care and social assistance. The fastest growing industry was information, with 54.6 percent growth from 1998 to 2004. The information industry ranked eleventh in terms of 2004 employment. The state's workforce is generally more educated than that of other

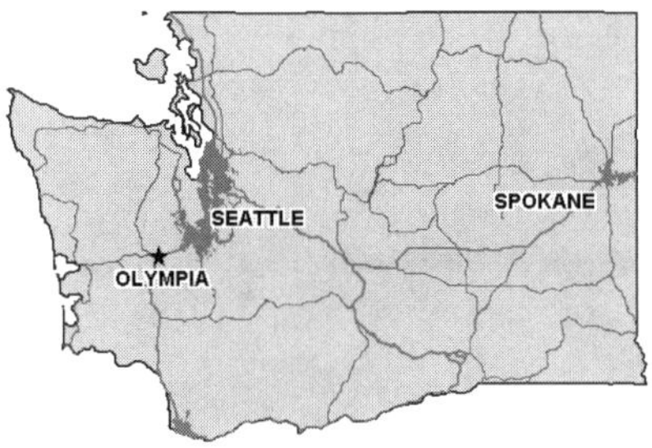

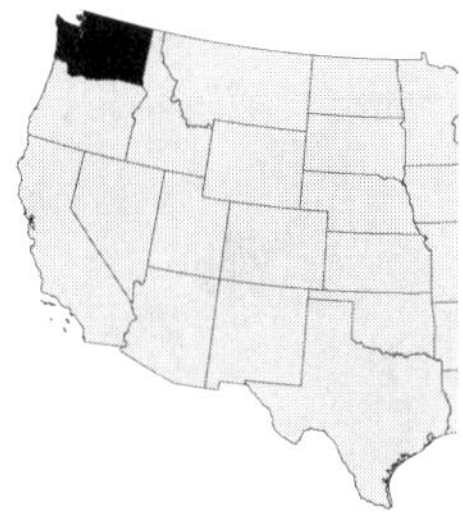

★ State Capitol

Major Urban Area

Major Roadway

Demographic and Socioeconomic Profile

Demographics and Socioeconomic Figures		
Population and Households	**2000**	**2005**
Total Population	5,894,121	6,146,338
Number of Households	2,271,398	2,450,474
Average Household Size	2.5	2.5
Age and Ethnicity		
Median Age	35.3	36.7
Population 18 Years of Age and Older	4,384,341	4,668,831
Population 65 Years of Age and Older	662,162	683,774
Caucasian Population	4,815,072	4,988,017
African-American Population	185,052	202,286
Hispanic Population	439,841	541,722
Asian Population	320,979	405,030
Foreign-Born Population	614,457	750,258
Income		
Per Capita Personal Income (USD)	$31,779	$35,234
Median Household Income (USD)	$45,776	$49,262
Individuals below Poverty Level	10.6%	11.9%

Data: U.S. Census, American Community Survey; U.S. Department of Commerce, Bureau of Economic Analysis

states: 88.8 percent of the state's adult population has graduated from high school, compared to an 84.2 percent national average; 30.1 percent hold a bachelor degree or higher (national average is 27.2 percent); and 10.5 percent hold professional or graduate degrees (national average is 10.0 percent).

Tax Profile and Business Climate. In fiscal year 2003–4 Washington had total tax revenues of $21.4 billion. The largest share was generated from sales and gross receipts taxes, followed by property taxes. There is not an individual or corporate income tax in Washington. The per capita tax burden in Washington was $3,452 for 2003–4, just above the national average of $3,447. In terms of business taxes, the state ranked thirtieth in a 2006 report by Anderson Economic Group. Forbes Magazine and the Tax Foundation ranked the state's business climate twelfth and eleventh, respectively.

Population Projections

	2010	2015	2020	2025
Total Population	6,541,963	6,950,610	7,432,136	7,996,400
Median Age	37.3	37.3	37.7	38.1
Population 18 Years of Age and Older	5,053,540	5,389,525	5,748,788	6,164,834
Population 65 Years of Age and Older	795,528	965,506	1,168,199	1,380,872

Data: U.S. Census Bureau

Workforce and Industry Profile

Workforce

	2000	2005
Civilian Labor Force	2,979,824	3,200,856
Labor Force Participation Rate	66.5%	66.8%
Unemployment Rate	5.0%	5.5%
Average Earnings per Job (USD)	$37,090	$41,460
Education Attainment (Population 25 Years and Older)	**(%)**	**(%)**
High School Graduate or Higher	87.1	88.8
Bachelors Degree or Higher	27.7	30.1
Graduate or Professional Degree	9.3	10.5

Data: U.S. Census Bureau, American Community Survey; U.S. Department of Labor, Bureau of Labor Statistics

Industry Overview

	1998	2004
Total Employees	2,134,598	2,268,913
Total Payroll ($1,000)	73,268,188	90,154,182
Total Establishments	161,473	171,529
Establishments with 1–19 Employees	142,096	150,587
Establishments with 20–49 Employees	12,485	13,527
Establishments with 50–249 Employees	6,136	6,560
Establishments with 250–999 Employees	667	744
Establishments with 1,000+ Employees	89	111

Data: U.S. Census Bureau, County Business Patterns

Major Industries (Ranked by 2004 Employment; Payroll in $1,000s)				
Industry	1998 Employment	2004 Employment	1998 Payroll	2004 Payroll
Retail Trade	288,387	318,753	6,107,356	7,642,173
Health Care and Social Assistance	269,465	309,627	7,767,349	11,349,615
Manufacturing	335,467	253,844	13,655,822	12,232,435
Accommodation and Food Services	195,249	206,951	2,165,493	2,995,883
Construction	143,168	152,990	5,224,593	6,658,471
Professional, Scientific, Technical Services	117,463	143,231	5,122,866	8,412,867
Admin., Support, Waste Mngt., Remediation Services	116,150	124,986	2,992,866	4,460,023
Wholesale Trade	120,196	124,686	4,704,938	5,995,231
Finance and Insurance	96,128	109,999	4,272,989	6,343,107
Other Services (except Public Admin.)	100,652	106,476	1,942,337	2,469,388

Data: U.S. Census Bureau, County Business Patterns

Taxes and Business Climate

State and Local Taxes		
Combined Revenues ($1,000)	2001–2	2003–4
Revenue from Property Taxes	5,790,556	6,386,346
Revenue from Sales and Gross Receipts Taxes	11,975,505	12,999,301
Revenue from Individual Income Taxes	0	0
Revenue from Corporate Income Taxes	0	0
Revenue from Other Taxes	1,747,442	2,039,281
Total Tax Revenue	19,513,503	21,424,928
Per Capita Taxes		
Property Tax per Capita	982	1,029
Sales and Gross Receipts Tax per Capita	2,032	2,094
Individual Income Tax per Capita	0	0
Corporate Income Tax per Capita	0	0
Other Taxes per Capita	296	329
Total Taxes per Capita	3,311	3,452

Data: U.S. Census Bureau; Anderson Economic Group, LLC

Business Climate Measures	
Anderson Economic Group: 2006 Business Tax Ranking (1 is Best)	30
Forbes Magazine: 2006 Best States for Business Ranking (1 is Best)	12
Tax Foundation: 2007 Business Tax Climate Ranking (1 is Best)	11
2002–3 Employer Firm Births	17,886
2002–3 Employer Firm Terminations	16,194

Data: Anderson Economic Group; Tax Foundation; Forbes Magazine; U.S. Census, Statistics of U.S. Businesses

Voting Behavior and Elected Officials

Voter Registration and Turnout (%)

	1992	1996	2000	2004
Registered Voters Who Voted	81.3	73.2	74.6	81.5
Citizens Age 18+ Who Voted	59.9	54.8	56.8	61.7

Data: Dave Leip's Atlas of U.S. Presidential Elections

Presidential Election Results (Nationwide Winner Listed First)

2004	Popular Vote (%)	Electoral Votes
George W. Bush (Republican, Incumbent)	45.6	0
John Kerry (Democrat)	52.8	11
Other	1.6	0
2000		
George W. Bush (Republican)	44.6	0
Albert Gore (Democrat)	50.2	11
Ralph Nader (Green)	4.1	0
Other	1.1	0
1996		
William Clinton (Democrat, Incumbent)	49.8	11
Robert Dole (Republican)	37.3	0
H. Ross Perot (Reformist)	8.9	0
Other	3.9	0
1992		
William Clinton (Democrat)	43.4	11
George H. W. Bush (Republican, Incumbent)	32.0	0
H. Ross Perot (Independent)	23.7	0
Other	1.0	0

Data: Dave Leip's Atlas of U.S. Presidential Elections

Governor and U.S. Congressional Seats				
Governor	Party	Year Term Began	Term	Max. Consecutive Terms
Christine Gregoire	D	2005	First	No limit
U.S. Senators	**Party**	**Year Elected**	**Term Expires**	
Maria Cantwell	D	2000	2013	
Patty Murray	D	1992	2011	
U.S. Representatives		**Republican**	**Democrat**	**Other**
		3	6	0

Data: National Governors Association, U.S. Senate, U.S. House of Representatives

Business and Economic Agencies

Agency	Website Address
Association of Washington Business	www.awb.org
Department of Community, Trade, and Economic Development	www.cted.wa.gov
Washington Small Business Dev. Center	www.wsbdc.org
Washington Secretary of State	www.secstate.wa.gov

Data: Various Agency Websites

West Virginia

Demographics and Socioeconomics. With a population of 1.8 million people, West Virginia was the fourteenth least populous state in the United States in 2005. From 2000 to 2005 the state's population decreased by 36,594 people, and is projected to decline by 0.02 percent a year, on average, through 2025. The state's 2005 per capita personal income of $26,029 was the third lowest in the United States, some $8,466 below the national average. Per capita income in West Virginia grew at an average annual rate of 3.5 percent from 2000 to 2005, compared to 2.9 percent nationally.

Workforce and Industry. The state's largest industry in terms of 2004 employment was health care and social assistance. The fastest growing major industry was professional, scientific, and technical services, with 27.4 percent growth from 1998 to 2004. The state's workforce is generally less educated than that of other states: 81.2 percent of the state's adult population has graduated from high school, compared to an 84.2 percent national average; 16.9 percent hold a bachelor degree or higher

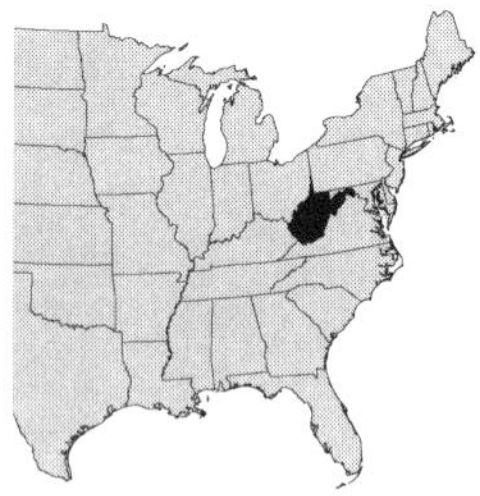

★ State Capitol
Major Urban Area
Major Roadway

Demographic and Socioeconomic Profile

Demographics and Socioeconomic Figures		
Population and Households	**2000**	**2005**
Total Population	1,808,344	1,771,750
Number of Households	736,481	740,702
Average Household Size	2.4	2.4
Age and Ethnicity		
Median Age	38.9	40.7
Population 18 Years of Age and Older	1,406,569	1,391,259
Population 65 Years of Age and Older	276,826	266,385
Caucasian Population	1,717,482	1,682,489
African-American Population	55,999	54,270
Hispanic Population	11,774	10,139
Asian Population	9,445	7,967
Foreign-Born Population	19,390	19,302
Income		
Per Capita Personal Income (USD)	$21,899	$26,029
Median Household Income (USD)	$29,696	$33,452
Individuals below Poverty Level	17.9%	18.0%

Data: U.S. Census, American Community Survey; U.S. Department of Commerce, Bureau of Economic Analysis

(national average is 27.2 percent); and 6.8 percent hold professional or graduate degrees (national average is 10.0 percent).

Tax Profile and Business Climate. West Virginia's total tax revenue was $5.0 billion for fiscal year 2003–4. The largest share of tax revenue was from sales and gross receipts taxes, followed by individual income taxes. West Virginia had per capita taxes of $2,740 in 2003–4, compared to the national average of $3,447. In terms of business taxes, the state ranked forty-third in a 2006 report by Anderson Economic Group. Forbes Magazine and the Tax Foundation ranked the state's business climate forty-nineth and thirty-fourth, respectively.

Population Projections

	2010	2015	2020	2025
Total Population	1,829,141	1,822,758	1,801,112	1,766,435
Median Age	41.4	42.7	43.9	45.4
Population 18 Years of Age and Older	1,446,830	1,450,163	1,443,442	1,428,017
Population 65 Years of Age and Older	292,402	329,775	372,024	408,533

Data: U.S. Census Bureau

Workforce and Industry Profile

Workforce

	2000	2005
Civilian Labor Force	790,694	802,850
Labor Force Participation Rate	54.5%	56.0%
Unemployment Rate	5.5%	5.0%
Average Earnings per Job (USD)	$26,887	$30,560
Education Attainment (Population 25 Years and Older)	**(%)**	**(%)**
High School Graduate or Higher	75.2	81.2
Bachelors Degree or Higher	14.8	16.9
Graduate or Professional Degree	5.9	6.8

Data: U.S. Census Bureau, American Community Survey; U.S. Department of Labor, Bureau of Labor Statistics

Industry Overview

	1998	2004
Total Employees	547,234	568,619
Total Payroll ($1,000)	13,278,895	15,608,156
Total Establishments	41,703	40,837
Establishments with 1–19 Employees	36,537	35,454
Establishments with 20–49 Employees	3,330	3,471
Establishments with 50–249 Employees	1,628	1,704
Establishments with 250–999 Employees	184	181
Establishments with 1,000+ Employees	24	27

Data: U.S. Census Bureau, County Business Patterns

Major Industries (Ranked by 2004 Employment; Payroll in $1,000s)				
Industry	1998 Employment	2004 Employment	1998 Payroll	2004 Payroll
Health Care and Social Assistance	99,695	114,182	2,520,213	3,326,293
Retail Trade	89,474	90,392	1,348,903	1,614,690
Manufacturing	74,424	66,877	2,595,303	2,597,601
Accommodation and Food Services	52,369	58,464	514,087	632,962
Construction	29,587	30,205	785,188	946,728
Admin., Support, Waste Mngt., Remediation Services	23,736	28,357	441,041	576,068
Other Services (except Public Admin.)	26,797	26,462	398,111	461,062
Professional, Scientific, Technical Services	18,472	23,527	487,462	796,812
Finance and Insurance	21,212	21,959	573,186	696,247
Wholesale Trade	23,082	20,792	689,794	795,019

Data: U.S. Census Bureau, County Business Patterns

Taxes and Business Climate

State and Local Taxes		
Combined Revenues ($1,000)	2001–2	2003–4
Revenue from Property Taxes	904,805	979,034
Revenue from Sales and Gross Receipts Taxes	1,979,834	2,150,048
Revenue from Individual Income Taxes	1,034,665	1,068,212
Revenue from Corporate Income Taxes	220,158	181,515
Revenue from Other Taxes	514,157	588,696
Total Tax Revenue	4,653,619	4,967,505
Per Capita Taxes		
Property Tax per Capita	500	540
Sales and Gross Receipts Tax per Capita	1,095	1,186
Individual Income Tax per Capita	572	589
Corporate Income Tax per Capita	122	100
Other Taxes per Capita	284	325
Total Taxes per Capita	2,574	2,740

Data: U.S. Census Bureau; Anderson Economic Group, LLC

Business Climate Measures	
Anderson Economic Group: 2006 Business Tax Ranking (1 is Best)	43
Forbes Magazine: 2006 Best States for Business Ranking (1 is Best)	49
Tax Foundation: 2007 Business Tax Climate Ranking (1 is Best)	34
2002–3 Employer Firm Births	3,433
2002–3 Employer Firm Terminations	3,537

Data: Anderson Economic Group; Tax Foundation; Forbes Magazine; U.S. Census, Statistics of U.S. Businesses

Voting Behavior and Elected Officials

Voter Registration and Turnout (%)

	1992	1996	2000	2004
Registered Voters Who Voted	71.5	65.6	60.8	64.7
Citizens Age 18+ Who Voted	50.6	44.9	46.1	53.3

Data: Dave Leip's Atlas of U.S. Presidential Elections

Presidential Election Results (Nationwide Winner Listed First)

2004	Popular Vote (%)	Electoral Votes
George W. Bush (Republican, Incumbent)	56.1	5
John Kerry (Democrat)	43.2	0
Other	0.7	0
2000		
George W. Bush (Republican)	51.9	5
Albert Gore (Democrat)	45.6	0
Ralph Nader (Green)	1.7	0
Other	0.8	0
1996		
William Clinton (Democrat, Incumbent)	51.5	5
Robert Dole (Republican)	36.8	0
H. Ross Perot (Reformist)	11.3	0
Other	0.5	0
1992		
William Clinton (Democrat)	48.4	5
George H. W. Bush (Republican, Incumbent)	35.4	0
H. Ross Perot (Independent)	15.9	0
Other	0.3	0

Data: Dave Leip's Atlas of U.S. Presidential Elections

Governor and U.S. Congressional Seats				
Governor	**Party**	**Year Term Began**	**Term**	**Max. Consecutive Terms**
Joe Manchin	D	2005	First	2
U.S. Senators	**Party**	**Year Elected**	**Term Expires**	
Jay Rockefeller	D	1984	2009	
Robert C. Byrd	D	1958	2013	
U.S. Representatives		**Republican**	**Democrat**	**Other**
		1	2	0

Data: National Governors Association, U.S. Senate, U.S. House of Representatives

Business and Economic Agencies

Agency	Website Address
West Virginia Chamber of Commerce	www.wvchamber.com
West Virginia Development Office	www.wvdo.org
West Virginia Small Business Dev. Center	www.sbdcwv.org
West Virginia Secretary of State	www.wv.gov/sec.aspx?pgID=1

Data: Various Agency Websites

Wisconsin

Demographics and Socioeconomics. With a population of 5.4 million people, Wisconsin was the twentieth most populous state in the United States in 2005. From 2000 to 2005 the state's population increased by 12,076 people, and is projected to increase to 6.1 million by 2025. This 0.6 percent projected annual growth rate compares to the projected national average of 1.0 percent. In 2005 Wisconsin had a per capita personal income of $33,251, which was $1,244 below the national average and the twenty-first highest in the country. The state's per capita income grew at an average annual rate of 3.1 percent from 2000 to 2005, compared to 2.9 percent nationally.

Workforce and Industry. The state's largest industry in terms of 2004 employment was manufacturing. The fastest growing major industry was transportation and warehousing, with 29.5 percent growth from 1998 to 2004. In terms of the education level of the workforce, 88.8 percent of Wisconsin's adult population has a high school diploma or the equivalent, compared to the national

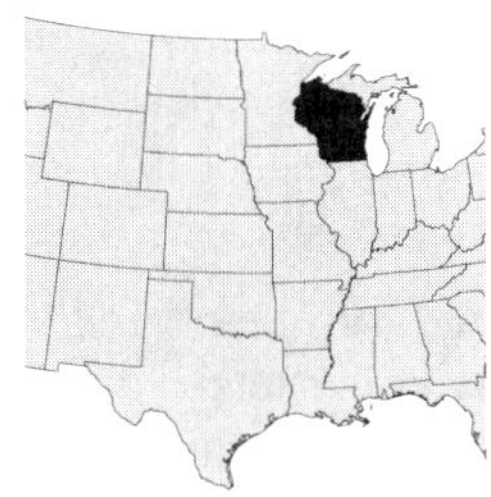

★ State Capitol

Major Urban Area

Major Roadway

Demographic and Socioeconomic Profile

Demographics and Socioeconomic Figures		
Population and Households	**2000**	**2005**
Total Population	5,363,675	5,375,751
Number of Households	2,084,544	2,219,571
Average Household Size	2.5	2.4
Age and Ethnicity		
Median Age	36.0	37.9
Population 18 Years of Age and Older	3,996,289	4,085,023
Population 65 Years of Age and Older	702,668	674,464
Caucasian Population	4,773,553	4,734,357
African-American Population	300,355	307,950
Hispanic Population	191,049	242,287
Asian Population	83,077	107,517
Foreign-Born Population	193,751	227,372
Income		
Per Capita Personal Income (USD)	$28,570	$33,251
Median Household Income (USD)	$43,791	$47,105
Individuals below Poverty Level	8.7%	10.2%

Data: U.S. Census, American Community Survey; U.S. Department of Commerce, Bureau of Economic Analysis

average of 84.2 percent. 25.0 percent of Wisconsin's adult population has a bachelor degree or higher (national average is 27.2 percent); and 8.1 percent hold professional or graduate degrees (national average is 10.0 percent).

Tax Profile and Business Climate. Wisconsin's total tax revenue was $20.4 billion for fiscal year 2003–4. The largest share of this was generated from property taxes, followed by sales and gross receipts taxes. Total Taxes per Capita in Wisconsin were $3,714, compared to the national average of $3,447 for 2003–4. In terms of business taxes, the state ranked twenty-fourth in a 2006 report by Anderson Economic Group. Forbes Magazine and the Tax Foundation ranked the state's business climate thirty-nineth and thirty-eighth, respectively.

Population Projections

	2010	2015	2020	2025
Total Population	5,727,426	5,882,760	6,004,954	6,088,374
Median Age	38.1	38.5	39.6	40.7
Population 18 Years of Age and Older	4,408,282	4,539,380	4,636,998	4,711,673
Population 65 Years of Age and Older	771,993	881,745	1,025,542	1,183,596

Data: U.S. Census Bureau

Workforce and Industry Profile

Workforce

	2000	2005
Civilian Labor Force	2,869,236	2,960,051
Labor Force Participation Rate	69.1%	69.9%
Unemployment Rate	3.4%	4.7%
Average Earnings per Job (USD)	$30,694	$35,660
Education Attainment (Population 25 Years and Older)	**(%)**	**(%)**
High School Graduate or Higher	85.1	88.8
Bachelors Degree or Higher	22.4	25.0
Graduate or Professional Degree	7.2	8.1

Data: U.S. Census Bureau, American Community Survey; U.S. Department of Labor, Bureau of Labor Statistics

Industry Overview

	1998	2004
Total Employees	2,319,343	2,435,143
Total Payroll ($1,000)	64,912,499	82,834,268
Total Establishments	138,635	144,116
Establishments with 1–19 Employees	117,738	121,865
Establishments with 20–49 Employees	12,751	13,660
Establishments with 50–249 Employees	7,060	7,442
Establishments with 250–999 Employees	943	1,015
Establishments with 1,000+ Employees	143	134

Data: U.S. Census Bureau, County Business Patterns

Major Industries (Ranked by 2004 Employment; Payroll in $1,000s)				
Industry	1998 Employment	2004 Employment	1998 Payroll	2004 Payroll
Manufacturing	566,219	489,281	19,872,068	20,479,413
Health Care and Social Assistance	291,781	346,114	7,935,213	12,091,444
Retail Trade	309,194	321,178	5,228,682	6,532,504
Accommodation and Food Services	191,531	213,765	1,722,956	2,255,623
Finance and Insurance	126,572	137,908	4,930,640	7,088,180
Construction	107,027	122,822	4,308,527	5,463,537
Admin., Support, Waste Mngt., Remediation Services	116,764	121,464	2,130,335	2,860,146
Wholesale Trade	114,445	119,884	4,131,194	5,368,268
Other Services (except Public Admin.)	104,798	114,234	1,696,610	2,156,632
Transportation and Warehousing	74,045	95,855	2,091,651	3,114,643

Data: U.S. Census Bureau, County Business Patterns

Taxes and Business Climate

State and Local Taxes		
Combined Revenues ($1,000)	2001–2	2003–4
Revenue from Property Taxes	6,466,173	7,429,001
Revenue from Sales and Gross Receipts Taxes	5,698,094	5,915,255
Revenue from Individual Income Taxes	4,973,615	5,251,190
Revenue from Corporate Income Taxes	445,016	681,990
Revenue from Other Taxes	1,027,018	1,163,552
Total Tax Revenue	18,609,916	20,440,988
Per Capita Taxes		
Property Tax per Capita	1,205	1,350
Sales and Gross Receipts Tax per Capita	1,062	1,075
Individual Income Tax per Capita	927	954
Corporate Income Tax per Capita	83	124
Other Taxes per Capita	191	211
Total Taxes per Capita	3,469	3,714

Data: U.S. Census Bureau; Anderson Economic Group, LLC

Business Climate Measures

Anderson Economic Group: 2006 Business Tax Ranking (1 is Best)	24
Forbes Magazine: 2006 Best States for Business Ranking (1 is Best)	39
Tax Foundation: 2007 Business Tax Climate Ranking (1 is Best)	38
2002–3 Employer Firm Births	11,726
2002–3 Employer Firm Terminations	11,490

Data: Anderson Economic Group; Tax Foundation; Forbes Magazine; U.S. Census, Statistics of U.S. Businesses

Voting Behavior and Elected Officials

Voter Registration and Turnout (%)

	1992	1996	2000	2004
Registered Voters Who Voted	n/a	n/a	n/a	n/a
Citizens Age 18+ Who Voted	69.0	57.4	65.0	72.4

Data: Dave Leip's Atlas of U.S. Presidential Elections

Presidential Election Results (Nationwide Winner Listed First)

2004	Popular Vote (%)	Electoral Votes
George W. Bush (Republican, Incumbent)	49.3	0
John Kerry (Democrat)	49.7	10
Other	1.0	0
2000		
George W. Bush (Republican)	47.6	0
Albert Gore (Democrat)	47.8	11
Ralph Nader (Green)	3.6	0
Other	0.9	0
1996		
William Clinton (Democrat, Incumbent)	48.8	11
Robert Dole (Republican)	38.5	0
H. Ross Perot (Reformist)	10.4	0
Other	2.4	0
1992		
William Clinton (Democrat)	41.1	11
George H. W. Bush (Republican, Incumbent)	36.8	0
H. Ross Perot (Independent)	21.5	0
Other	0.6	0

Data: Dave Leip's Atlas of U.S. Presidential Elections

Governor and U.S. Congressional Seats				
Governor	**Party**	**Year Term Began**	**Term**	**Max. Consecutive Terms**
Jim Doyle	D	2003	Second	No limit
U.S. Senators	**Party**	**Year Elected**	**Term Expires**	
Russell Feingold	D	1992	2011	
Herb Kohl	D	1988	2013	
U.S. Representatives		**Republican**	**Democrat**	**Other**
		3	5	0

Data: National Governors Association, U.S. Senate, U.S. House of Representatives

Business and Economic Agencies

Agency	Website Address
Wisconsin Chamber of Commerce Foundation	www.wischamberfoundation.org
Wisconsin Housing and Economic Development Authority	www.wheda.com
Wisconsin Small Business Dev. Center	www.wisconsinsbdc.org
State of Wisconsin, Department of Financial Institutions	www.wdfi.org/corporations

Data: Various Agency Websites

Wyoming

Demographics and Socioeconomics. Wyoming, located in the Mountain region of the United States, has a population of 495,226 people, making it the least populous state in 2005. The state's population increased by 1,444 people from 2000 to 2005, and is projected to increase to 529,031 by 2025. This 0.3 percent projected annual growth rate compares to the projected national average of 1.0 percent. The state's 2005 per capita personal income of $37,270 was the tenth highest in the United States, some $2,775 above the national average. Per capita income in Wyoming grew at an average annual rate of 5.5 percent from 2000 to 2005, compared to 2.9 percent nationally.

Workforce and Industry. In 2004 the state's largest industry in terms of employment was retail trade, followed by health care and social assistance. The fastest growing major industry was transportation and warehousing, with 43.2 percent growth from 1998 to 2004. In terms of the education level of the workforce, 91.3 percent of Wyoming's adult population has a high school diploma or the equivalent, compared to

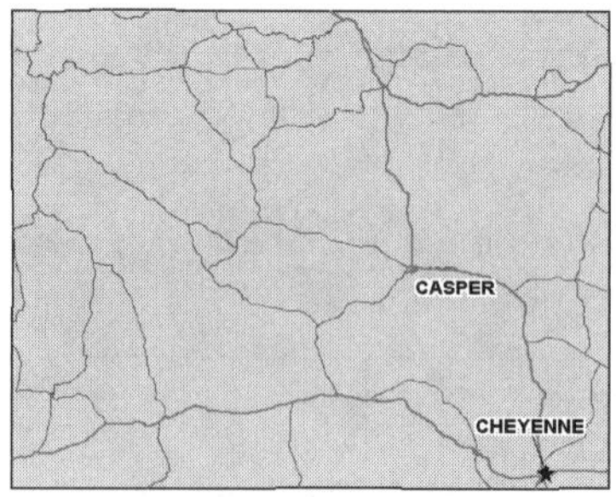

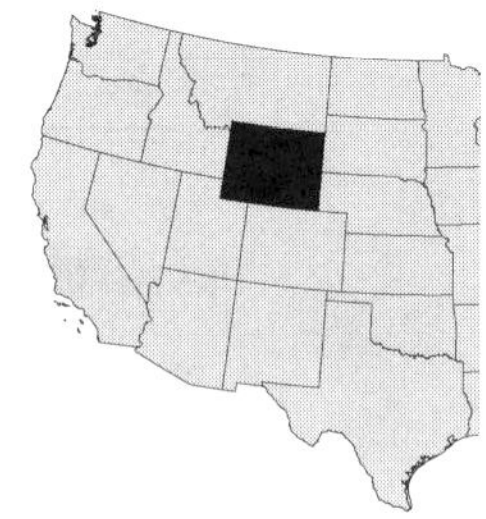

★ State Capitol

Major Urban Area

Major Roadway

Demographic and Socioeconomic Profile

Demographics and Socioeconomic Figures		
Population and Households	**2000**	**2005**
Total Population	493,782	495,226
Number of Households	193,608	204,935
Average Household Size	2.5	2.4
Age and Ethnicity		
Median Age	36.2	39.1
Population 18 Years of Age and Older	365,685	382,349
Population 65 Years of Age and Older	57,467	59,221
Caucasian Population	454,095	457,681
African-American Population	3,126	3,317
Hispanic Population	31,384	33,437
Asian Population	2,972	3,148
Foreign-Born Population	11,205	11,235
Income		
Per Capita Personal Income (USD)	$28,460	$37,270
Median Household Income (USD)	$37,892	$46,202
Individuals below Poverty Level	11.4%	9.5%

Data: U.S. Census, American Community Survey; U.S. Department of Commerce, Bureau of Economic Analysis

the national average of 84.2 percent: 23.2 percent of Wyoming's adult population has a bachelor degree or higher (national average is 27.2 percent); and 7.7 percent hold professional or graduate degrees (national average is 10.0 percent).

Tax Profile and Business Climate. In fiscal year 2003–4 Wyoming had total tax revenues of $2.2 billion, with other taxes generating the largest share of total revenue. The per capita tax burden in Wyoming was $4,437 for 2003–4, some $990 above the national average. In terms of business taxes, the state was ranked forty-seventh in a 2006 report by Anderson Economic Group. Forbes Magazine and the Tax Foundation ranked the state's business climate twenty-third and first, respectively.

Population Projections

	2010	2015	2020	2025
Total Population	519,886	528,005	530,948	529,031
Median Age	39.5	40.9	42.4	44.3
Population 18 Years of Age and Older	403,613	412,506	418,436	422,797
Population 65 Years of Age and Older	72,658	88,842	109,655	128,605

Data: U.S. Census Bureau

Workforce and Industry Profile

Workforce

	2000	2005
Civilian Labor Force	254,508	280,019
Labor Force Participation Rate	67.5%	71.3%
Unemployment Rate	3.8%	3.6%
Average Earnings per Job (USD)	$26,837	$32,940
Education Attainment (Population 25 Years and Older)	**(%)**	**(%)**
High School Graduate or Higher	87.9	91.3
Bachelors Degree or Higher	21.9	23.2
Graduate or Professional Degree	7.0	7.7

Data: U.S. Census Bureau, American Community Survey; U.S. Department of Labor, Bureau of Labor Statistics

Industry Overview

	1998	2004
Total Employees	163,791	187,360
Total Payroll ($1,000)	3,980,094	5,696,419
Total Establishments	17,888	19,330
Establishments with 1–19 Employees	16,231	17,439
Establishments with 20–49 Employees	1,160	1,338
Establishments with 50–249 Employees	453	491
Establishments with 250–999 Employees	42	59
Establishments with 1,000+ Employees	2	3

Data: U.S. Census Bureau, County Business Patterns

Major Industries (Ranked by 2004 Employment; Payroll in $1,000s)				
Industry	1998 Employment	2004 Employment	1998 Payroll	2004 Payroll
Retail Trade	26,974	30,057	443,320	631,049
Health Care and Social Assistance	23,694	27,645	556,515	856,703
Accommodation and Food Services	22,882	24,972	236,920	313,071
Construction	13,265	15,613	383,677	536,727
Manufacturing	8,916	10,244	283,720	431,613
Other Services (except Public Admin.)	7,894	8,726	128,223	183,960
Transportation and Warehousing	5,313	7,606	141,255	277,194
Professional, Scientific, Technical Services	6,096	7,605	170,895	268,859
Finance and Insurance	6,130	7,445	200,139	264,138
Admin., Support, Waste Mngt., Remediation Services	4,684	6,587	79,550	141,096

Data: U.S. Census Bureau, County Business Patterns

Taxes and Business Climate

State and Local Taxes		
Combined Revenues ($1,000)	2001–2	2003–4
Revenue from Property Taxes	692,341	683,963
Revenue from Sales and Gross Receipts Taxes	691,457	734,105
Revenue from Individual Income Taxes	0	0
Revenue from Corporate Income Taxes	0	0
Revenue from Other Taxes	434,570	827,197
Total Tax Revenue	1,818,368	2,245,265
Per Capita Taxes		
Property Tax per Capita	1,402	1,352
Sales and Gross Receipts Tax per Capita	1,400	1,451
Individual Income Tax per Capita	0	0
Corporate Income Tax per Capita	0	0
Other Taxes per Capita	880	1,635
Total Taxes per Capita	3,681	4,437

Data: U.S. Census Bureau; Anderson Economic Group, LLC

Business Climate Measures	
Anderson Economic Group: 2006 Business Tax Ranking (1 is Best)	32
Forbes Magazine: 2006 Best States for Business Ranking (1 is Best)	23
Tax Foundation: 2007 Business Tax Climate Ranking (1 is Best)	1
2002–3 Employer Firm Births	1,885
2002–3 Employer Firm Terminations	1,693

Data: Anderson Economic Group; Tax Foundation; Forbes Magazine; U.S. Census, Statistics of U.S. Businesses

Voting Behavior and Elected Officials

Voter Registration and Turnout (%)

	1992	1996	2000	2004
Registered Voters Who Voted	85.3	87.9	99.2	104.7
Citizens Age 18+ Who Voted	62.1	59.4	59.7	64.1

Data: Dave Leip's Atlas of U.S. Presidential Elections

Presidential Election Results (Nationwide Winner Listed First)

2004	Popular Vote (%)	Electoral Votes
George W. Bush (Republican, Incumbent)	68.9	3
John Kerry (Democrat)	29.1	0
Other	2.1	0
2000		
George W. Bush (Republican)	67.8	3
Albert Gore (Democrat)	27.7	0
Ralph Nader (Green)	2.1	0
Other	2.4	0
1996		
William Clinton (Democrat, Incumbent)	36.8	0
Robert Dole (Republican)	49.8	3
H. Ross Perot (Reformist)	12.3	0
Other	1.1	0
1992		
William Clinton (Democrat)	34.0	0
George H. W. Bush (Republican, Incumbent)	39.6	3
H. Ross Perot (Independent)	25.6	0
Other	0.9	0

Data: Dave Leip's Atlas of U.S. Presidential Elections

Governor and U.S. Congressional Seats				
Governor	**Party**	**Year Term Began**	**Term**	**Max. Consecutive Terms**
David Freudenthal	D	2003	Second	2
U.S. Senators	**Party**	**Year Elected**	**Term Expires**	
Michael B. Enzi	R	1996	2009	
Craig Thomas	R	1994	2013	
U.S. Representatives		**Republican**	**Democrat**	**Other**
		1	0	0

Data: National Governors Association, U.S. Senate, U.S. House of Representatives

Business and Economic Agencies

Agency	Website Address
Buffalo Chamber of Commerce	www.buffalowy.com
Wyoming Business Council	www.wyomingbusiness.org
Wyoming Small Business Dev. Center	www.uwyo.edu/sbdc
Wyoming Secretary of State, Corporations	soswy.state.wy.us/corporat/corporat.htm

Data: Various Agency Websites

Ranking the States

Total Population in 2005

Rank	State Name	Population	Rank	State Name	Population
1	California	35,278,768	*26*	Kentucky	4,058,633
2	Texas	22,270,165	*27*	Oregon	3,560,109
3	New York	18,655,275	*28*	Oklahoma	3,433,496
4	Florida	17,382,511	*29*	Connecticut	3,394,751
5	Illinois	12,440,351	*30*	Iowa	2,862,541
6	Pennsylvania	11,979,147	*31*	Mississippi	2,824,156
7	Ohio	11,155,606	*32*	Arkansas	2,701,431
8	Michigan	9,865,583	*33*	Kansas	2,662,616
9	Georgia	8,821,142	*34*	Utah	2,427,350
10	New Jersey	8,521,427	*35*	Nevada	2,381,281
11	North Carolina	8,411,041	*36*	New Mexico	1,887,200
12	Virginia	7,332,608	*37*	West Virginia	1,771,750
13	Massachusetts	6,182,860	*38*	Nebraska	1,706,976
14	Washington	6,146,338	*39*	Idaho	1,395,634
15	Indiana	6,093,372	*41*	Maine	1,283,673
16	Arizona	5,829,839	*41*	New Hampshire	1,272,486
17	Tennessee	5,810,590	*42*	Hawaii	1,238,158
18	Missouri	5,631,910	*43*	Rhode Island	1,032,662
19	Maryland	5,461,318	*44*	Montana	910,651
20	Wisconsin	5,375,751	*45*	Delaware	818,587
21	Minnesota	4,989,848	*46*	South Dakota	746,033
22	Colorado	4,562,244	*47*	Alaska	641,724
23	Alabama	4,442,558	*48*	North Dakota	609,645
24	Louisiana	4,389,747	*49*	Vermont	602,290
25	South Carolina	4,113,961	*50*	Wyoming	495,226

Population Projections for 2025

Rank	State Name	Population	Rank	State Name	Population
1	California	44,305,177	26	Oregon	4,536,418
2	Texas	30,865,134	27	Kentucky	4,489,662
3	Florida	25,912,458	28	Nevada	3,863,298
4	New York	19,540,179	29	Oklahoma	3,820,994
5	Illinois	13,340,507	30	Connecticut	3,691,016
6	Pennsylvania	12,801,945	31	Utah	3,225,680
7	Ohio	11,605,738	32	Arkansas	3,151,005
8	North Carolina	11,449,153	33	Mississippi	3,069,420
9	Georgia	11,438,622	34	Iowa	2,993,222
10	Michigan	10,713,730	35	Kansas	2,919,002
11	New Jersey	9,636,644	36	New Mexico	2,106,584
12	Arizona	9,531,537	37	Idaho	1,852,627
13	Virginia	9,364,304	38	Nebraska	1,812,787
14	Washington	7,996,400	39	West Virginia	1,766,435
15	Tennessee	7,073,125	41	New Hampshire	1,586,348
16	Massachusetts	6,938,636	41	Hawaii	1,438,720
17	Maryland	6,762,732	42	Maine	1,414,402
18	Indiana	6,721,322	43	Rhode Island	1,157,855
19	Missouri	6,315,366	44	Montana	1,037,387
20	Minnesota	6,108,787	45	Delaware	990,694
21	Wisconsin	6,088,374	46	Alaska	820,881
22	Colorado	5,522,803	47	South Dakota	801,845
23	South Carolina	4,989,550	48	Vermont	703,288
24	Alabama	4,800,092	49	North Dakota	620,777
25	Louisiana	4,762,398	50	Wyoming	529,031

Percent Foreign-Born Population, 2005

Rank	State Name	Foreign Born	Rank	State Name	Foreign Born
1	California	27.2%	*26*	New Hampshire	5.7
2	New York	21.4	*27*	Nebraska	5.6
3	New Jersey	19.5	*28*	Idaho	5.5
4	Florida	18.5	*29*	Alaska	5.4
5	Nevada	17.4	*30*	Pennsylvania	5.0
6	Hawaii	17.2	*31*	Oklahoma	4.5
7	Texas	15.9	*T32*	Wisconsin	4.2
8	Arizona	14.5	*T32*	South Carolina	4.2
9	Massachusetts	14.4	*34*	Indiana	4.0
10	Illinois	13.6	*35*	Tennessee	3.8
11	Rhode Island	12.6	*36*	Arkansas	3.7
12	Connecticut	12.5	*37*	Vermont	3.6
13	Washington	12.2	*38*	Iowa	3.6
14	Maryland	11.7	*39*	Ohio	3.5
15	Colorado	10.1	*41*	Missouri	3.4
16	Virginia	9.9	*41*	Maine	3.0
17	Oregon	9.7	*42*	Louisiana	2.8
18	Georgia	9.0	*43*	Alabama	2.7
19	New Mexico	8.9	*44*	Kentucky	2.4
20	Utah	7.9	*T45*	South Dakota	2.3
21	Delaware	7.7	*T45*	Wyoming	2.3
22	North Carolina	6.7	*47*	North Dakota	2.0
23	Minnesota	6.3	*48*	Montana	1.8
24	Michigan	6.1	*49*	Mississippi	1.5
25	Kansas	5.8	*50*	West Virginia	1.1

Median Age of Population in 2005

Rank	State Name	Median Age	Rank	State Name	Median Age
1	Maine	41.2	*T25*	South Carolina	37.1
T2	Vermont	40.7	*T27*	Arkansas	37.0
T2	West Virginia	40.7	*T27*	Oregon	37.0
4	Montana	40.2	*T27*	South Dakota	37.0
5	Pennsylvania	39.7	*30*	Michigan	36.9
T6	Florida	39.5	*T31*	Minnesota	36.7
T6	New Hampshire	39.5	*T31*	Washington	36.7
8	Connecticut	39.3	*33*	Oklahoma	36.5
T9	North Dakota	39.1	*T34*	Nebraska	36.2
T9	Wyoming	39.1	*T34*	New Mexico	36.2
11	Iowa	38.6	*T34*	North Carolina	36.2
12	Hawaii	38.5	*T37*	Indiana	36.1
13	Rhode Island	38.4	*T37*	Kansas	36.1
14	Massachusetts	38.2	*39*	Illinois	35.6
15	New Jersey	38.0	*41*	Mississippi	35.5
T16	Delaware	37.9	*41*	Louisiana	35.4
T16	Wisconsin	37.9	*42*	Nevada	35.2
18	Ohio	37.6	*43*	Colorado	34.7
T19	Kentucky	37.5	*44*	Idaho	34.6
T19	New York	37.5	*45*	Arizona	34.5
T21	Alabama	37.4	*46*	California	34.4
T21	Missouri	37.4	*47*	Georgia	34.3
23	Tennessee	37.3	*48*	Alaska	33.9
24	Virginia	37.2	*49*	Texas	33.2
T25	Maryland	37.1	*50*	Utah	28.5

Unemployment Rate in 2005

Rank	State Name	Unemployed	Rank	State Name	Unemployed
1	Hawaii	2.8%	*T25*	Connecticut	4.9
2	North Dakota	3.4	*T27*	Colorado	5.0
T3	Vermont	3.5	*T27*	New York	5.0
T3	Virginia	3.5	*T27*	Pennsylvania	5.0
T5	New Hampshire	3.6	*T27*	Rhode Island	5.0
T5	Wyoming	3.6	*T27*	West Virginia	5.0
T7	Florida	3.8	*32*	Kansas	5.1
T7	Idaho	3.8	*33*	North Carolina	5.2
T7	Nebraska	3.8	*T34*	Georgia	5.3
10	South Dakota	3.9	*T34*	New Mexico	5.3
T11	Alabama	4.0	*T34*	Texas	5.3
T12	Minnesota	4.0	*T37*	California	5.4
T13	Montana	4.0	*T37*	Indiana	5.4
T14	Maryland	4.1	*T37*	Missouri	5.4
T14	Nevada	4.1	*41*	Washington	5.5
16	Delaware	4.2	*41*	Tennessee	5.6
17	Utah	4.3	*42*	Illinois	5.7
T18	New Jersey	4.4	*43*	Ohio	5.9
T18	Oklahoma	4.4	*T44*	Kentucky	6.1
20	Iowa	4.6	*T44*	Oregon	6.1
T21	Arizona	4.7	*46*	Michigan	6.7
T21	Wisconsin	4.7	*T47*	Alaska	6.8
T23	Maine	4.8	*T47*	South Carolina	6.8
T23	Massachusetts	4.8	*49*	Louisiana	7.1
T25	Arkansas	4.9	*50*	Mississippi	7.9

Change in Per Capita Income from 2000 to 2005

Rank	State Name	Change (%)	Rank	State Name	Change (%)
1	Wyoming	31.0	*26*	Arizona	17.5
2	South Dakota	26.9	*27*	Pennsylvania	17.4
T3	New Mexico	26.1	*28*	Minnesota	16.6
T3	Montana	26.1	*29*	Wisconsin	16.4
5	Alabama	24.7	*30*	Kentucky	16.0
6	North Dakota	24.4	*31*	Massachusetts	15.7
7	Maryland	22.6	*32*	South Carolina	15.5
8	Oklahoma	22.5	*T33*	Utah	15.2
9	Arkansas	21.5	*T33*	Texas	15.2
10	Hawaii	21.3	*35*	Missouri	14.9
11	Virginia	20.8	*T36*	New York	14.8
12	Rhode Island	20.6	*T36*	Indiana	14.8
13	Delaware	20.1	*38*	North Carolina	14.6
14	Iowa	19.7	*T39*	Connecticut	14.5
15	Florida	19.6	*T39*	Oregon	14.5
16	Nebraska	19.4	*41*	New Jersey	14.2
17	Kansas	19.0	*42*	California	13.6
18	West Virginia	18.9	*43*	New Hampshire	13.3
19	Mississippi	18.7	*44*	Ohio	13.0
T20	Alaska	18.6	*45*	Illinois	12.7
T20	Maine	18.6	*46*	Colorado	12.3
T20	Tennessee	18.6	*47*	Georgia	11.4
23	Vermont	18.2	*48*	Washington	10.9
24	Idaho	18.0	*49*	Michigan	10.8
25	Nevada	17.6	*50*	Louisiana	6.5

Population Age 25+ with Bachelors Degree of Higher					
Rank	**State Name**	**% Age 25+**	***Rank***	**State Name**	**% Age 25+**
1	Massachusetts	36.9	*T25*	Maine	25.6
2	Colorado	35.5	*27*	North Dakota	25.5
3	Connecticut	34.9	*T28*	Florida	25.1
4	Maryland	34.5	*T28*	New Mexico	25.1
5	New Jersey	34.2	*T28*	North Carolina	25.1
6	Virginia	33.2	*T28*	Texas	25.1
7	Vermont	32.5	*32*	Wisconsin	25.0
8	New Hampshire	31.8	*T33*	Michigan	24.7
9	New York	31.3	*T33*	South Dakota	24.7
10	Minnesota	30.7	*35*	Missouri	24.0
11	Washington	30.1	*36*	Iowa	23.8
12	California	29.5	*T37*	Idaho	23.3
13	Rhode Island	29.3	*T37*	Ohio	23.3
14	Illinois	29.2	*39*	Wyoming	23.2
15	Kansas	28.2	*41*	South Carolina	23.0
T16	Hawaii	27.9	*41*	Oklahoma	22.4
T16	Utah	27.9	*42*	Tennessee	21.8
18	Oregon	27.7	*43*	Alabama	21.4
19	Delaware	27.6	*44*	Indiana	21.3
T20	Alaska	27.3	*T45*	Louisiana	20.6
T20	Nebraska	27.3	*T45*	Nevada	20.6
22	Georgia	27.1	*47*	Kentucky	19.3
23	Montana	26.5	*48*	Arkansas	18.9
24	Pennsylvania	25.7	*49*	Mississippi	18.7
T25	Arizona	25.6	*50*	West Virginia	16.9

State and Local Taxes per Capita in 2003–4

Rank	State Name	Taxes Per Capita	Rank	State Name	Taxes Per Capita
1	New York	$5,260	26	New Hampshire	$3,133
2	Connecticut	$4,921	27	Florida	$3,094
3	New Jersey	$4,555	28	Iowa	$3,054
4	Wyoming	$4,437	29	Indiana	$2,999
5	Massachusetts	$4,217	30	North Dakota	$2,989
6	Maryland	$4,016	31	North Carolina	$2,929
7	Rhode Island	$3,891	32	Oregon	$2,917
8	Hawaii	$3,813	33	Louisiana	$2,899
9	Minnesota	$3,811	34	Texas	$2,881
10	Maine	$3,789	35	Georgia	$2,877
11	California	$3,736	36	Arizona	$2,871
12	Wisconsin	$3,714	37	New Mexico	$2,861
13	Vermont	$3,681	38	Missouri	$2,822
14	Alaska	$3,610	39	Kentucky	$2,767
15	Nebraska	$3,609	41	West Virginia	$2,740
16	Delaware	$3,608	41	Utah	$2,735
17	Illinois	$3,555	42	Idaho	$2,728
18	Washington	$3,452	43	Oklahoma	$2,677
19	Pennsylvania	$3,447	44	South Carolina	$2,662
20	Ohio	$3,419	45	Montana	$2,623
21	Nevada	$3,417	46	South Dakota	$2,615
22	Kansas	$3,380	47	Tennessee	$2,536
23	Virginia	$3,342	48	Arkansas	$2,536
24	Michigan	$3,313	49	Mississippi	$2,444
25	Colorado	$3,169	50	Alabama	$2,328

Participation of Citizens Age 18+, 2004 Presidential Election

Rank	State Name	Voted (%)	Rank	State Name	Voted (%)
1	Minnesota	74.2	*26*	Florida	58.1
2	Wisconsin	72.4	*27*	Maryland	57.8
3	Maine	72.2	*28*	Utah	57.7
4	New Hampshire	69.1	*29*	Kentucky	57.5
5	South Dakota	68.2	*30*	Virginia	57.2
6	Alaska	68.0	*31*	Illinois	56.0
7	Oregon	67.8	*32*	Oklahoma	55.6
8	Iowa	66.9	*T33*	New Jersey	55.5
9	Ohio	65.3	*T33*	Alabama	55.5
10	Vermont	64.8	*35*	North Carolina	55.4
T11	North Dakota	64.2	*36*	New Mexico	55.1
T11	Montana	64.2	*37*	Tennessee	54.8
T11	Michigan	64.2	*38*	Mississippi	54.4
14	Wyoming	64.1	*39*	Indiana	53.7
15	Missouri	63.6	*41*	West Virginia	53.3
16	Colorado	62.7	*41*	Rhode Island	52.5
17	Washington	61.7	*42*	South Carolina	51.8
18	Delaware	60.6	*43*	Georgia	51.7
19	Pennsylvania	60.5	*44*	Arkansas	51.6
20	Idaho	60.2	*45*	New York	50.4
21	Nebraska	60.0	*46*	Nevada	50.0
22	Connecticut	59.6	*47*	Arizona	49.6
23	Massachusetts	58.9	*48*	California	47.7
24	Kansas	58.6	*49*	Texas	46.7
25	Louisiana	58.5	*50*	Hawaii	44.7

About the Data

The majority of the data presented in this book comes from government agencies, including the Census Bureau, the Department of Labor, and the Department of Commerce. These agencies provide the most reliable estimates available at the time the data is released. However, as new information becomes available, these agencies will occasionally refine their estimates. As a result, researchers should be aware that data may vary slightly based on when it was retrieved.

Below is more information on the sources used for each section of the state profiles.

Demographic and Socioeconomic Data. The population, household, age, and ethnicity, data is from the U.S. Census Bureau's 2005 American Community Survey, and the 2000 Census Summary File 1 and Summary File 3. The household income and poverty data is also from these sources, while the per capita income data in this section is from the U.S. Department of Commerce's Bureau of Economic Analysis (BEA), table SA1-3. Population projection's are from the Census Bureau's April 2005 interim projections consistent with Census 2000.

Workforce and Industry Data. Labor force and educational attainment data is from the U.S. Census Bureau's 2005 American Community Survey and the 2000 Census Summary File 3. Unemployment rates for 2000 and 2005 are from the Department of Labor's Bureau of Labor Statistics' (BLS) Local Area Unemployment Statistics, and are annualized rates without seasonal adjustment. The data on average earnings per job are from the BLS. Average earnings data for 2000 was obtained from the BLS Quarterly Census of Employment and Wages, and average earnings for 2005 were obtained from the Bureau of Labor Statistics' May 2005 National Occupational Employment and Wage Estimates using the mean annual wage estimates for all occupations. The industry data is from the U.S. Census Bureau's County Business Patterns.

Tax and Business Climate Data. Data for state and local tax revenues were collected from the survey of State and Local Government Finances, and provided by the Census Bureau's Government's Division. In general we include tax revenue from state and local sources to allow valid comparison among states. Anderson Economic Group, LLC calculated the per capita taxes using population figures from the Census Bureau, as available at the time the data were collected. Employer firm birth and employer firm termination data were collected from the Census Bureau's Statistics of U.S. Businesses.

Measures of business climates are from Anderson Economic Group, *Forbes* Magazine, and the Tax Foundation. Please see the glossary for a description of how each group assesses a state's business climate. Further information on the business climate rankings is available on the websites of *Forbes* Magazine, the Tax Foundation, and Anderson Economic Group.

Voter Behavior and Elected Official Data. The data on voter registration and turnout, as well as the presidential election results, is from Dave Leip's Atlas of U.S. Presidential Elections, available at www.uselectionatlas.org. This site was also useful in verifying the gubernatorial and congressional section, data for which was collected from a variety of sources, but mainly the websites for the National Governor's Association, the United States Senate, and the United States House of Representatives.

Business and Economic Agencies. This information was collected by Anderson Economic Group. The first agency listed for each state is a state-level chamber of commerce, or similar. The second agency listed is the state's economic development agency or office. Third listed is an agency that promotes and provides resources for small businesses in each state, and the last listed is the agency or office that businesses should contact for information on registering and filing to do business in the state.

These agencies are only a few of many that are available in each state. There are many local chambers of commerce and economic development organizations that can serve as excellent resources as well.

Glossary of Terms

African-American Population. Persons having origins in any of the black racial groups of Africa. It includes people who indicate their race as "African American or Black," or provide written entries such as African American, Afro-American, Kenyan, Nigerian, or Haitian.

Definition: U.S. Census Bureau, American Community Survey

Anderson Economic Group 2006 Business Tax Burden Ranking. A ranking of business tax burdens in all 50 states. This ranking measures actual taxes paid by businesses in 2004 as a percentage of profits earned within each state's borders. "Business" taxes are defined as taxes with an initial incidence on a business, rather than an individual. Included are corporate income, gross receipts, value-added, and property taxes; but not taxes on employee wages, residential property, or consumer spending.

Definition: Anderson Economic Group, LLC

Asian Population. Persons having origins in any of the original peoples of the Far East, Southeast Asia, or the Indian subcontinent including, for example, Cambodia, China, India, Japan, Korea, Malaysia, Pakistan, the Philippine Islands, Thailand, and Vietnam. It includes "Asian Indian," "Chinese," "Filipino," "Korean," "Japanese," "Vietnamese," and "Other Asian."

Definition: U.S. Census Bureau, American Community Survey

Average Wage per Job. Average wage and salary disbursements are wage and salary disbursements divided by the number of wage and salary jobs (total wage and salary employment). Wage and salary disbursements consists of the monetary remuneration of employees, including the compensation of corporate officers; commissions, tips, and bonuses; and receipts in kind, or pay-in-kind, such as the meals furnished to the employees of restaurants. It reflects the amount of payments disbursed, but not necessarily earned during the year.

Definition: U.S. Department of Commerce, Bureau of Economic Analysis

Average Household Size. The total number of occupants in a household, divided by the total number of household units.

Definition: U.S. Census Bureau, American Community Survey

Bachelors Degree of Higher. Respondents who have completed a bachelors, masters, or professional degree were classified as having a "bachelors degree or higher." Associates degrees were included in this category only if the coursework could be transferred into a complete bachelors degree.

Definition: U.S. Census Bureau, American Community Survey

Caucasian Population. The U.S. Census Bureau defines "Caucasian" as a person having origins in any of the original peoples of Europe, the Middle East, or North Africa. It includes people who indicate their race as "White" or report entries such as Irish, German, Italian, Lebanese, Near Easterner, Arab, or Polish.

Definition: U.S. Census Bureau, Summary of Social, Economic, and Housing Characteristics

Civilian Labor Force. The civilian, noninstitutional population, age 16 and over, who may be classified as employed or unemployed.

Definition: U.S. Census Bureau, American Community Survey

Corporate Income Tax. Taxes on corporations and unincorporated businesses (when taxed separately from individual income), measured by net income, whether on corporations in general or on specific kinds of corporations, such as financial institutions. Some other business activity taxes, such as Michigan's Single Business Tax (a value-added tax), are also included in this category.

Definition: U.S. Census Bureau, Quarterly Summary of State and Local Government Tax Revenue

Employees. The total number of persons on establishment payrolls employed full or part time who received pay for any part of the pay period that includes the twelfth day of the month.

Definition: U.S. Department of Labor, Bureau of Labor Statistics

Employer Firm Births and Deaths. Births are establishments that have zero employment in the first quarter of the initial year and positive employment in the first quarter of the subsequent year. Deaths are establishments that have positive employment in the first quarter of the initial year and zero employment in the first quarter of the subsequent year.

Definition: U.S. Census Bureau, Statistics of U.S. Businesses

Establishment. The physical location of a certain economic activity—for example, a factory, mine, store, or office. A single establishment generally produces a single good or provides a single service. An enterprise (a private firm, government, or nonprofit organization) can consist of a single establishment or multiple establishments.

Definition: U.S. Census Bureau, County Business Patterns

Forbes Magazine: 2006 Best States for Business Ranking. A ranking of the business climates of all 50 states based on 30 metrics in 6 main categories: business costs, economic climate, growth prospects, labor, quality of life, and regulatory environment.

Definition: Forbes, The Best States for Business

Foreign-Born Population. The foreign-born population includes all people who were not U.S. Citizens at birth. Foreign-born people are people who indicated they were either a U.S. citizen by naturalization or that they were not a citizen of the United States. Immigration status is not relevant in determining the foreign-born population.

Definition: U.S. Census Bureau, Summary of Social, Economic, and Housing Characteristics

Graduate Degree or Higher. This category includes people who hold at least one graduate degree. A graduate degree includes masters of arts, masters of science, field specific masters degrees, professional, and doctorate degrees.

Definition: U.S. Census Bureau, American Community Survey

High School Graduate or Higher. This category includes people whose highest degree was a high school diploma or its equivalent (for example, passed the test of General Educational Development), people who attended college but did not receive a degree, and people who received an associates, bachelors, masters, or professional doctorate degree. People who reported completing the twelfth grade but not receiving a diploma are not included.

Definition: U.S. Census Bureau, American Community Survey

Hispanic Population. Since the 2000 Census, the U.S. Census Bureau has defined "Hispanic" as any population identifying themselves as "Spanish," "Hispanic origin," or "Latino." Some respondents identified with all three terms, while others may have identified with only one, or none of the three terms. In addition, all write-in responses to the "other Spanish/Hispanic/Latino" category were coded as "Hispanic," beginning with the 2000

Census. Currently, the U.S. Census Bureau defines "Hispanic" as a population that may be of any race. This handbook used all census classifications of "Hispanic" or "other Hispanic."

Definition: U.S. Census Bureau, Summary of Social, Economic, and Housing Characteristics

Household Income. The sum of all monetary income received in a calendar year by all household members 15 years old and over, including household members not related to the householder, people living alone, and other nonfamily household members. Household income may include nonwage income as well.

Definition: U.S. Department of Labor, Bureau of Labor Statistics

Individual Income Tax. The U.S. government classifies income taxes as taxes on individuals measured by net income and taxes on special types of income (e.g., interest, dividends, income from intangible property, etc.).

Definition: U.S. Census Bureau, Quarterly Summary of State and Local Government Tax Revenue, Quarterly Summary of Technical Documentation

Labor Force Participation Rate. The proportion of the total number of persons in the labor force to the total population 16 years old and over.

Definition: U.S. Department of Labor, Bureau of Labor Statistics

Median. The middle value in a distribution, with an equal number of values above and below the median (sometimes called "midpoint").

Number of Households. A household includes all people residing in a housing unit. A household may consist of family members and or lodgers, foster children, wards, or employees who share the housing unit. A person living alone in a housing unit is also counted as a household. The count of households excludes group quarters.

Definition: U.S. Census Bureau, American Community Survey

Other Taxes. Taxes that are not listed separately or specifically accounted for in a tax category. These taxes most commonly include inheritance and estate taxes; taxes on recording, registering, or transferring documents; and taxes on the value or quantity of natural resource extraction.

Definition: U.S. Census Bureau, Government Finance and Employment Classification Manual

Personal Income. The sum of wages, rental income of persons, personal dividend income, personal interest income, and personal current transfer receipts.

Definition: U.S. Department of Commerce, Bureau of Economic Analysis

Popular Vote. The number of votes from citizens, independent of the electoral college.

Definition: U.S. National Archives and Records Administration

Poverty. Poverty thresholds are determined by the amount of income necessary for self-sustenance. Poverty thresholds determine the government's official poverty definition and may vary based on family size and age of family members. Thresholds are adjusted annually for inflation, but they do not vary geographically.

Definition: U.S. Census Bureau

Poverty Rate. The number of people in a given area living under the poverty threshold, divided by the total number of people in that area. (*See poverty).*

Definition: U.S. Census Bureau

Property Tax. General property taxes, relating to property as a whole, taxed at a single rate or at classified rates according to the class of property. Property may refer to real property (i.e., land and structures), or personal property (i.e., automobiles and boats).

Definition: U.S. Census Bureau, Quarterly Summary of State and Local Government Tax Revenue, Quarterly Summary Technical Documentation

Sales and Gross Receipts Taxes. Taxes on goods and services, measured on the basis of the volume or value of their transfer. Depending on the good, sales taxes may be based upon gross receipts or gross income accrued from the sale of the good, or as an amount per unit sold (gallon, package, etc.). The Census Bureau also includes related taxes based upon use, storage, production, importation, or consumption of goods and services. Few states levy gross receipts taxes, which are included in this category by Census Bureau convention.

Definition: U.S. Census Bureau, Quarterly Summary of State and Local Government Tax Revenue, Quarterly Summary Technical Documentation

State and Local Taxes. In Census Bureau data, "State and Local Taxes" include the State-imposed taxes collected or received by the state and subsequently distributed to local governments. Locally collected and retained tax amounts are excluded from the data.

Definition: U.S. Census Bureau, Quarterly Summary of State and Local Government Tax Revenue, Quarterly Summary Technical Documentation

Tax Foundation: 2007 Business Tax Climate Ranking. An index of each state's tax friendliness to all business activity. The overall index is based on a composite of five specific tax indices; the corporate tax, the individual income tax, the sales tax, the unemployment insurance tax, and the property tax.

Definition: Tax Foundation

Taxes. Taxes are comprised of all compulsory contributions exacted by a government for public purposes, except employer and employee assessments for retirement and social insurance purposes, which are classified as insurance trust revenue. Included are all receipts from licenses and compulsory fees, in addition to those that are imposed for regulatory purposes and those designed to provide revenue.

Definition: U.S. Census Bureau, Quarterly Summary of State and Local Government Tax Revenue, Quarterly Summary Technical Documentation

Tax Revenue. Revenue from taxes generated in a given area includes related penalty and interest receipts but excludes protested amounts and refunds.

Definition: U.S. Census Bureau, Quarterly Summary of State and Local Government Tax Revenue, Quarterly Summary Technical Documentation

Total Payroll. The total amount of money paid to employees in wages.

Definition: U.S. Department of Labor, Bureau of Labor Statistics

Total Population. All people, male and female, child and adult, living in a given geographic area.

Definition: U.S. Census Bureau, American Community Survey

Unemployment. According the U.S. Census Bureau, all civilians 16 years old and over are classified as unemployed if they (1) were neither "at work" nor "with a job but not at work" during the reference week, and (2) were actively looking for work during the past four weeks, and (3) were available to accept a job.

Definition: U.S. Bureau of Labor Statistics

Unemployment Rate. The proportion of the total number of persons considered "unemployed" to the total population 16 years and over (*See unemployment).*

Definition: U.S. Bureau of Labor Statistics

Index